India-Africa Relations

INDIA-AFRICA RELATIONS

S.K. Singh

PRASHANT PUBLISHING HOUSE
DELHI-110094

Published by :
Prashant Publishing House
C-34, 28 Foota Road, Gali-3,
West Karwal Nagar, Delhi-110094
Phone : 011-22963970, Mob. : 9810396373
e-mail.: prashantpublishinghouse@gmail.com

India-Africa Relations

First Published 2016

ISBN 978-93-80565-64-4

PRINTED IN INDIA
Published by Mr. R.K. Jha M/s Prashant Publishing House and Published at H.S. Offset House Press, Delhi.

Contents

Preface

Africa–India relations refers to the historical, political, economic, military, helper and cultural connections between the India and the African continent.

The Indo-African partnership has been rooted in the spirit of the Afro-Asian conference held at Bandung, Indonesia, in 1955. Cemented by a common stand against colonization and racism, today this partnership is at a turning point motored by the stellar economic growth in the two regions and the growing exchange between them. The goal of shared development through cooperation between the two regions is a perspective that is in line with the reduction of world poverty as enshrined in the Sustainable Development Goals.

Understandably, the third edition of the Africa-India Forum Summit generates a lot of interest. The Summit this year was much larger than in previous years, with participation from 54 African countries.

Participation in the previous two summits, held in 2008 and 2011, was limited to Regional Economic Communities (RECs) in accord with the Banjul Agreement. The 2015 Summit has given greater privilege to bilateral endeavours. That said, the implication of regional actors is an asset of the India-Africa partnership and should continue, in the interest of promoting regional development in Africa. Additionally, regional cooperation provides a platform for opinion building and sharing common positions in international organizations.

The 3rd India-Africa Forum Summit is scheduled to be held in New Delhi from 26th to 29th October 2015, with all 54 heads of African nations having been invited for the Summit. This is the most significant diplomatic outreach by the Government of India underlining the importance of Africa in India's growth trajectory. A closer India-Africa partnership is important for the security and development of both India and Africa. In the coming years, Africa will play an increasing role in shaping global norms and institutions. The India-Africa connectivity, therefore, presents immense opportunities for exploring strategies for mutual cooperation and growth.

Africa and India are separated by the Indian Ocean. The geographical proximity between the Horn of Africa and the Indian subcontinent has played an important role in the development of the relationship since ancient times.

By the end of the 20th Century India and Africa witnessed new turn in their relations. These were many dimensions of old linkages that continue. Many drivers and rallying points of 20th century like decolonization and racial discrimination disappeared. Many others like Afro- Asian resurgence, Non- Aligned Movement (NAM) and Collective Self Reliance of South were subsumed by new forces and post cold war architecture emerged.

Two new developments at the global level impacted indo-African relations in a significant ways. The first was the advent of globalization. It drastically affected the domestic scenario of both India and Africa. It also threw the new directions, imperatives and parameters of international relations. Both India and Africa underwent Structural Adjustment Programme (SAP) and both shifted their priorities from South-South linkages to global integration. The second factor was the rise of China and India as fast growing economies and rising global powers.

As the book addresses this crucial issue quite deftly, it is hoped that it would prove to be a source of great information for the reader.

—*Editor*

1

Introduction

Africa–India relations refers to the historical, political, economic, military, helper and cultural connections between the India and the African continent.

Historical relations concerned mainly India and Eastern Africa. However, in modern days —and with the expansion of diplomatic and commercial representations,— India has now developed ties with most of the African nations. In 2013 trade between India & Africa stood at US$ 72 billion making India the fourth largest trading partner of Africa.

HISTORICAL BACKGROUND

Africa and India are separated by the Indian Ocean. The geographical proximity between the Horn of Africa and the Indian subcontinent has played an important role in the development of the relationship since ancient times.

Ancient trade relations

Little is known about contacts made between Indians and Africans before the first century CE. The only surviving source, *Periplus Maris Erythraei* (*Periplus of the Erythraean Sea*),—which dates to mid-first century—refers to trade relations between the Kingdom of Aksum and Ancient India around the first millennium. Helped by the monsoon winds, merchants traded cotton, glass beads and other goods in exchange for gold and soft-carved ivory. The influence of the Indian architecture on the African kingdom shows the level of trade development between the two civilizations.

Under Ptolemaic rule, Ancient Egypt dispatched two trade delegations to India. The Greek Ptolemaic dynasty and India had developed bilateral trade using the Red Sea and Indian ports. Controlling the western and northern end of other trade routes to Southern Arabia and India, the Ptolemies had begun to exploit trading opportunities with India prior to the Roman involvement but according to the historian Strabo the volume of commerce between India and Greece was not comparable to that of later Indian-Roman trade. The *Periplus Maris Erythraei* mentions a time when sea trade between India and Egypt did not involve direct sailings. The cargo under these situations was shipped to Aden:

"Eudaimon Arabia was called fortunate, being once a city, when, because ships neither came from India to Egypt nor did those from Egypt dare to go further but only came as far as this place, it received the cargoes from both, just as Alexandria receives goods brought from outside and from Egypt."

The trade started by Eudoxus of Cyzicus in 130 BCE kept increasing, and according to Strabo (II.5.12.):

"At any rate, when Gallus was prefect of Egypt, I accompanied him and ascended the Nile as far as Syene and the frontiers of Kingdom of Aksum, and I learned that as many as one hundred and twenty vessels were sailing from Myos Hormos to India, whereas formerly, under the Ptolemies, only a very few ventured to undertake the voyage and to carry on traffic in Indian merchandise."

In India, the ports of Barbaricum (modern Karachi), Barygaza, Muziris, Korkai, Kaveripattinam and Arikamedu on the southern tip of India were the main centers of this trade. The *Periplus Maris Erythraei* describes Greco-Roman merchants selling in Barbaricum "thin clothing, figured linens, topaz, coral, storax, frankincense, vessels of glass, and silver and gold plate" in exchange for "costus, bdellium, lycium, nard, turquoise, lapis lazuli, Seric skins, cotton cloth, silk yarn, and indigo". In Barygaza, they would buy wheat, rice, sesame oil, cotton and cloth.

With the establishment of Roman Egypt, the Romans took over and further developed the already existing trade. Roman trade with India played an important role in further developing the Red Sea route. Starting around 100 BCE a route from Roman Egypt to India was established, making use of the Red Sea to cross the Arabian Sea directly to southern India. Traces of Indian influences are visible in Roman works of silver and ivory, or in Egyptian cotton and silk fabrics. The Indian presence in Alexandria may have influenced the culture but little is known about the manner of this influence. Clement of Alexandria mentions the Buddha in his writings and other Indian religions find mentions in other texts of the period.

Medieval period relations

Relations attained stronger levels during medieval times due to the development of trade routes between the Mediterranean and Asia, through Arabia.

African heritage in India

The presence of Africans in India dates back to the eighth century CE.

Under the rule of the British Empire

During the British colonial rule in the Indian Subcontinent and large parts of Africa, the Indian city of Mumbai was already a centre of ivory trade between East Africa and Britain.

The stay of Mohandas Gandhi in South Africa between 1893 and 1915 remains one of the main events which paved the road to the modern-day political relations.

Modern-day relations

Political

The development of modern-day relations has gone through two main periods. During the period of colonialism and liberation wars, political relations became stronger. At the wake of the Cold War, many African countries joined the non-aligned movement pioneered by Egypt, Ghana, India, Indonesia and Yugoslavia.

During the years of decolonisation, India exerted considerable political and ideological influence in Africa as a role model and a leader of the Non-Aligned Movement. But India's ability to develop a broader strategic role in Africa during the 20th century was subject to several constraints. India's influence was limited by financial weakness and inward-looking economic policies. Its commitment to decolonisation through nonviolent means made it relatively reluctant to provide military assistance to national liberation movements. India's role in East Africa was also constrained by the large Indian ethnic population that was often resented by black African nationalists.

The India-Africa Forum Summit, which was held from April 4 to April 8, 2008 in New Delhi, India for the first time, constitutes the basic framework for the relations under the South-South Cooperation platform.

There are numerous of Indians and Africans of Indian descent living in Africa, mainly in the eastern and southern coast in places such as Mauritius, Kenya and South Africa.

Business

Indian firms are conducting numerous takeovers abroad and are venturing into Africa. In June 2008, Bharti Airtel, an Indian telecommunications giant, purchased Zain Africa for US$9 billion. Trade between India & Africa has grown exponentially during the past decade. Indo-African trade volume reached US$ 53.3 billion in 2010-11 & US$ 62 billion in 2011-12. It is expected that it would further go up to US$ 90 billion by 2015. As of 2011, India has emerged as Africa's fourth largest trade partner behind China, EU & USA whilst Africa has emerged as India's sixth largest trading partner behind EU, China, UAE, USA & ASEAN. It is to be noted that this volume was at a meager US$ 3 billion in 2001. In November 2012 FICCI President led a business delegation to Ethiopia to meet the new Prime Minister Hailemariam Desalegn and reaffirm India's commitment to the growth and development of Africa. Indian companies have already invested more than US$ 34 billion in the resource-rich continent as of 2011 & further investments worth US$ 59.7 billion are in the pipeline. Among the proposals that CII (Confederation of Indian Industry) received from the African nations are 126 agricultural projects worth an investment of $4.74 billion, 177 infrastructure projects worth $34.19 billion, and 34 energy sector plans costing $20.74 billion (337 projects totalling

US$ 59.7 billion). Ex-Prime Minister of India, Dr.Manmohan Singh while expressing his country's support to Africa, said in an Indo-African trade summit that "Africa possesses all the prerequisites to become a major growth pole of the world in the 21st century. We will work with Africa to enable it to realise this potential". The Indian government has promised to extend loans worth US$ 5.4 billion (during 2011-14) to several African nations in order to nurture growth in those nations.

INDIA–SOUTH AFRICA RELATIONS

The bilateral relations between the Republic of India and the Republic of South Africa have grown strong since the end of apartheid in South Africa in 1994. Both countries have since developed close strategic, cultural and economic ties. Both are former British colonies and full member states of the Commonwealth of Nations as Commonwealth republics.

India and South Africa also share an extensive energy partnership. In 2010, India imported 1.4 million tonnes of South African coal in February, making it the largest purchaser of coal from the country. Ties with further solidified with South Africa's 2011 acceptance into the BRICS group.

Background

There is a major resident Indian community in South Africa. Mohandas Karamchand Gandhi (more commonly known as Mahatma Gandhi) had commenced his political-legal career in South Africa, experimenting with civil disobedience in the 1890s and 1900s, to improve the quality of living of the Indians living there. A statue to him was unveiled in Pietermaritzburg by Saurav Ganguly, the captain of the Indian national cricket team during the 2003 Cricket World Cup.

Indians also contributed to the African National Congress's struggle against the Apartheid regime. The Indian government was an outspoken critic of the apartheid-era South African government, refusing to maintain diplomatic relations. India's support evoked goodwill in South Africa and other African countries.

South African Minister for Human Settlement Lindiwe Nonceba Sisulu during her visit to Delhi to join the celebration of 20 years of South African independence has said "India is our closest ally in the Asian continent" also added "The purpose of this visit is a gesture from the South African government to thank its Indian counterpart for all the help and support it has extended in our struggle for liberation".

Development of bilateral relations

Both countries established diplomatic relations after the end of apartheid in 1994. South African leader Nelson Mandela was awarded the Mahatma Gandhi Peace Prize and Bharat Ratna by the Indian government. Both nations have also promoted sporting ties, with the Indian national cricket team and the South Africa national cricket team frequently exchanging visits and participating in cricket tournaments hosted by either country.

Economic ties

Bilateral trade grew exponentially from USD 3 million in 1992-93 to USD 4 billion in 2005-06, and the two governments have targeted increasing bilateral trade to USD 12 billion by 2010. Gold bullion constitute one-third of India's imports from South Africa, while India polishes and processes diamonds from South African mines. South Africa has promoted signing a free trade agreement with India and the Southern Africa Customs Union (SACU), which includes Botswana, Lesotho, Namibia and Swaziland along with South Africa. Bharti Airtel was scheduled to acquire MTN to make one of the world's largest telecommunications companies, and also touted as step inSouth-South cooperation. The deal was, however, rejected by the South African government of Jacob Zuma on the grounds that MTN would not be as South African anymore amid concerns of dual-listing on the Indian and South African stock exchanges.

Military ties

India and South Africa have also developed military cooperation, trading arms and joint exercises and programs to train forces. Some analysts have argued that while there are some strategic commonalities between India and South Africa, this has not always translated into common perspectives.

IBSA

On June 6, 2003 India and South Africa signed an agreement with Brazil, known as the Brasília Declaration, establishing "South-South" cooperation, based on the premise of the three nations beingregional powers of South Asia, Southern Africa and South America. The declaration called for extensive tripartite cooperation on strategic, commercial and cultural affairs, development of a tripartite free trade agreement and a united front in negotiating with Western nations in the World Trade Organization(WTO), calling for reform of the U.N. Security Council and supporting each other's bid for permanent membership with veto rights. The IBSA Dialogue Forum was created to promote cooperation and consensus on issues of trade, poverty alleviation, intellectual property rights, social development, agriculture, climate change, culture, defence, education, energy, health-care, information society, science and technology, peaceful nuclear energy, tourism and transport. The fourth summit was held in Brasília. The three nations pledged to boost trilateral trade to USD 15 billion by 2010. The three nations have also expanded military cooperation and conducted joint naval exercises in 2008.

INDIA'S ENGAGEMENTS WITH AFRICA

By the end of the 20th Century India and Africa witnessed new turn in their relations. These were many dimensions of old linkages that continue. Many drivers and rallying points of 20th century like decolonization and racial discrimination disappeared. Many others like Afro- Asian resurgence, Non- Aligned Movement (NAM) and Collective Self Reliance of South were subsumed by new forces and post cold war architecture emerged.

Two new developments at the global level impacted indo-African relations in a significant ways. The first was the advent of globalization. It drastically affected the domestic scenario of both India and Africa. It also threw the new directions, imperatives and parameters of international relations. Both India and Africa underwent Structural Adjustment Programme (SAP) and both shifted their priorities from South-South linkages to global integration. The second factor was the rise of China and India as fast growing economies and rising global powers.

Rapid growth of India changed Indian priorities, imperatives and needs. Another is India's growing clout in international affairs that has led the search for fruitful economic engagement everywhere. Moreover, India's improved relations with the West since the 1990's has created the space for rearranging its relations with the extended neighborhood in South Asia, South-East Asia, Africa, Central Asia and the Middle East, on a completely different framework. This framework emphasizes economic relations and energy diplomacy rather than the impulse of Third World solidarity.

In the recently held India-Africa Forum Summit in New Delhi (8-9 April 2008), a framework for cooperation between Africa and India was spelt out. It emphasized the rich history of Africa-India relationship and the existing close and multi-layered ties between the two sides. Both agreements offer a direction to Indo-African relations in the coming years, and provide a framework for the establishment of a new-type, long-term and stable partnership of equality and mutual benefit between India and Africa, as well as a blueprint for India-Africa co-operation in political, economic, social development and other fields in future. The Summit marked the culmination of India's renewed focus on Africa. It was spurred largely by India's desire to change the world's perception of it - away from being a recipient to being a donor - in order to boost its global-political position. The Framework for Co-operation lists several areas (and sub-areas) for co-operation such as economic co-operation, political co-operation, science, technology and research, social development, tourism, and infrastructure, and energy and environment. It lists a number of focus areas therein, for instance, agriculture, trade, regional integration, peace and security, ICT, and culture.

INDIA-SOUTH AFRICA RELATIONS

India's links with the struggle for freedom and justice in South Africa date back to the period during which Mahatma Gandhi started his Satyagraha movement in South Africa over a century ago. India was at the forefront of the international community in its support to the anti-apartheid movement; it was the first country to sever trade relations with the apartheid Government (in 1946) and subsequently imposed a complete — diplomatic, commercial, cultural and sports — embargo on South Africa. India worked consistently to put the issue of apartheid on the agenda of the UN, NAM and other multilateral organizations and for the imposition of comprehensive international sanctions against South Africa. The ANC maintained a representative office in New Delhi from the 1960s onwards.

Following talks between the then South African Government and the ANC, India's relations with South Africa were restored after a gap of over four decades with the opening of a Cultural Centre in Johannesburg in May 1993. Formal diplomatic and consular relations with South Africa were restored in November 1993 during the visit to India of the then South African Foreign Minister Pik Botha. A Consulate General was thereafter established in Johannesburg. The Indian High Commission in Pretoria was opened in May 1994, followed by the opening of the Consulate General in Durban the same month. Since Parliament in South Africa meets in Cape Town, a permanent office of the High Commission was opened there in 1996, which has been re-designated as Consulate General of India with effect from January 2011. In addition to its High Commission in Delhi, South Africa has a Consulate General in Mumbai.

POLITICAL RELATIONS

Development of political relations since 1994

Against the background of India's consistent support to the anti-apartheid struggle, there has been a steady consolidation of our close and friendly ties with South Africa, both bilaterally and through the trilateral IBSA Dialogue Forum. A number of bilateral agreements have been concluded between the two countries since the assumption of diplomatic relations in 1993 in diverse areas ranging from economic and commercial cooperation, defence, culture, heath, human settlements, public administration, science and technology and education. India's Technical and Economic Cooperation Programme (ITEC) has been a useful medium of promoting cooperation in development of human resources.

Recent High Level visits

Prime Minister Dr Manmohan Singh visited South Africa in March 2013 to attend 5th BRICS Summit held in Durban. PM's official delegation included Finance Minister Shri P.Chidambaram, Commerce and Industry Minister Shri Anand Sharma; and other senior officials. President Smt. Pratibha Devisingh Patil paid a State Visit to South Africa in May 2012. President of South Africa, Mr Jacob Zuma paid a visit to India in March 2012 for 4th BRICS Summit. President Zuma, accompanied by Mrs Nompumelelo Ntuli-Zuma, had earlier paid a State Visit to India from 02 to 05 June 2010. President Zuma's delegation included 7 Cabinet Ministers [Ministers of International Relations and Cooperation, Defence, Public Enterprises, Trade & Industry, Agriculture, Forestry & Fisheries, Transport and Communications]. Three MOUs/ Agreements were signed during the visit: (i) MOU on 2 Cooperation in the Field of Agriculture and Allied Sectors, (ii) Air Services Agreement and (iii) MoU on cooperation between the Foreign Service Institute of India and the Diplomatic Academy of South Africa. A 200-member strong business delegation as well as senior officials accompanied President Zuma on his visit. President Zuma met President, Vice President and Prime Minister; MOS for External Affairs as well as Chairperson of UPA and Leader of the Opposition in the Lok Sabha called on him. Discussions reflected the fraternal warmth and affection as well as the strategic partnership that characterize bilateral relations. President Zuma and his delegation also met Indian business leaders in Mumbai on June 2,

2010. The regular Parliamentary exchanges between India and South Africa continued. From South Africa, a joint Parliamentary delegation led by Speaker Mr. Max Sisulu and Chairperson, National Council of Provinces, Mr. M.J. Mahlangu, visited India on 8-14 July, 2012. A goodwill Parliamentary delegation led by Hon'ble Minister for Parliamentary Affairs and Water Resources Shri Pawan Bansal, visited South Africa in October, 2012. There has been regular exchanges at Ministerial level including visit of

Shri Pratik Prakashbapu Patil, MOS(Coal) in October 2012 and Shri Anand Sharma, Minister of Commerce, Industry and Textile in January 2013. Secretary, Ministry of Overseas Indian Affairs addressed Indian Diaspora during his visit to South Africa at Johannesburg, Cape Town and Durban in April 2013.

Joint Commission and Foreign Office Consultations

The India-South Africa Joint Commission at the level of Foreign Ministers was set up in 1994 to identify areas of mutually beneficial cooperation. The 7 th session of the JMC was held in Pretoria in February 2008. During the visit, three Agreements on Customs Cooperation, S&T and visa free travel for diplomatic and official passport holders were signed. India hosted the 8th session of the JMC in March 2011 in New Delhi. EAM Shri S.M. Krishna headed the Indian delegation, while Minister Mashabane led the South African side. Four rounds of Foreign Office Consultations have also been held; the latest in Pretoria in May 2010. Secretary (West), MEA, Shri Vivek Katju headed the Indian delegation.

IBSA & BRICS Initiative

On June 6, 2003, the Foreign Ministers of India, Brazil and South Africa met in Brasilia and agreed to set up a Dialogue Forum for regular consultations on such matters. Subsequently, in 2006, this was upgraded to Summit level; five Summits have been held so far, the last in Pretoria in October 2011. IBSA Trilateral Ministerial meeting was held in New Delhi in March 2011. 16 Sectoral Working Groups have been established in areas such as health, agriculture, education, human settlements, S&T and defence. South Africa has also been admitted as a member of the BRICS grouping and attended the BRICS meeting held in April

2011 at Sanya, BRICS Summit held in March 2012 in New Delhi and South Africa hosted the 5th Summit at Durban in March 2013.

SOUTH AFRICA'S FOREIGN RELATIONS DURING APARTHEID, 1948

The position of South Africa in international affairs remained important throughout apartheid. The South African government needed to rely on the external community for certain products and as a market for South African products. Security was also provided by Western powers, and South Africa did not want complete isolation, although sometimes it seemed the easier option for the Prime Ministers. Over the years South Africa did become increasingly isolated, but this was also not the best thing for the Western powers. The western powers remained aware that, although apartheid was unacceptable, South Africa was still important to them. South Africa's importance was both strategic and economic. During the Cold War, South Africa was of strategic importance in the fight against communism, and South African propaganda focused on this Western fear. The country was also of strategic importance as a route to the east. Financially, South Africa provided the West with important commodities, such as gold and coal, and provided an important market for Western products. For this reason, the West was not prepared to break all relations with South Africa, and Britain and the USA in particular were very against sanctions against South Africa. The international community did never the less criticise apartheid, and anti-apartheid groups existed in many countries to increase this criticism.

Initial opposition to South Africa's racial policies

In 1948 apartheid was introduced in South Africa in a post-World War II political climate that was very against racial discrimination. The world increasingly moved away from ideas of racial superiority after the horrors of WWII, but South Africa introduced a more institutionalised form of racism. South Africa's racial polices were placed on the agenda of the first meeting of the United Nations by India, and various countries criticised the policy of apartheid. However, it was not until later that the true nature of apartheid became known, and for this reason there was initially not that much severe criticism of apartheid. Most countries, and especially those in the west, felt there was no need to change their relations with South Africa.

The U.N.O. and its actions against South Africa: Committees formed, sanctions, suspension from U.N.O.

South Africa was placed on the agenda of the United Nations

for the first time in 1946 regarding the treatment of people of Indian origin living in South Africa. In 1952 apartheid was again raised, this time in connection with the wider question of race conflict in the country in reaction to the ANC Defiance Campaign. The South West African question was also on the agenda annually as from 1946. Initially the South African government responded to comments on its policy by saying that apartheid was part of the internal affairs of the country, and for this reason fell beyond the scope of the United Nations. Many Western countries agreed with this claim, but nonetheless continued to hold discussions and appealed to South Africa to change its policies year after year.

In 1960 the worldwide view changed as a result of the Sharpeville Incident. As from this point many Western countries no longer held the view that apartheid fell within internal affairs and they began to openly criticise South Africa. On 1 April 1960 the Security Council also discussed the issue, and recognised that it might be a threat to world peace and security. They called upon the government to introduce measures to bring about racial harmony. The South African government instead reacted with banning the ANC and PAC. From this point on the UN decided to follow steps to try and ensure the following of the UN Charter inside South Africa.

In 1961 United Nations Secretary-General, Dag Hammarskjold visited South Africa, but reported back that he could not come to an acceptable agreement with the Prime Minister. In the same year H.F. Verwoerd announced South Africa's withdrawal from the Commonwealth of Nations as a result of criticism from this organisation, and the Foreign Minister was criticized for his speech in the General Assembly. In 1966, the first of many UN seminars on apartheid was held in Brazil, and later in the same year the General Assembly proclaimed 21 March to be International Day for the Elimination of Racial Discrimination in remembrance of the Sharpeville Incident. A 1971 General Assembly resolution condemned the establishment of homelands. In 1974 there was a resolution to expel South Africa from the United Nations as a result of human rights violations, but it was not accepted as France, the UK and the USA did not support it.

The one possible form of action against South Africa was the introduction of economic sanctions and the isolation of South Africa. Sanctions were often discussed and supported in the UN, and many recognised them as an effective and peaceful means of pressure. However, the main trading partners of South Africa continually voted against the introduction of mandatory sanctions in the Security Council. In 1962 the General Assembly asked that member states break diplomatic, trade and transport relations in an attempt to convince South Africa to abandon apartheid, and again in 1968 they asked for the suspension of all cultural, educational and sporting exchanges. In 1963 the Security Council called upon states to stop the sale of arms to South Africa, and repeated the call in 1970 (when only France, the UK and the USA abstained from voting) and again in 1972. It was however only in 1977 that the arms embargo became mandatory, and other sanctions were still not in place. The year 1982 was decaled International Year of Mobilisation for Sanctions against South Africa by the General Assembly, with a new programme of action being introduced the following year. In 1985 the Security Council called on members to introduce more far reaching economic measures against South Africa, but a draft resolution of selective sanctions was vetoed by the UK and USA in 1988.

Another form of possible assistance from the UN revolved around assisting the victims of apartheid. In 1963 the General Assembly passed a resolution calling on states to contribute to funds assisting victims of apartheid. The Special Committee Against Apartheid was set up in the same year, with a Centre Against Apartheid being established in 1976 and 1978-9 being declared International Anti-Apartheid Year. Many countries did adhere to this call, and some private contributions had even been provided prior to the United Nations call. In 1972 the Security Council made a similar call for contributions and recognised the legitimacy of the struggle against apartheid. The next year they recognised the freedom movements as the true representatives of the majority of the South African people. In 1989 the General Assembly adopted the "Declaration on Apartheid and its Destructive Consequences in Southern Africa," calling for negotiations to end apartheid.

It can be seen from the above discussion that the UN continually failed to take steps to being apartheid to an end. Despite continuous condemnation and criticism of the policy, mandatory sanctions were never introduced. The main reason for this lies in the fact that the five permanent members of the Security Council have the right to veto, and Britain and the USA were not in favour of mandatory sanctions and so could continually veto this move. The role of the Cold War in decisions is also evident. Sanctions needed to go through the Security Council rather than through the General Assembly.

The Lusaka Manifesto and other policies and statements from exile

In 1963 the Organisation of African Unity (OAU) was formed, introducing a period of increased criticism of apartheid. The OAU immediately called for sanctions against South Africa and Portuguese goods and also agreed that each member state would contribute 1% of their budget to the OAU fund for liberation. They even promised to provide volunteer liberation fighters and set up a Liberation Committee to give aid to the liberation movements. However by the end of the 1960s this support seemed to be unreliable. It was only Tanzania, Zambia and the Congo that gave constant support, and then in 1969 after the signing of the Lusaka Manifesto even this support seemed uncertain.

In April 1969 fourteen independent black states from Central and East Africa met in Zambia to discuss African issues. The meeting resulted in the formulation of the Lusaka Manifesto, which was signed by thirteen of the states present, excluding Malawi, on 13 April. The Lusaka Manifesto was later also accepted and adopted by both the OAU and the United Nations (UN).

The Lusaka Manifesto, which was mainly drafted by the Tanzanian and Zambian leaders, was a statement outlining the diplomatic position of independent African states. It called for black majority rule for all states in Africa and for human equality and dignity throughout Africa and rejected racism. However at the same time it took a conciliatory approach towards South Africa. The states decided that South Africa should be accepted as an independent country. Although they still wanted the liberation of

South Africa, they wanted to achieve this through peaceful means, dialogue and negotiation rather then through armed struggle. It also offered compromises regarding the time period for change as long as South Africa accepted the principle of human equality and dignity. The countries signing the Manifesto were themselves concerned about South African military action and for this and economic reasons did not really want to involve themselves in an armed struggle.

African National Congress First National Consultative Conference Morogoro, Tanzania, 25 April - 1 May 1969

The ANC and PAC were both quite upset by the Lusaka Manifesto, which was drawn up without consulting them. They saw that support for their operations would decrease and were not sure what position they would find themselves in exile. The manifesto also did not give the freedom movements an important position in the solution for South Africa, and even spoke of trying to convince them to turn away from armed struggle if South Africa agreed to certain conditions. The ANC decided to discuss these problems and their new position at the Morogoro Conference also held in 1969. This was the first National Consultative Conference of the ANC. The ANC and PAC however felt unable to criticise the Manifesto openly as they relied on support from the signatories of the Manifesto.

The South African government welcomed the policy of dialogue and détente, which Vortser had already turned to as a way of reducing South Africa's isolation in his outward looking policy. The government also insisted that separate development focused on human equality and dignity and that this was a form of decolonisation. The government however still rejected the Lusaka Manifesto, largely because the Manifesto did still say that if there was no other choice the African sates would support the struggle for freedom by whatever methods they could find.

The rejection of the Lusaka Manifesto by the South African government and the lack of change in South Africa led to another declaration in 1971. The Magadishu Declaration of the OAU stated that, as South Africa would not accept the Manifesto, the African states were justified in rejecting dialogue. It also stated that Southern

Africa could only be liberated by force, and that African states should not enter into dialogue with South Africa. This declaration led to the intensification of the struggle for independence in Southern Africa and especially in Angola and Mozambique. From this time on it was up to South Africa to try and keep what contact she could with African states.

The "Outward-Looking" policy of the S.A. government and its strengthening of relations with the West

When BJ Vorster came to power in 1966 people were not quite sure which direction he would move in, but it was expected that he was a 'verkrampte' (conservative NP). However, in a speech in February 1967 he showed himself to be with the 'verligtes' - that is the liberal school of the National Party. In his speech Vorster spoke of taking South Africa out of isolation and the laager mentality. Vorster wanted to improve South Africa's image overseas and its foreign relations, even with the other black states in Africa. The reaction inside South Africa to his new policy varied, with the liberal newspapers fully supporting the move by Vorster, and saying that the laager mentality was not actually the mentality of the Afrikaner.

One of the first moves by Vorster to alleviate isolation was in the sports field. Verwoerd's sport policy had said that another country with a multi-racial sports team could not play in South Africa. This meant that a New Zealand team that contained a Maori player was not allowed to play in South Africa. Vorster now decided that South Africa could not tell other countries what their sports teams should look like. This meant that from 1967 onwards countries with mixed sports teams could play in South Africa, and international sporting events could be held in South Africa, although anti-apartheid movements were by this time trying to get people to boycott South Africa with regards to sport. Vorster had the support of the verligtes in this move, but the verkramptes did not want to go against Verwoerd's policy in any way. This led to some division between vekramptes and verligtes in the NP and in the government.

On the issue of black states in Africa, Verwoerd had already realised that it would be necessary to establish cordial relations with as many black states as possible. In Verwoerd's term the number of independent black states increased considerably, and together with this negative feelings towards South Africa also increased. Verwoerd realised that cooperation and friendship was the only choice in the face of the complete isolation in Africa. Cooperation on the economic level would be the first step.

Vorster carried on with this policy and executed it by forming relations with independent African counties. The policy became known as one of 'dialogue and détente' or as the 'outward looking policy'.

In 1967 Vorster offered free technical and economic advice to any African country that would like it, saying there were no political strings attached. He focused on economic aspects first knowing that many African countries were very poor and would need economic assistance despite their rejection of South Africa's racial policy. Vorster decided to try and attract the more conservative African states first. It was mainly Malawi, the ex-Portuguese territories and the ex- British protectorates in southern Africa that formed relations with South Africa although there were also some connections in West Africa.

For Vorster the first step was to arrange meetings with some African leaders. Here again he was going against the policy followed by Verwowerd who had even rejected a request by Abubakar Tafawa Balewa of Nigeria to visit South Africa in 1962 and an offer by Kuanda of Zambia in 1964 to establish diplomatic relations because the offer had been made from a political platform. Vorster set up a meeting with Chief Leabua Jonathan of Lesotho in 1966, with Sir Sereste Khama of Botswana in 1968 and with Prince Makhosini Dlamini of Swaziland in 1971. These contacts were however still characterised by mistrust and the distance between them was seen in Vorster's rejection of the Lusaka Manifesto of April 1969 and with the way he tried to score points against Kuanda.

Botswana, Lesotho and Swaziland remained openly critical of apartheid, but had to rely on South Africa for economic reasons as a result of their geographical position. Many workers from these countries worked in South Africa on the mines, and there was a customs union between the countries. Postal, telegraphic and monetary ties were also firmly established. Relations with Lesotho involved loans to Lesotho, assistance with stimulating the wool industry in Lesotho and the Oxbow irrigation scheme. Botswana was given assistance with increasing agricultural production.

The first country not bordering on South Africa to accept Voster's offer was Malawi and its President Hastings Banda. Malawi recognised the economic advantage it would get from the deal, especially as a loan of R6 million had been extended to the country in 1966. During 1967 visits to South Africa began with three Malawian Ministers visiting South Africa and a trade mission visiting Cape Town and meeting with Vorster. A trade agreement was entered into later in 1967 and South Africa gave the country another loan of R8 million to move its capital city and R11 million to build a railway. South Africa also employed Malawians on the mines, and by 1967 the number stood at 30 000, a number that was set to increase.

The first official visit by a South African minister to Malawi took place in 1968 when the Minister of Foreign Affairs, H. Muller, paid them a visit. The year also saw the setting up of diplomatic relations as consulates were established in the capitals of both countries. This was a very important link for South Africa and gave the illusion of shrinking isolation.

South Africa had historical relations with Mozambique and continued to focus on these relations as part of the outward looking policy. In the 1960s South Africa continued to employ many Mozambiqueans on the mines and tried to keep close relations. This was quite easy in both Mozambique and Angola considering the fact that these counties only achieved independence in the mid-1970s. Close ties with Mozambique were built up in the Cabora Bassa dam project on the Zambezi River. This provided hydro- electric power and irrigation water. A loan was provided to Angola for the development of the Kunene scheme on the Ruacana Falls.

After independence relations between South Africa and Mozambique actually continued. In 1984 South Africa and

Mozambique signed the Nkomati Accord, an Accord of good neighbourliness between the two countries. The Accord said that neither county would support the opposition movements of the other country. This meant that South Africa was to stop material aid to RENAMO and that the ANC could no longer use Mozambique as an entry point back into South Africa. Most of the ANC forces needed to leave Mozambique as a result of the Accord, which was a victory for South Africa. South Africa never fully obeyed the accord, and continued to supply RENAMO. Mozambique on the other hand was forced to sign and listen to the treaty as a result of economic interests, and the Accord was later reaffirmed and a joint security commission was set up to monitor the situation. In 1986 Mozambique's President, Samora Machel, was killed in a strange aeroplane crash just over the South African border in which the South African government was involved.

Vorster also wanted to form relations with other African states so that South Africa could have allies on the continent. In 1969 the government started a fund with the purpose of promoting economic relations with other African countries. This led to the policy of dialogue and détente of the 1970s. Vorster declared himself willing to talk to any African leader. The OAU rejected such dialogue, saying that the South African government should enter into dialogue with the South African blacks before other countries would form relations. The OAU also called on South Africa to move away from apartheid, and in 1971 it decided that as a result of South Africa's rejection of the Lusaka Manifesto they were justified in abandoning dialogue with the county.

During 1971 and 1972 talks were held with representatives from 12 African states and 43 groups of representatives from Africa visited South Africa. In 1974 and 1975 Vorster went on African tours to talk to leaders, and among others visited and held talks with the leaders of Liberia, President Houphouet-Boigny of the Ivory Coast who also encouraged others to talk to South Africa and Senegal. These more conservative countries were aware of the economic advantage of forming relations with South Africa and many feared the military power of South Africa should action be taken against them. They also listened when the West called for compromise. South Africa was also over the years able to enter into relations with Madagascar, Mauritius, Gabon, Ivory Coast, Zaire (Democratic Republic of Congo), Liberia, Ghana and the Central African Republic.

South Africa was however not very successful at breaking the isolation. Those countries that did forge relations with South Africa did so out of economic and military concern and despite the antagonism that they had for apartheid. The government tried to implement the policy as quickly as possible so as improve the image of South Africa, but by this time international resistance was growing, as was resistance inside the country in the form of the Black Consciousness Movement. From the 1980s onwards isolation only increased as more and more Western countries turned towards sanctions and breaking relations. The small successes that the government did achieve were seen as huge breakthroughs, but this only highlights the real position of South Africa and the extent of the growing isolation.

Cultural and sporting isolation

During the apartheid period one of the main ways that the international community showed their rejection of apartheid was through boycotting South Africa in various spheres. Boycotts included economic or consumer boycotts, academic, cultural and sport boycotts. These boycotts were very effective in isolating South Africa and making the public aware of the international opinion. The boycotts also showed the black community that they had international support and, although some boycotts did affect the black community negatively, the ANC still called for such boycotts as the positive effects outweighed the negative effects. In most cases there were still who argued against boycotts and attempted to keep relations with South Africa. The Anti – Apartheid Movements (AAMs) tried to change the public's view and to encourage the governments to introduce boycotts and sanctions.

On 13 November 1959 the British government made the following resolution regarding the importing of South African goods:

Boycotts against Apartheid

"This Committee condemns the Government of the Union of South Africa for its action against Ronald Segal, editor of Africa South, as further evidence of that Government's contempt for the freedom of the Press; calls on all in the United Kingdom who reprobate the evil policy of apartheid to join in boycotting Nationalist South African goods; and especially urges the people of other territories of the Commonwealth to demonstrate solidarity by similar action."

Boycotts regarding sport and culture affected the average white South African. In a sport-crazy South Africa, the sport boycott brought home to the average South African the negative effects of international isolation as a result of apartheid. These boycotts also did not have as much effect on the black population, especially as relations with black teams were sometimes maintained and even strengthened. By bringing the debate on apartheid into sport and cultural circles it also meant that more people were made aware of apartheid and with the problems surrounding the situation. International action against sport relations started in the mid-1950s and began to have real effect in the 1960s. The situation regarding segregated sport and segregated watching of sport was brought up by those directly affected by the South African policy. Black sportsmen began to ask for a break in relations with white South Africa, which also refused to play any non-white team, in favour of relations with non-racial teams.

An important step towards changing relations was taken in 1956 by the International Table Tennis Federation, which decided to stop links with the all-white South African Table Tennis Union in favour of links with the non- racial South African Table Tennis Board. The South African government responded by taking away the passports of these players so that they still could not play in the international games. After this first step other sports slowly began to follow, although there was often a problem as the top people in the federations did not want change and did not want confrontation. This led to the changes being slow in most sports.

In 1959 the South Africa Sports Association (SASA) was formed as a non-racial organisation to secure the rights for these players in the international field. SASA first tried to get recognition by working together with the white organisations, but by 1962 realised this was not going to be effective and it approached the International Olympic Committee (IOC). It asked that South Africa be expelled from the Olympics for their racial policy, and South Africa received a warning that if there were no changes it would be suspended in 1963. This led to the creation of the South African Non-Racial Olympic Committee (SAN-ROC) in January 1963 as changes were introduced. Problems however persisted and AAMs continued to campaign for the exclusion of apartheid South Africa, resulting in South Africa's exclusion from the Tokyo Games in 1964.

In 1967 an International Olympic Committee visited South Africa, and the visit concluded with a favourable report on changes in South African sport. The IOC saw that South Africa had a multi-racial team that had been selected on merit for the next Olympic Games, and decided to invite South Africa to participate in the 1968 Mexico Olympics. This however resulted in much criticism from AAMs and black states who threatened that they would stay away from the games if South Africa participated. This meant that in April 1968 the Olympic Committee withdrew their invitation to South Africa.

Other campaigns by AAMs were also taking place in the 1960s. Demonstrations began in 1960 in New Zealand after Verwoerd refused to allow a Moari player to tour together with the rest of the All Blacks team to South Africa. The tour was cancelled in the end. A change of policy however came about when Vorster replaced Verwoerd and stated that South Africa would no longer dictate to other countries what their teams should look like. This opened the door to international sporting events, but led to a lot of problems within the National Party as many did not support the change. Amid these problems Vorster refused to allow the coloured cricketer, Basil D'Oliveria, an ex-South African, to join the English cricket team on tour in 1968. D' Oliveria had initially been excluded from the team, but after demonstrations by the AAM and another player being found unfit, he was included. Vorster said that that the team had not been chosen on merit but because of the critics of apartheid, and that he was not prepared to accept such a cricket team.

In 1969 - 1970 a South African rugby team visited Britain, but the tour was disrupted by AAM demonstrations. The AAM had some success at convincing groups to break ties with South Africa, and another 1970 tour was cancelled. As sport isolation continued it became clear that South Africa would need to make more changes to her sport policy if she wanted to be accepted internationally. As this began to affect the players more and more stood up against apartheid in sport. In 1971 Vosrter differentiated between multiracial and multinational sport. Multiracial sport was still forbidden, but multinational, where people of different races compete against each other but in separate teams, would now be allowed at international level.

In 1977 the Commonwealth Countries, calling for an end to sporting ties with South Africa as long as apartheid continued, accepted the Gleneagles Agreement. In December 1977 and again in December 1985 the UN accepted resolutions Against Apartheid in Sport, and called for an end to segregated sport. This stopped links between the countries that signed the resolution and apartheid South Africa both on a national and individual basis. Money would not be given to a team that tried to maintain links with South Africa and action would be taken against such teams. Visas and entry documents would be denied to segregated sports teams trying to visit these countries. A Commission Against Apartheid Sports was also formed, and although some contact did continue, the UN continually looked at the policy and tried to stop the interaction.

Boycotts in the cultural field became important in the 1960s and AAMs started to campaign for the boycott. The boycott included music, plays and other forms of art. People were called on not to perform in South Africa or to allow their plays to be performed in South Africa unless it was before a non-segregated audience. In 1963 forty-five British playwrights signed a declaration in favour of the boycott and in 1964 Marlon Brando called for a similar declaration by actors and directors regarding all films. In 1965 the British Screenwriters Guild called for a ban on the distribution of films in South Africa and then more than sixty American cultural personalities signed a declaration against apartheid and professional association with South Africa. Various other declarations over the next years stopped the selling of films to South Africa and the selling of films containing certain British actors to South Africa. The performing of certain South African plays in America and Britain was also stopped.

These boycotts did not have the same negative effect on the South African economy as the consumer boycotts did, but did bring home to the average South African the international view of apartheid. These boycotts were disrupting everyday life, and were seen as embarrassing. Although the boycotts alone could not bring an end to apartheid, they were effective in isolating South Africa and in encouraging small changes to policy.

HISTORICAL CLOTH TRADE CEMENTS INDIA-AFRICA RELATIONS

African leaders at the India-Africa Forum Summit held from October 26-29 in New Dehli posed for a photo op decked out in Prime Minister Narendra Modi's signature kurta and pyjama with the lone exception of President Robert Mugabe who steadfastly remained in Western clothing.

The aim of the photo op was to stitch together, symbolically and actually, ties between the 54 invited African nations and India.

Cloth has been a tie that binds people from Africa and India together since at least the 13th century when Ethiopian rulers prized cotton and silk produced in India and imported huge amounts. In fact this cloth trade was the foundation of the slave trade between India and Africa that, by 1550, saw more than 10,000 Ethiopians leaving Ethiopia in exchange for Indian cloth on a yearly basis.

Because of this trade, India saw the rise of Ethiopian armies throughout the Deccan, in Hyderabad, and Gujarat most eloquently symbolised in the form of Malik Ambar, the Ethiopian who became Prime Minister of Ahmadnagar Sultanate in the 16th Century, and the Ethiopian naval might based in Janjira on the coast of western India.

In the 19th century, African consumer demands for high quality cloth had a transformational effect in India.

East African consumers were a fussy lot and they could afford it. By 1850, East Africans highly valued unbleached cotton from Salem, Massachusetts, in the United States imported through Zanzibar, known as *merikani*. However, with the civil war and abolition of slavery in the United States in 1865, the textile industry of Salem was destroyed.

Bombay textile industry filled the vacuum and Zanzibar became Bombay's biggest market. East African demand for textiles changed Bombay's economy making it India's most important port for foreign trade at the turn of the 20th century.

Around the same time, a new fashion came up in Mombasa — the creation of the *leso* or *kanga*. This patterned cloth was originally produced through block prints in Mombasa or Zanzibar on *merikani* cloth but soon was printed and sold out of Bombay. Today, *kangas* sold in East Africa are still often printed in India although mainly designed in East Africa. The *kanga* has for nearly 150 years sustained a market of Indian textile produced specifically for East Africa.

Symbolic power of clothing

In the 1960s, many African leaders used attire to make statements about how they represented their newly independent nations, not unlike Gandhi's clothing statements at India's independence.

The leaders had to both reject (culturally) and appropriate (symbolically) western dress while at the same time signify they represent the whole of their diverse countries rather than just the part from which they came. Thus, President Jomo Kenyatta wore, along with his western suit to symbolise equal power to those he displaced, a beaded Luo cap to draw in his most threatening rivals and carried a Maasai fly-whisk to include others.

President Muammar Gaddafi of Libya outdid almost every African leader in sartorial statements. Once he rejected Arab nationalism for African nationalism — he chose to wear clothing that symbolised this rejection and alliance. He indicated unity with other African nations, usually in the style of West African *agbada*, or with the outline of Africa repeatedly printed onto the fabric of his clothing.

One fashion, a slim long shirt with short round collars and long sleeves, became worn, and is still worn, across Africa. It is embellished differently in each country, sometimes plain with printed trim, or with embroidery or with a printed pattern. This shirt became a symbol of Africa in everyday men's clothing and a rejection of western attire. The best example of this style is President Goodluck Jonathan of Nigeria whose constant attire was this shirt in somber dark colours in the fashion of the Niger Delta.

On release from prison in 1994, Mandela would transform politician's attire in East and Southern Africa showing another kind of formal was possible with a shirt that became known as the "Madiba shirt." These Madiba shirts became popular after he was pictured wearing one at the dress rehearsal for the opening of Parliament in 1994. This informal formal shirt ushered in a trend in symbolic dressing of the new millennium — politician shirts. While symbolising Africa, many of the prints of the shirts are Indonesian demonstrating another Indian Ocean connection that has been domesticated in Africa.

Today, in the middle of the growing disparities across the continent, many African Leaders do not even attempt the pretense of looking one with the people and have largely, in this decade, opted for the very well tailored and expensive western suit and all its associated trappings of power.

India-Africa Forum Summit

African leaders, not only familiar with Indian clothing and material but well cognizant of the power of symbolic dress, might pause to wonder why this particular display of cordiality and unity in a photo op and why now? The third India Africa Forum Summit is unique in that all 54 African countries were invited to attend while less than 15 attended any of the prior two summits, and then only as representatives of the African Union. This can be seen as an indication of Africa's increased importance to India and the increasing importance of Indian Ocean trade and connections more generally.

However, it is also an interesting moment where the rising power of China in the Indian Ocean region and the rising close ties of China to Africa have made many other areas of the world, including the United States and the European Union, suddenly pay more attention to Africa. The photo op might signal a long history of trade, transformation and connections between Africa and India but it might also be a symbolic attempt to hold onto that history against the growing influence of China.

ZAMBIA - INDIA RELATIONS

Political: The leaders of Zambian freedom struggle, such as Dr. Kenneth Kaunda, drew inspiration from India's struggle for freedom, particularly from Mahatma Gandhi. While India gave support to the economic and technical development of Zambia, the latter reciprocated by supporting India on issues of importance to it, such as India's nuclear tests in 1998, terrorism, the issue of J&K and India's admission as a Permanent Member in the expanded UN Security Council.

High level visits: During his stay in power, Dr. Kenneth Kaunda paid more than ten visits to India, beginning 1967. From the Indian side Smt. Indira Gandhi, paid three visits to Zambia in 1964 (as Information & Broadcasting Minister), and in 1970 and 1976 as Prime Minister. Presidents V.V. Giri and Sanjiva Reddy visited Zambia in 1974 and 1981 respectively followed by Prime Minister Rajiv Gandhi in 1986 and President Venkataraman in 1989. President Chiluba paid a state visit to India in October 1993.

Late President Mwanawasa paid a state visit to India from April 20-25, 2003. Thereafter, several high level visits have taken place from Zambia, which include: Energy Minister George Mpombo in March 2005 to attend the CII Conclave on "India-Africa Project Partnership"; Finance Minister Ng'andu Mgande in September 2005 for the Joint Permanent Commission meeting in New Delhi; visit of the First Lady, Mrs. Maureen Mwanawasa to India from October 8-15, 2005 under ICCR's Distinguished Visitors' Programme; Agriculture Minister Mundia Sikatana visited India in March 2006; Lt Gen I.S.A. Chisuzi, Army Commander in May 2006 and the Zambian Parliamentary Delegation led by Speaker of National Assembly in September, 2007 to attend 53rd Commonwealth Parliamentary Conference. In 2008, Mr. Felix Mutati, Zambia's Commerce, Trade & Industry Minister visited

Delhi to participate in CII's India Africa Conclave, on March 19-21,2008 and again on 17th September, 2008 on way to China. President Rupiah Banda, then in capacity of Vice President, visited India from 4-9th April, 2008, to participate in India Africa Forum summit.

The India Africa Forum summit in April, 2008 has given a new thrust to India's engagement with Africa with increase in existing credit lines to Africa from US$ 2.15 billion to US$ 5.4 billion till 2012; duty free access to 85% of India's total tariff lines as well as preferential duty access to 9% of India's total tariff lines by Africa's 33 LDCs; grant of US$ 500 million to Africa in next 5-6 years and; increase in ITEC training slots from 1100 to 1600 a year to African countries. The Second India Africa Forum Summit (IAFS-II) held in Addis Ababa in May 2011 built upon the foundations of the historical relationship that existed between India and Africa, and designed a new architecture for a structured engagement, interaction and cooperation between India and our African partners in the 21st century. The Summit celebrated our friendship and renewed our commitment to Africa. At the Summit, Prime Minister Manmohan Singh said: "the India-Africa partnership rests on three pillars of capacity building and skill transfer, trade and infrastructure development". Under the decisions of the IAFS, three institutions viz. a Human Settlement Centre, an Entrepreneurship Development Institute and a Cluster of Biomass Gassifier Systems are proposed to be established in Zambia.

In recent years from Indian side, the Speaker of Lok Sabha, Shri Manohar Joshi paid an official visit to Zambia with a 7-member Parliamentary delegation from February 9-13, 2003. During the visit, then Zambian President Levy P. Mwanawasa publicly assured our Speaker on February 13, 2003 that Zambia would support India in her admission as a Permanent Member of the expanded UN Security Council and on the terrorism issue. Smt. Shashi Tripathi, Secretary (West), Ministry of External Affairs paid an official visit to Zambia from February 27-March 1, 2005 for Foreign Office Consultations. During this visit, India and Zambia signed an agreement to institutionalize Annual Foreign Office Consultations. Shri. Suresh Reddy, Speaker Andhra Pradesh

Assembly, visited Zambia in January, 2007. Hon'ble Vice President of India, Shri M. Hamid Ansari, paid an Official visit to Zambia from 5-7 January, 2010. During the visit, Hon'ble Vice President announced a new line of credit of US$75 million for developmental projects in Zambia and a grant of US$5 million for projects in health, education and social sectors. A Loan Agreement between EXIM Bank of India and the Zambian Ministry of Finance and National Planning was signed to extend to Zambia a US$50 million line of credit for the Itezhi Tezhi hydropower project in which TATA and ZESCO are joint venture partners.

Ministerial meeting of LDCs in New Delhi: Hon. Fashion Phiri, Deputy Minister of Foreign Affairs, represented Zambia at the Ministerial Meeting of LDCs in New Delhi from 18-19 February 2011. Highlight of this Conference was showcasing by India of its own national instruments of mutually beneficial cooperation that are in the forefront of assisting the LDCs – (i) ITEC, (ii) Duty Free, Quota Free (DFQF) regime for LDC's exports to India, (iii) E-connectivity Project; and (iv) Government of India's credit line Programme.

Cooperation in Defence field: Several Zambian defence chiefs and about 300 other defence officers have been trained in the Indian defence institutions. Several Indian army and air force training teams were deputed to Zambia in the 1970s and 1980s for training of the Zambian Armed Forces. India had deputed, since 1994, a Military Advisory Team comprising four officers (reduced to three officers in 2008) in Defence Services Command and Staff College in Zambia. This deputation came to an end with the departure of the team in March 2010. In 2006-07, India gave ten training slots, and in 2007-08, seven slots to the Zambian Armed Forces, under the ITEC programme. In 2008-09 two slots were utilized including one course at DSSC, Wellington. In 2009-10 seven slots were utilized and in 2010-11 India offered 16 training slots out of which 9 were utilized. The recent visits by Indian side to Zambia include that of Maj. Gen. R.P.S. Malhan, ADG (Staff Duties) 31st August- 2nd September, 2006; Lt. Gen Susheel Gupta, DCOAS (IS&T) 15-17th March 2007; Major General Vinay Bhatnagar, DG (Staff Duties) 28th November- 1st December, 2007; Lt. Gen SPS Dhillon, Deputy Chief of Army Staff (IS&T) (March

18- 21, 2009); National Defence College (NDC) delegation from 10-15 May, 2009 and; Maj.Gen Chander Prakash, Additional Director General (Staff Duties) from 3-6 June, 2009.

Economic cooperation: Over the years, India has provided considerable economic assistance to Zambia. In 1979 and 1982, India extended government and EXIM Bank credits to Zambia totaling Rs. 25 crores. In 1989, India provided railway wagons costing about Rs.8 crores to Zambia under the Africa Fund. Approval of the GoI for the Zambian proposal for a LoC of US$50 million for setting up of pre-fabricated health posts in the rural areas of Zambia has been conveyed to the Government of Zambia in January 2012. Around 2400 civilian Zambians have been trained in India under ITEC in various disciplines so far. In February, 2008 India extended a grant of Rs. 1 crore for flood relief.

During President Mwanawasa's visit to India in April 2003, India extended a credit line of $ 10 million (out of which $ 8.5 million were utilized for purchase of Tata trucks and $1.5 million for procurement of vocational tool kits), grant assistance of US $ 100,000 for donation of anti-HIV/AIDs medicines and another grant of Rs. 25 million for donation of agricultural equipment to Zambia. India also waived off the inter-governmental credit amounting to about $ 3 million outstanding against Zambia. Similarly, it donated 10,000 tons of non-basmati rice to Zambia to alleviate the food shortage. During the visit the number of ITEC slots available to Zambia was increased from 30 to 50. This was further increased to 60 in 2007-08 and subsequent to India Africa Forum summit was further increased to 80 in 2008-09. 75 in 2009-10, 86 in 2010-11, and 91 in 2011-12.

Bilateral Trade: India's exports to Zambia are at US$132.27 million (2007-08), US$ 107.43 million (2008-09), US$ 88.34 (2009-2010) and India's imports from Zambia are at US$74.84 million (2007-08), US$ 208.40 million (2008-09) and US$102.67 (2009-10). India's export items include drug and pharmaceuticals, machinery and instruments, transport equipment, cotton yarn and fabrics, plastic, rubber, chemicals, and electronic goods. India's imports from Zambia include non-ferrous metals, ores (copper and cobalt), semi-precious stones and raw cotton. India and Zambia have set up a Joint Permanent Commission at the Ministerial level, its last meeting was held in New Delhi on September 9-10, 2005.

ITPO led the participation of Indian companies in the Zambian Agricultural and Commercial Show in Lusaka in August 2002-2003. Zambia has sent private sector led trade delegations to India to participate in trade fairs. CII Conclaves on India-Africa Partnership have been held in New Delhi, (March 2005); in Lusaka (April 24-25, 2006); in New Delhi (October 9 – 11, 2006); and again in New Delhi on March 19-21, 2008. An UNCTAD-EXIM Bank of India Investment Forum was held in Lusaka on 11-12th June, 2007 on ICT and pharmaceuticals. Subsequently, a CHEMEXCIL delegation visited Lusaka from 11-14th November, 2007 and took part in Buyer Seller Meet along with local chemical industry. A 25-member delegation of the Pharmaceuticals Export Promotion Council (PHARMEXCIL), representing 21 pharmaceutical companies visited Zambia from 3 to 6 August, 2009. A Buyer-Seller Meeting (BSM) was held on August 4, 2009 which was inaugurated by Zambia's Deputy minister of Commerce, Trade and Industry, Mr. Richard Taima. About 30 local companies participated in the BSM. Ms. Esnat Mwape, Director General, Pharmaceutical Regulatory Authority of Zambia and two representatives of pharmaceutical industry, Rakesh N. Shah, MD, Pharmnova Zambia Limited and M. Krishna Swamy, MD, Alliance Pharmaceuticals Ltd. participated in the Indo-Africa Pharma Business Meet held in Hyderabad from September 25-27, 2009 at the invitation of Pharmaceuticals Export Promotion Council.

More recently, there has been renewed interest in India for trade and investment with Zambia.

(i) An 18 member business delegation, which included government officials, participated in the 7th CII-EXIM Bank Conclave on India Africa Project Partnership 2011 held in New Delhi from March 27-29, 2011.

(ii) Zambian Government delegation visited India for seeking investments from India under the Public-Private Partnership (PPP) – Zambian government delegation visited India from July 29-August 5, 2010 with the objective of attracting investments from India through the (PPP) concept. The delegation included Deputy Minister of Finance and National Planning David Phiri and Deputy Minister of Commerce Trade and Industry Lwipa Puma. They visited Delhi and Mumbai. Around 30 Indian companies took advantage of the Public Private Partnership concept and entered into various investment portfolios. Deputy Minister of Finance and National Planning David Phiri met Secretary (West) in the Ministry of External Affairs.

(iii) An MoU was signed between Zambia International Trade and Investment Centre (ZITIC), Lusaka and Indo-African Chamber of Commerce & Industries (IACCI) for a working partnership on May 13, 2010, during the Africa Day Symposium organized by IACCI in Mumbai on May 13 & 14, 2010.

(iv) Pan African e-networking project : The e-networking project was completed by the TCIL – Patient End Location (PEL) Centre at University Teaching Hospital, Lusaka and was commissioned on November 05, 2009; Learning Centre at Mulungusi University, Kabwe on November 06, 2009; and VVIP Centre (video conferencing) at State House on November 17, 2009. The Pan-African e-Netowrk Project for Zambia was successfully inaugurated through Video Conferencing at the Mulungushi University in Kabwe on August 16, 2010. Zambian Minister of Communications and Transport, Hon. Professor Geoffrey Lungwangwa interacted with Hon'ble EAM at the Tele-education facility installed under the project at Mulungushi University in the town of Kabwe.

(v) An MoU was signed on October 5, 2009 in New Delhi between the Golden Valley Agricultural Research Trust (GART) of Zambia and the Indian Council for Agricultural Research (ICAR) for professional cooperation and collaboration in Agricultural Research and Education in the field of (a) exchange of scientists and technologists, (b) exchange of germplasma and breeding material (c) exchange of scientific literature information and methodology and (d) exchange of scientific equipment as available and required in the programme of common interest. A four member team from ICAR led by Secretary ICAR proposes to visit Zambia in the first week of June, 2011 to discuss technical programmes of interest of both the countries.

(vi) Hole in the Wall Computer Literacy Project - Under this programme HiWEL, Delhi (Hole in the Wall Education Limited) commissioned two Hole in the Wall learning stations in two schools (Vera Chiluba Basic & Ngwelele Basic School) in Lusaka on December 12, 2008. The expenditure of USD 60,000/- incurred on this project was wholly funded by India. The MoU was signed between GoI and GoZ on Hole – in - the - Wall Project on September 12, 2007.

(vii) An exhibition and seminar on low cost housing was organised by Building Materials and Technology promotion Council (BMTPC), Ministry of Housing & Urban Poverty Alleviation (HUPA), Govt. of India was in Lusaka on 9-10th April, 2008. In December 2010, a detailed questionnaire and a draft MoU was received from BMTPC seeking inputs from the Government of Zambia which was forwarded by the High Commission to Zambian Foreign Office with the request to identify the agency for the said project and also furnish its response on the MoU. A response from the Zambia side is awaited.

(viii) Health Minister, Kapembwa Simbao launched the Vision Care Appasamy Eye Hospital in Lusaka on 25th June, 2009 – a joint venture between Vision Care Centre of Zambia and Appasmy Associates of India. The Hospital provides both minor and major eye services locally.

Investments from India

(i) Phase-1 of the Konkola Deep Mining Project (KDMP) and the ultramodern Nchanga Smelter of the Konkola Copper Mines (KCM) were launched by President Rupiah Banda on April 20, 2010 at Chingola. KCM is a subsidiary of the

Vedanta Resources group (the parent company M/s Sterlite Industries in India). While Vedanta Resources is India-owned, they are registered in UK. M/s Vedanta Resources, had invested $ 48 million in 2004 in Konkola Copper Mine (KCM) to acquire a majority stake. With the launch of these two projects, KCM aims to reach the target of producing 500,000 tonnes of finished copper per annum by 2013. Their combined investment in Konkola Deep Water Copper Mining Project, Sulphuric Acid plant and new Smelter has touched US$2.2 billion. KCM's investment is expected to reach US$3 billion in the next three years.

(ii) RJ Corporation, an Indian firm, has pledged to invest US$30 million over the period of six years. The company would spend US$15 million on manufacturing plant for Pepsi in Phase I of the project. In Phase II, the firm would construct another plant for manufacturing fruit drinks at a cost of another US$15 million. President Rupiah Banda, laid the foundation of Pepsi Plant in Lusaka on January 17, 2000 and it started its bottling production in October 2010.

(iii) M/s Nava Bharat Singapore Limited, a subsidiary of Nava Bharat Ventures Ltd. Hyderabad, has purchased 65% equity shares in Mamba Colleries Ltd. Government of Zambia retains the remaining 35% shares through Zambia Consolidated Copper Mine Investment Holdings (ZCCM-IH). Nava Bharat will invest US$108 million in the recapitalization of Mamba Colleries and the installation of the new coal handling and washing plant. Nava Bharat would also develop a coal fired power plant of a minimum generating capacity of 270 megawatts using the low grade coal of Mamba Colleries.

(iv) Taurian Manganese Ltd, one of the group of companies of Dharni Sampada Pvt. Ltd. In India, has invested about US$20 million in 2010 in manganese mining and plans to invest another US$300 million in construction of a manganese processing plant in Serenje district in Central Province. It will be one of the biggest manganese processing plants in Africa.

(v) Bharti Airtel launched its new brand, Airtel Zambia, in November 2010. The new brand comes with a promise to meet the emerging needs of customers with innovative, affordable and relevant solutions to empower consumers and will provide low tariffs and roll out deep in rural areas and bridge the digital divide.

(vi) The other major Indian investments include a joint venture – Indo-Zambia Bank - with 60% equity held by three Indian public sector banks – Bank of India, Bank of Baroda and Central Bank of India – and remaining by the Zambian government.

(vii) EXIM Bank of India has a 34% share in Development Bank of Zambia after a debt settlement agreement with the Government of Zambia, who owed $18.8 million to EXIM Bank. Out of $18.8 million, $9.4 million was written off, $8 million paid by the Government of Zambia in six installments to EXIM Bank and $1.4 million invested in DBZ and EXIM Bank given 34% equity. Now the EXIM Bank's equity stands at 20%, due to increase in the equity subscribed/paid up by other institutions.

(viii) An agreement was signed by EXIM Bank of India and Indo-Zambia Bank (IZB) in Lusaka under which the former would provide a credit of US$5 million to IZB to be utilized for import of capital goods from India.

Investments of TATA:

a) TATA invested about $8 million in renovation of a five-star hotel called Taj Pamodzi, which is being managed by the Taj Hotels group.

b) In October, 2006 TATA set up a vehicle & bicycle assembly plant in Ndola with investment of US$ 10 million.

c) Zambia Electricity Supply Company (ZESCO) and TATA Africa Holdings have formed a joint venture company called Itezhi Tezhi Power Corporation Limited (ITPC) to carry out Itezhi-Tezhi ($200 million) power project. India has provided a Line of Credit (LOC) of US$ 50 million to Government of Zambia for this power project.

d) TATA is also collaborating with the Copperbelt Energy Corporation (CEC) for 36 MW power project in the Copperbelt.

e) TATA acquired a leather tannery from Zambia Development Agency (ZDA) in February 2009 for US$1.164 million at Kabwe. The company plans to upgrade the tannery with further investment of about US$4 million in the next five years. The Tannery has been operational for 2 years and is making steady progress. The export has doubled in the year 2010-11 and the company is taking aggressive steps to double its production in the year 2011-12 and upgrading the facility to become one of the best in the industry which will result in further increase in investment. The company has invested about $100,000 in the water effluent system and to further equip and upgrade the tannery and are also investing in the samming and splitting machinery which is worth nearly $150,000.

f) Hindustan Syringes and Medical Devices Limited (HMD), one of the largest producers of single use syringes in India, entered into a partnership with TATA-Zambia to promote prevention of Injection safety and Infection prevention by the use of Auto-Disable (AD) Syringes in Zambia. TATA-Zambia have donated 10,000 AD syringes to Ministry of Health to do a field trial as the government is working towards making a policy decision on the use of AD syringes. Tata Consultancy Engineering (TCE) is providing consultancy services to ZESCO for the Kariba North Power Plant.

Many persons of Indian Origin, who settled down in Zambia many years back, have taken local nationality and have invested in precious stones mining, agriculture, horticulture and chemicals. President Rupiah Banda on 11thMarch, 2009 inaugurated a US$10 million mobile phone assembly plant in Lusaka of Melcome Group – a company owned by a local Person of Indian Origin. This investment was under Japan's "Triangle of Hope" initiative, which promoted economic development of third world countries. Trade Kings, a company owned by Zambian Indians, have invested over

US$125 million and have set up the first ever integrated steel plant in the country at Kafue.

Bilateral Agreements

(i) On 17th August, 2007, India and Zambia successfully concluded review of Convention between India and Zambia for Avoidance of Double Taxation. The draft Agreement has been approved by both sides and is awaiting to be signed.

(ii) Keeping in view the ever growing economic and commercial exchanges between India and Zambia, the increase in volume of Indian investments in Zambia and the continuing efforts by both the countries to further increase these exchanges, India's Ministry of Finance has proposed to conclude the Bilateral Investment Promotion and Protection Agreement (BIPPA) with Zambia. It has been pending with Zambia since February 2005. Certain amendments proposed by us were under consideration by the Zambian side. However, due to changes/inclusion of articles in the Draft model text necessitated by changes in the global business environment, another Draft model Agreement was submitted by GoZ in May 2008. Another model text was sent to GoZ in December 2010 which is reportedly pending with the Zambian Ministry of Commerce, Trade and Industry for their comments.

(iii) Zambian Minister of Communications and Transport, Prof. Geoffery Lungwangwa attended the 4th Connecting Rural Communities Asia Forum 2011 held in Jaipur in January 2011. During the visit he had meeting with our Ministers of Communications & IT and Transport and also with the Chairman of Telecom Regulatory Authority of India. During the meetings, it was agreed to establish the following MoUs: (a) An MoU between the Ministry of Communications & IT, (GoI) and the Ministry of Communications & Transport (GoZ) for collaboration in e-governance roll out, to share experience and best practices as well as training; (b) An MoU between Telecom Regulatory Authority of India and the Ministry of

Communications & Transport (GoZ). Now Zambian Foreign Office requested us through a Note Verbale to inform the appropriate Indian authorities to initiate these MoUs for the consideration of the Government of Zambia. The request was forwarded to MEA.

(iv) The two countries signed an Agreement for Cooperation in Trade and an MOU for Cooperation in Agriculture on April 21, 2003 during the visit of the Zambian President to India. The two countries signed on February 28, 2005 a Protocol for Institutionalization of the Annual Foreign Office Consultations during the visit of Secretary (West), MEA to Zambia. No further meeting has taken place.

UNCTAD : A high level meeting on Trade Capacity Building and Competition Policy for African LDCs, under the theme "Competitiveness : Key to economic prosperity" was held in Lusaka on May 10-12, 2010 with the support of UNCTAD, Zambian Ministry of Commerce, Trade and Industry and Indian Ministry of Commerce and Industry. The Indian Delegation made presentations on DFTP, India's aid for trade profile including technical cooperation and other capacity building programmes, India's business perspective vis-à-vis LDCs and UNCTAD India Case Study with relevance to African LDCs.

Duty Free Tariff Preference Scheme (DFTP) - Zambian Minister for Commerce, Trade and Industry signed the Letter of Intent to utilize India's Duty Free Tariff Preference Scheme (DFTP) in May 2010. With the signing of this Letter and on completion of documentation, Zambian products will be able to access up to 94 % of the Indian market under this Scheme.

2

History of Africa

The history of Africa begins with the emergence of *Homo sapiens* in East Africa, and continues into the present as a patchwork of diverse and politically developing nation states. The recorded history of early civilization arose in Egypt, and later in Nubia, the Sahel, the Maghreb and the Horn of Africa.

During the Middle Ages, Islam spread through the regions. Crossing the Maghreb and the Sahel, a major centre of Muslim culture was Timbuktu. Some notable pre-colonial states and societies in Africa include the Nok culture, Mali Empire, Ashanti Empire, Kingdom of Mapungubwe, Kingdom of Sine, Kingdom of Sennar, Kingdom of Saloum, Kingdom of Baol, Kingdom of Zimbabwe, Kingdom of Kongo, Ancient Carthage, Numidia, Mauretania, the Aksumite Empire, the Ajuran Sultanate and the Adal Sultanate.

From the late 15th century, Europeans and Arabs transported enslaved West, Central and South Africaoverseas in the African slave trade. European colonization of Africa developed rapidly in the Scramble for Africa of the late 19th and early 20th centuries. It is widely believed that Africa had up to 10,000 different states and autonomous groups with distinct languages and customs before it was colonized. Following struggles for independence in many parts of the continent, as well as a weakened Europe after the Second World War, decolonization took place.

Africa's history has been challenging for researchers in the field of African studies because of the scarcity of written sources in large parts of the continent. Scholarly techniques such as the recording of oral history, historical linguistics, archaeology and genetics have been crucial.

Prehistory

Paleolithic

The first known hominids evolved in Africa. According to paleontology, the early hominids' skull anatomy was similar to that of the gorilla and chimpanzee, great apes that also evolved in Africa, but the hominids had adopted a bipedal locomotion and freed their hands. This gave them a crucial advantage, enabling them to live in both forested areas and on the open savanna at a time when Africa was drying up and the savanna was encroaching on forested areas. This occurred 10 to 5 million years ago.

By 3 million years ago, several australopithecine hominid species had developed throughout southern, eastern and central Africa. They were tool users, and makers of tools. They scavenged for meat and were omnivores.

By approximately 2.3 million years ago, primitive stone tools were first used to scavenge kills made by other predators and to harvest carrion and marrow from their bones. In hunting, *Homo habilis* was probably not capable of competing with large predators and was still more prey than hunter. *H. habilis* probably did steal eggs from nests and may have been able to catch small game and weakened larger prey (cubs and older animals). The tools were classed as Oldowan.

Around 1.8 million years ago, *Homo ergaster* first appeared in the fossil record in Africa. From *Homo ergaster, Homo erectus* evolved 1.5 million years ago. Some of the earlier representatives of this species were still fairly small-brained and used primitive stone tools, much like *H. habilis*. The brain later grew in size, and *H. erectus* eventually developed a more complex stone tool technology called the Acheulean. Possibly the first hunters, *H. erectus* mastered the art of making fire and was the first hominid to leave Africa, colonizing most of the Old World and perhaps later giving rise to *Homo floresiensis*. Although some recent writers suggest that *Homo georgicus* was the first and most primitive hominid ever to live outside Africa, many scientists consider *H. georgicus* to be an early and primitive member of the *H. erectus* species. The fossil record shows *Homo sapiens* living in southern and eastern Africa at least 100,000 and possibly 150,000 years ago. Around 40,000 years ago, the species' expansion out of Africa launched the colonization of the planet by modern human beings. By 10,000 BCE, *Homo sapiens* had spread to all corners of the old world. Their migration is traced by linguistic, cultural and genetic evidence. The earliest physical evidence of astronomical activity appears to be a lunar calendar found on the Ishango bone dated to between 23,000 and 18,000 BC.

Emergence of agriculture

Around 16,000 BCE, from the Red Sea hills to the northern Ethiopian Highlands, nuts, grasses and tubers were being collected for food. By 13,000 to 11,000 BCE, people began collecting wild grains. This spread to Western Asia, which domesticated its wild grains, wheat and barley. Between 10,000 and 8000 BCE, northeast Africa was cultivating wheat and barley and raising sheep and cattle from southwest Asia. A wet climatic phase in Africa turned the Ethiopian Highlands into a mountain forest. Omotic speakers domesticated enset around 6500–5500 BCE. Around 7000 BCE, the settlers of the Ethiopian highlands domesticated donkeys, and by 4000 BCE domesticated donkeys had spread to southwest Asia. Cushitic speakers, partially turning away from cattle herding, domesticated teff and finger millet between 5500 and 3500 BCE.

In the steppes and savannahs of the Sahara and Sahel in Northern West Africa, the Nilo-Saharan speakers and Mandé peoples started to collect and domesticate wild millet, African rice and sorghum between 8000 and 6000 BCE. Later, gourds, watermelons, castor beans, and cotton were also collected and domesticated. The people started capturing wild cattle and holding them in circular thorn hedges, resulting in domestication. They also started making pottery and built stone settlements. Fishing, using bone-tipped harpoons, became a major activity in the numerous streams and lakes formed from the increased rains.

In West Africa, the wet phase ushered in expanding rainforest and wooded savannah from Senegal to Cameroon. Between 9000 and 5000 BCE, Niger–Congo speakers domesticated the oil palm and raffia palm. Two seed plants, black-eyed peas and voandzeia (African groundnuts), were domesticated, followed by okra and kola nuts. Since most of the plants grew in the forest, the Niger–Congo speakers invented polished stone axes for clearing forest.

Most of southern Africa was occupied by pygmy peoples and Khoisan who engaged in hunting and gathering. Some of the oldest rock art was produced by them.

Just prior to Saharan desertification, the communities that developed south of Egypt in what is now Sudan were full participants in the Neolithic revolution and lived a settled to semi-nomadic lifestyle, with domesticated plants and animals. It has been suggested that megaliths found at Nabta Playa are examples of the world's first known archaeoastro nomical devices, predating Stonehenge by some 1,000 years. The sociocultural complexity observed at Nabta Playa and expressed by different levels of authority within the society there has been suggested as forming the basis for the structure of both the Neolithic society at Nabta and the Old Kingdom of Egypt. By 5000 BCE, Africa entered a dry phase, and the climate of the Sahara region gradually became drier. The population trekked out of the Sahara region in all directions, including towards the Nile Valley below the Second Cataract, where they made permanent or semipermanent settlements. A major climatic recession occurred, lessening the heavy and persistent rains in central and eastern Africa. Since then, dry conditions have prevailed in eastern Africa.

Metallurgy

The first metals to be smelted in Africa were lead, copper, and bronze in the fourth millennium BCE.

Copper was smelted in Egypt during the predynastic period, and bronze came into use not long after 3000 BCE at the latest in Egypt and Nubia. Nubia was a major source of copper as well asgold. The use of gold and silver in Egypt dates back to the predynastic period.

In the Aïr Mountains, present-day Niger, copper was smelted independently of developments in the Nile valley between 3000 and 2500 BCE. The process used was unique to the region, indicating that it was not brought from outside the region; it became more mature by about 1500 BCE.

By the 1st millennium BCE, iron working had been introduced in northwestern Africa, Egypt, and Nubia. In 670 BC, Nubians were pushed out of Egypt by Assyrians using iron weapons, after which the use of iron in the Nile valley became widespread.

The theory of iron spreading to Sub-Saharan Africa via the Nubian city of Meroe is no longer widely accepted. Metalworking in West Africa has been dated as early as 2500 BCE at Egaro west of the Termit in Niger, and iron working was practiced there by 1500 BCE. In Central Africa, there is evidence that Iron working may have been practiced as early as the 3rd millennium BCE. Iron smelting was developed in the area between Lake Chad and the African Great Lakes between 1000 and 600 BCE, long before it reached Egypt. Before 500 BCE, the Nok culture in the Jos Plateau was already smelting iron.

Antiquity

The ancient history of North Africa is inextricably linked to that of the Ancient Near East. This is particularly true of Ancient Egypt and Nubia. In the Horn of Africa the Kingdom of Aksum ruled modern-day Eritrea, northern Ethiopia and the coastal area of the western part of the Arabian Peninsula. The Ancient Egyptians established ties with the Land of Punt in 2350 BC. Punt was a trade partner of Ancient Egypt and it is believed that it was located in modern-day Somalia, Djibouti or Eritrea. Phoenician cities such as Carthage were part of the Mediterranean Iron Age and classical antiquity. Sub-Saharan Africa developed more or less independently in those times.

Ancient Egypt

After the desertification of the Sahara, settlement became concentrated in the Nile Valley, where numerous sacral chiefdoms appeared. The regions with the largest population pressure were in the delta region of Lower Egypt, in Upper Egypt, and also along the second and third cataracts of the Dongola reach of the Nile in Nubia. This population pressure and growth was brought about by the cultivation of southwest Asian crops, including wheat and barley, and the raising of sheep, goats, and cattle. Population growth led to competition for farm land and the need to regulate farming. Regulation was established by the formation of bureaucracies among sacral chiefdoms. The first and most powerful of the chiefdoms was Ta-Seti, founded around 3500 BCE. The idea of sacral chiefdom spread throughout upper and lower Egypt.

Later consolidation of the chiefdoms into broader political entities began to occur in upper and lower Egypt, culminating into the unification of Egypt into one political entity by Narmer (Menes) in 3100 BCE. Instead of being viewed as a sacral chief, he became a divine king. The henotheism, or worship of a single god within a polytheistic system, practiced in the sacral chiefdoms along upper and lower Egypt, became the polytheistic religion of ancient Egypt. Bureaucracies became more centralized under the pharaohs, run by viziers, governors, tax collectors, generals, artists, and technicians. They engaged in tax collecting, organizing of labor for major public works, and building irrigation systems, pyramids, temples, and canals. During the Fourth Dynasty (2620-2480 BCE), long distance trade was developed, with the Levant for timber, with Nubia for gold and skins, with Punt for frankincense, and also with the western Libyan territories. For most of the Old Kingdom, Egypt developed her fundamental systems, institutions and culture, always through the central bureaucracy and by the divinity of the Pharaoh.

After the fourth millennium BCE, Egypt started to extend direct military and political control over her southern and western neighbours. By 2200 BCE, the Old Kingdom's stability was undermined by rivalry among the governors of the nomes who challenged the power of pharaohs and by invasions of Asiatics into the delta. The First Intermediate Period had begun, a time of political division and uncertainty.

By 2130, the period of stagnation was ended by Mentuhotep, the first Pharaoh of the Eleventh Dynasty, and the emergence of the Middle Kingdom. Pyramid building resumed, long-distance trade re-emerged, and the centre of power moved from Memphis to Thebes. Connections with the southern regions of Kush, Wawat and Irthet at the second cataract were made stronger. Then came the Second Intermediate Period, with the invasion of the Hyksos on horse-drawn chariots and utilizing bronze weapons, a technology heretofore unseen in Egypt. Horse-drawn chariots soon spread to the west in the inhabitable Sahara and North Africa. The Hyksos failed to hold on to their Egyptian territories and were absorbed by Egyptian society. This eventually led to one of Egypt's most powerful phases, the New Kingdom (1580–1080 BCE), with the Eighteenth Dynasty. Egypt became a superpower controlling Nubia and Judea while exerting political influence on the Libyans to the West and on the Mediterranean.

As before, the New Kingdom ended with invasion from the west by Libyan princes, leading to the Third Intermediate Period. Beginning with Shoshenq I, the Twenty-second Dynasty was established. It ruled for two centuries.

To the south, Nubian independence and strength was being reasserted. This reassertion led to the conquest of Egypt by Nubia, begun by Kashta and completed by Piye (Pianhky, 751–730 BCE) and Shabaka (716–695 BCE). This was the birth of the Twenty-fifth Dynasty of Egypt. The Nubians tried to re-establish Egyptian traditions and customs. They ruled Egypt for a hundred years. This was ended by an Assyrian invasion, with Taharqa experiencing the full might of Assyrian iron weapons. The Nubian pharaoh Tantamani was the last of the Twenty-fifth dynasty.

When the Assyrians and Nubians left, a new Twenty-sixth Dynasty emerged from Sais. It lasted until 525 BCE, when Egypt was invaded by the Persians. Unlike the Assyrians, the Persians stayed. In 332, Egypt was conquered by Alexander the Great. This was the beginning of the Ptolemaic dynasty, which ended with Roman conquest in 30 BCE. Pharaonic Egypt had come to an end.

Nubia

Around 3500 BCE, one of the first sacral kingdoms to arise in the Nile was Ta-Seti, located in northern Nubia. Ta-Seti was a powerful sacral kingdom in the Nile Valley at the 1st and 2nd cataracts that exerted an influence over nearby chiefdoms. Based on its pictorial representation, it claimed to have ruled over Upper Egypt. Ta-Seti traded as far as Syro-Palestine, as well as with Egypt. Ta-Seti exported gold, copper, ostrich feathers, ebony and ivory to the Old Kingdom. By the 32nd century BCE, Ta-Seti was in decline. After the unification of Egypt by Narmer in 3100 BCE, Ta-Seti was invaded by the Pharaoh Hor-Aha of the First Dynasty, destroying the final remnants of the kingdom. Ta-Seti is affiliated with A-Group culture known to archaeology.

Small sacral kingdoms continued to dot the Nubian portion of the Nile for centuries after 3000 BCE. Around the latter part of the third millennium, there was further consolidation of the sacral kingdoms. Two kingdoms in particular emerged: the Sai kingdom, immediately south of Egypt, and Kingdom of Kerma at the third cataract. Sometime around the 18th century BCE, the Kingdom of Kerma conquered the Kingdom of Sai, becoming a serious rival to Egypt. Kerma occupied a territory from the first cataract to the confluences of the Blue Nile, White Nile, and Atbarah River. About 1575 to 1550 BCE, during the latter part of the Seventeenth Dynasty, the Kingdom of Kerma invaded Egypt. The Kingdom of Kerma allied itself with the Hyksos invasion of Egypt.

Egypt eventually re-energized under the Eighteenth Dynasty and conquered the Kingdom of Kerma or Kush, ruling it for almost 500 years. The Kushites were Egyptianized during this period. By 1100 BCE, the Egyptians had withdrawn from Kush. The region regained independence and reasserted its culture. Kush built a new religion around Amun and made Napata its spiritual centre. In 730 BCE, the Kingdom of Kush invaded Egypt, taking over Thebes and beginning the Nubian Empire. The empire extended from Palestine to the confluences of the Blue Nile, the White Nile, and River Atbara.

In 760 BCE, the Kushites were expelled from Egypt by iron-wielding Assyrians. Later, the administrative capital was moved from Napata to Meröe, developing into a new Nubian culture. Initially Meroites were highly Egyptianized, but they subsequently began to take on distinctive features. Nubia became a centre of iron-making and cotton cloth manufacturing. Egyptian writing was replaced by the Meroitic alphabet. The lion god Apedemak was added to the Egyptian pantheon of gods. Trade links to the Red Sea increased, linking Nubia with Mediterranean Greece. Its architecture and art became more unique, with pictures of lions, ostriches, giraffes, and elephants. Eventually with the rise of Aksum,

Nubia's trade links were broken and it suffered environmental degradation from the tree cutting required for iron production. In 350 CE, the Aksumite king Ezana brought Meröe to an end.

Carthage

The Egyptians referred to the people west of the Nile, ancestral to the Berbers, as Libyans. The Libyans were agriculturalists like the Mauri of Morocco and the Numidians of central and eastern Algeria and Tunis. They were also nomadic, having the horse, and occupied the arid pastures and desert, like the Gaetuli. Berber desert nomads were typically in conflict with Berber coastal agriculturalists.

The Phoenicians were seamen of the Mediterranean. They were in constant search for valuable metals like copper, gold, tin, and lead. Soon they began to populate the North African coast with settlements, trading and mixing with the native Berber population. In 814 BCE, Phoenicians from Tyre established the city of Carthage. By 600 BCE, Carthage had become a major trading entity and power in the Mediterranean, largely through trade with tropical Africa. Carthage's prosperity fostered the growth of the Berber kingdoms, Numidia and Mauretania. Around 500 BCE, Carthage provided a strong impetus for trade with sub-Saharan Africa. Berber middlemen, who had maintained contacts with sub-Saharan Africa since the desert had desiccated, utilized pack animals to transfer products from oasis to oasis. Danger lurked from the Garamantes of Fez, who raided caravans. Salt and metal goods were traded for gold, slaves, beads, and ivory.

The Carthaginians were rivals to the Greeks and Romans. Carthage fought three wars with Rome: the First Punic War (264 to 241 BCE), over Sicily; the Second Punic War (218 to 201 BCE), in which Hannibal invaded Europe; and the Third Punic War (149 to 146 BCE). Carthage lost the first two wars, and in the third it was destroyed, becoming the Roman province of Africa, with the Berber Kingdom of Numidia assisting Rome. The Roman province of Africa became a major agricultural supplier of wheat, olives, and olive oil to imperial Rome via exorbitant taxation. Two centuries later, Rome brought the Berber kingdoms of Numidia and Mauretania under its authority. In the 420s CE, Vandals invaded

North Africa and Rome lost her territories. The Berber kingdoms subsequently regained their independence.

Christianity gained a foothold in Africa at Alexandria in the 1st century CE and spread to northwest Africa. By 313 CE, with the Edict of Milan, all of Roman North Africa was Christian. Egyptians adopted Monophysite Christianity and formed the independent Coptic Church. Berbers adopted Donatist Christianity. Both groups refused to accept the authority of the Roman Catholic Church.

Role of the Berbers

As Carthaginian power grew; its impact on the indigenous population increased dramatically. Berber civilization was already at a stage in which agriculture, manufacturing, trade, and political organization supported several states. Trade links between Carthage and the Berbers in the interior grew, but territorial expansion also resulted in the enslavement or military recruitment of some Berbers and in the extraction of tribute from others. By the early 4th century BC, Berbers formed one of the largest element, with Gauls, of the Carthaginian army. In the Revolt of the Mercenaries, Berber soldiers participated from 241 to 238 BC after being unpaid following the defeat of Carthage in the First Punic War. Berbers succeeded in obtaining control of much of Carthage's North African territory, and they minted coins bearing the name Libyan, used in Greek to describe natives of North Africa. The Carthaginian state declined because of successive defeats by the Romans in the Punic Wars; in 146 BC the city of Carthage was destroyed. As Carthaginian power waned, the influence of Berber leaders in the hinterland grew. By the 2nd century BC, several large but loosely administered Berber kingdoms had emerged. Two of them were established in Numidia, behind the coastal areas controlled by Carthage. West of Numidia lay Mauretania, which extended across the Moulouya River in Morocco to the Atlantic Ocean. The high point of Berber civilization, unequaled until the coming of the Almohads and Almoravids more than a millennium later, was reached during the reign of Masinissa in the 2nd century BC. After Masinissa's death in 148 BC, the Berber kingdoms were divided and reunited several times. Masinissa's line survived until AD 24, when the remaining Berber territory was annexed to the Roman Empire.

Somalia

The ancestors of the Somali people were an important link in the Horn of Africa connecting the region's commerce with the rest of the ancient world. Somali sailors and merchants were the main suppliers of frankincense, myrrh and spices, all of which were valuable luxuries to the Ancient Egyptians, Phoenicians, Mycenaeans and Babylonians.

In the classical era, several flourishing Somali city-states such as Opone, Mosylon, Cape Guardafui, and Malao competed with the Sabaeans, Parthians and Axumites for the rich Indo-Greco-Roman trade.

Roman North Africa

Increases in urbanization and in the area under cultivation during Roman rule caused wholesale dislocations of the Berber society, forcing nomad tribes to settle or to move from their traditional rangelands. Sedentary tribes lost their autonomy and connection with the land. Berber opposition to the Roman presence was nearly constant. The Roman emperor Trajan established a frontier in the south by encircling the Aurès and Nemencha mountains and building a line of forts from Vescera (modern Biskra) to Ad Majores (Hennchir Besseriani, southeast of Biskra). The defensive line extended at least as far as Castellum Dimmidi (modern Messaâd, southwest of Biskra), Roman Algeria's southernmost fort. Romans settled and developed the area around Sitifis (modern Sétif) in the 2nd century, but farther west the influence of Rome did not extend beyond the coast and principal military roads until much later.

The Roman military presence of North Africa remained relatively small, consisting of about 28,000 troops and auxiliaries in Numidia and the two Mauretanian provinces. Starting in the 2nd century AD, these garrisons were manned mostly by local inhabitants.

Aside from Carthage, urbanization in North Africa came in part with the establishment of settlements of veterans under the

Roman emperors Claudius (reigned 41-54), Nerva (96-98), and Trajan (98-117). In Algeria such settlements included Tipasa, Cuicul or Curculum (modern Djemila, northeast of Sétif), Thamugadi (modern Timgad, southeast of Sétif), and Sitifis (modern Sétif). The prosperity of most towns depended on agriculture. Called the "granary of the empire", North Africa became one of the largest exporters of grain in the empire, shipping to the provinces which did not produce cereals, like Italy and Greece. Other crops included fruit, figs, grapes, and beans. By the 2nd century AD, olive oil rivaled cereals as an export item.

The beginnings of the Roman imperial decline seemed less serious in North Africa than elsewhere. However, uprisings did take place. In AD 238, landowners rebelled unsuccessfully against imperial fiscal policies. Sporadic tribal revolts in the Mauretanian mountains followed from 253 to 288. The towns also suffered economic difficulties, and building activity almost ceased.

The towns of Roman North Africa had a substantial Jewish population. Some Jews had been deported from Judea or Palestine in the 1st and 2nd centuries AD for rebelling against Roman rule; others had come earlier with Punic settlers. In addition, a number of Berber tribes had converted to Judaism.

Christianity arrived in the 2nd century and soon gained converts in the towns and among slaves. More than eighty bishops, some from distant frontier regions of Numidia, attended the Council of Carthage in 256. By the end of the 4th century, the settled areas had become Christianized, and some Berber tribes had converted *en masse*.

A division in the church that came to be known as the Donatist heresy began in 313 among Christians in North Africa. The Donatists stressed the holiness of the church and refused to accept the authority to administer the sacraments of those who had surrendered the scriptures when they were forbidden under the Emperor Diocletian (reigned 284-305). The Donatists also opposed the involvement of Emperor Constantine (reigned 306-337) in church affairs in contrast to the majority of Christians who welcomed official imperial recognition. The occasionally violent Donatist controversy has been characterized as a struggle between opponents and supporters of the Roman system. The most articulate North African critic of the Donatist position, which came to be called a heresy, was Augustine, bishop of Hippo Regius. Augustine maintained that the unworthiness of a minister did not affect the validity of the sacraments because their true minister was Christ. In his sermons and books Augustine, who is considered a leading exponent of Christian dogma, evolved a theory of the right of orthodox Christian rulers to use force against schismatics and heretics. Although the dispute was resolved by a decision of an imperial commission in Carthage in 411, Donatist communities continued to exist as late as the 6th century.

A decline in trade weakened Roman control. Independent kingdoms emerged in mountainous and desert areas, towns were overrun, and Berbers, who had previously been pushed to the edges of the Roman Empire, returned.

Belisarius, general of the Byzantine emperor Justinian I based in Constantinople, landed in North Africa in 533 with 16,000 men and within a year destroyed the Vandal kingdom. Local opposition delayed full Byzantine control of the region for twelve years, however, and when imperial control came, it was but a shadow of the control exercised by Rome. Although an impressive series of fortifications were built, Byzantine rule was compromised by official corruption, incompetence, military weakness, and lack of concern in Constantinople for African affairs, which made it an easy target for the Arabs during for Muslim conquests . As a result, many rural areas reverted to Berber rule.

Aksum

The earliest state in Eritrea and northern Ethiopia, Dmt, dates from around the 8th and 7th centuries BCE. D'mt traded through the Red Sea with Egypt and the Mediterranean, providing frankincense. By the 5th and 3rd centuries, D'mt had declined, and several successor states took its place. Later there was greater trade with southern Arabia, mainly with the port of Saba. Adulis became an important commercial centre in the Ethiopian Highlands. The interaction of the peoples in the two regions, the southern Arabia Sabaeans and the northern Ethiopians, resulted in the Ge'ez culture and language and eventual development of the Ge'ez script. Trade links increased and expanded from the Red Sea to the Mediterranean, with Egypt, Greece, and Rome, to the Black Sea, and to Persia, India, and China. Aksum was known throughout those lands. By the 5th century BCE, the region was very prosperous, exporting ivory, hippopotamus hides, gold dust, spices, and live elephants. It imported silver, gold, olive oil, and wine. Aksum manufactured glass crystal, brass, and copper for export. A powerful Aksum emerged, unifying parts of eastern Sudan, northern Ethiopia (Tigre), and Eritrea. Its kings built stone palatial buildings and were buried under megalithic monuments. By 300 CE, Aksum was minting its own coins in silver and gold.

In 331 CE, King Ezana (320–350 CE) was converted to Monophysite Christianity, supposedly byFrumentius and Aedesius, who became stranded on the Red Sea coast. Some scholars believed the process was more complex and gradual than a simple conversion. Around 350, the time Ezana sacked Meroe, the Syrian monastic tradition took root within the Ethiopian church.

In the 6th century Aksum was powerful enough to add Saba on the Arabian peninsula to her empire. At the end of the 6th century, the Persians pushed Aksum out of the peninsula. With the spread of Islam through western Asia and northern Africa, Aksum's trading networks in the Mediterranean faltered. The Red Sea trade diminished as it was diverted to the Persian Gulf and dominated by Arabs, causing Aksum to decline. By 800 CE, the capital was moved south into the interior highlands, and Aksum was much diminished.

West Africa

In the western Sahel, the rise of settled communities was largely the result of domestication of millet and sorghum. Archaeology points to sizable urban populations in West Africa beginning in the 2nd millennium BCE. Symbiotic trade relations developed before the trans-Saharan trade, in response to the opportunities afforded by north-south diversity in ecosystems across deserts, grasslands, and forests. The agriculturists received salt from the desert nomads. The desert nomads acquired meat and other foods from pastoralists and farmers of the grasslands and from fishermen on the Niger River. The forest dwellers provided furs and meat. Dhar Tichitt and Oualata were prominent among the early urban centers, dated to 2000 BCE, in present-dayMauritania. About 500 stone settlements litter the region in the former savannah of the Sahara. Its inhabitants fished and grew millet. It has been found that the Soninke of the Mandé peoples were responsible for constructing such settlements. Around 300 BCE, the region became more desiccated and the settlements began to decline, most likely relocating to Koumbi Saleh. From architectural evidence and from comparison of pottery styles, it is believed that Dhar Tichitt was related to the subsequent Ghana Empire. Djenné-Djenno in what is now Mali was settled around 300 BCE, and the town grew to a sizable Iron Age population, as evidenced by crowded cemeteries. Living structures were made of sun-dried mud. By 250 BCE, Djenné-Djenno was a large, thriving market town.

Farther south, in central Nigeria, around 1000 BCE, the Nok culture developed on the Jos Plateau. It was a highly centralized community. The Nok people produced lifelike representations in terracotta, including human heads, elephants, and other animals. By 500 BCE, they were smelting iron. By 200 CE, the Nok culture had vanished. Be this as it may, based on stylistic similarities with the Nok terracottas, the bronze figurines of the Yoruba kingdom ofIfe and the Bini kingdom of Benin are now believed to be continuations of the traditions of the earlier Nokite culture.

Bantu expansion

The Bantu expansion was a critical movement of people in African history and the settling of the continent. People speaking Bantu languages (a branch of the Niger–Congo family) began in the second millennium BC to spread from Cameroon eastward to the Great Lakes region. In the first millennium BCE, Bantu languages spread from the Great Lakes to southern and east Africa. An early expansion was south to the upper Zambezi valley in the 2nd century BCE. Then, Bantu speakers pushed westward to the savannahs of present-day Angola and eastward into Malawi,Zambia, and Zimbabwe in the 1st century CE. The second thrust from the Great Lakes was eastward, 2,000 years ago, expanding to the Indian Ocean coast, Kenya and Tanzania. The eastern group eventually met the southern migrants from the Great Lakes in Malawi, Zambia, and Zimbabwe. Both groups continued southward, with eastern groups continuing to Mozambique and reaching Maputo in the 2nd century CE, and expanding as far as Durban. By the later first millennium CE, the expansion had reached the Great Ke River of South Africa. Sorghum, a major Bantu crop, could not thrive under the winter rainfall of Namibia and the western Cape. Khoisan people inhabited the remaining parts of southern Africa.

MEDIEVAL & EARLY MODERN AFRICA 500 TO 1800

Central Africa

Prehistory

Archeological finds in Central Africa have been discovered dating back to over 100,000 years. According to Zangato and Holl, there is evidence of iron-smelting in the Central African Republic and Cameroon that may date back to 3000 to 2500 BCE. Extensive walled sites and settlements have recently been found in Zilum, Chad approximately 60 km (37 mi) southwest of Lake Chad dating to the first millennium BCE.

Trade and improved agricultural techniques supported more sophisticated societies, leading to the early civilizations of Sao, Kanem, Bornu, Shilluk, Baguirmi, and Wadai.

Around 1000 BCE, Bantu migrants had reached the Great Lakes Region in Central Africa. Halfway through the first millennium BCE, the Bantu had also settled as far south as what is now Angola.

Sao civilization

The Sao civilization flourished from ca. the sixth century BCE to as late as the sixteenth century CE in Middle Africa. The Sao lived by the Chari River south of Lake Chad in territory that later became part of Cameroon and Chad. They are the earliest people to have left clear traces of their presence in the territory of modern Cameroon. Today, several ethnic groups of northern Cameroon and southern Chad but particularly the Sara people claim descent from the civilization of the Sao. Sao artifacts show that they were skilled workers in bronze, copper, and iron. Finds include bronze sculptures and terra cotta statues of human and animal figures, coins, funerary urns, household utensils, jewelry, highly decorated pottery, and spears. The largest Sao archaeological finds have been made south of Lake Chad.

Kanem Empire

The Kanem Empire was centered in the Chad Basin. It was known as the Kanem Empire from the 9th century CE onward and lasted as the independent kingdom of Bornu until 1900. At its height it encompassed an area covering not only much of Chad, but also parts of modern southern Libya, eastern Niger, northeastern Nigeria, northern Cameroon, parts of South Sudanand the Central African Republic.

The history of the Empire is mainly known from the Royal Chronicle or *Girgam* discovered in 1851 by the German traveller Heinrich Barth. Kanem rose in the 8th century in the region to the north and east of Lake Chad. The Kanem empire went into decline, shrank, and in the 14th century was defeated by Bilala invaders from the Lake Fitriregion.

Around the 9th century CE, the central Sudanic Empire of Kanem, with its capital at Njimi, was founded by the Kanuri-speaking nomads. Kanem arose by engaging in the trans-Saharan trade. It exchanged slaves captured by raiding the south for horses from North Africa, which in turn aided in the acquisition of slaves. By the late 11th century, the Islamic Sayfawa (Saifawa) dynasty was founded by Humai (Hummay) ibn Salamna.

The Sayfawa Dynasty ruled for 771 years, making it one of the longest-lasting dynasties in human history. In addition to trade, taxation of local farms around Kanem became a source of state income. Kanem reached its peak under *Mai* (king) Dunama Dibalemi ibn Salma (1210–1248). The empire reportedly was able to field 40,000 cavalry, and it extended from Fezzan in the north to the Sao state in the south. Islam became firmly entrenched in the empire. Pilgrimages to Mecca were common; Cairo had hostels set aside specifically for pilgrims from Kanem.

Bornu Empire

The Kanuri people led by the Sayfuwa migrated to the west and south of the lake, where they established the Bornu Empire. By the late 16th century the Bornu empire had expanded and recaptured the parts of Kanem that had been conquered by the Bulala.

Satellite states of Bornu included the Damagaram in the west and Baguirmi to the southeast of Lake Chad. Around 1400, the Sayfawa Dynasty moved its capital to Bornu, a tributary state southwest of Lake Chad with a new capital Birni Ngarzagamu. Overgrazing had caused the pastures of Kanem to become too dry. In addition, political rivalry from the Bilala clan was becoming intense. Moving to Bornu better situated the empire to exploit the trans-Saharan trade and to widen its network in that trade. Links to the Hausa states were also established, providing horses and salt from Bilma for Akan gold.

Mai Ali Gazi ibn Dunama (c. 1475–1503) defeated the Bilala, reestablishing complete control of Kanem. During the early 16th century, the Sayfawa Dynasty solidified its hold on the Bornu population after much rebellion. In the latter half of the 16th century, *Mai* Idris Alooma modernized its military, in contrast to the Songhai Empire. Turkish mercenaries were used to train the military. The Sayfawa Dynasty were the first monarchs south of the Sahara to import firearms. The empire controlled all of the Sahel from the borders of Darfur in the east to Hausaland to the west. Friendly relationship was established with the Ottoman Empirevia Tripoli. The *Mai* exchanged gifts with the Ottoman sultan.

During the 17th and 18th centuries, not much is known about Bornu. During the 18th century, it became a centre of Islamic learning. However, Bornu's army became outdated by not importing new arms, and Kamembu had also begun its decline. The power of the *mai* was undermined by droughts and famine that were becoming more intense, internal rebellion in the pastoralist north, growing Hausa power, and the importation of firearms which made warfare more bloody. By 1841, the last *mai*was deposed, bringing to an end the long-lived Sayfawa Dynasty.

Shilluk Kingdom

The Shilluk Kingdom was centered in South Sudan from the 15th century from along a strip of land along the western bank of White Nile, from Lake No to about 12° northlatitude. The capital and royal residence was in the town of Fashoda. The kingdom was founded during the mid-fifteenth century CE by its first ruler, Nyikang. During the nineteenth century, the Shilluk Kingdom faced decline following military assaults from the Ottoman Empire and later British and Sudanese colonization in Anglo-Egyptian Sudan.

Baguirmi Kingdom

The Kingdom of Baguirmi existed as an independent state during the 16th and 17th centuries southeast of Lake Chad in what is now the country of Chad. Baguirmi emerged to the southeast of the Kanem-Bornu Empire. The kingdom's first ruler was Mbang Birni Besse. Later in his reign, the Bornu Empire conquered and made the state a tributary.

Wadai Empire

The Wadai Empire was centered on Chad and the Central African Republic from the 17th century. TheTunjur people founded the Wadai Kingdom to the east of Bornu in the 16th century. In the 17th century there was a revolt of the Maba people who established a Muslim dynasty.

At first Wadai paid tribute to Bornu and Durfur, but by the 18th century Wadai was fully independent and had become an aggressor against its neighbours. To the west of Bornu, by the 15th century theKingdom of Kano had become the most powerful of the Hausa Kingdoms, in an unstable truce with the Kingdom of Katsina to the north. Both were absorbed into the Sokoto Caliphate during the Fulani Jihad of 1805, which threatened Bornu itself.

Luba Empire

Sometime between 1300 to 1400 CE, Kongolo Mwamba (Nkongolo) from the Balopwe clan unified the various Luba peoples, near Lake Kisale. He founded the Kongolo Dynasty, which was later ousted by Kalala Ilunga. Kalala expanded the kingdom west of Lake Kisale. A new centralized political system of spiritual kings (*balopwe*) with a court council of head governors and sub-heads all the way to village heads. The *balopwe* was the direct communicator with the ancestral spirits and chosen by them. Conquered states were integrated into the system and represented in the court, with their titles. The authority of the *balopwe* resided in his spiritual power rather than his military authority. The army was relatively small. The Luba was able to control regional trade and collect tribute for redistribution. Numerous offshoot states were formed with founders claiming descent from the Luba. The Luba political system spread throughout Central Africa, southern Uganda, Rwanda, Burundi, Malawi, Zambia, Zimbabwe, and the western Congo. Two major empires claiming Luba descent were the Lunda Empire and Maravi Empire. The Bemba people of northern Zambia were descended from Luba migrants who arrived in Zambia during the 17th century.

Lunda Empire

In the 1450s, a Luba from the royal family Ilunga Tshibinda married Lunda queen Rweej and united all Lunda peoples. Their son *mulopwe* Luseeng expanded the kingdom. His son Naweej expanded the empire further and is known as the first Lunda emperor, with the title *mwato yamvo* (*mwaant yaav, mwant yav*), the Lord of Vipers. The Luba political system was retained, and conquered peoples were integrated into the system. The *mwato yamvo*assigned a *cilool* or *kilolo* (royal adviser) and tax collector to each state conquered.

Numerous states claimed descent from the Lunda. The Imbangala of inland Angola claimed descent from a founder, Kinguri, brother of Queen Rweej, who could not tolerate the rule of *mulopwe* Tshibunda. *Kinguri*became the title of kings of states founded by Queen Rweej's brother. The Luena (Lwena) and Lozi (Luyani) in Zambia also claim descent from Kinguri. During the 17th century, a Lunda chief and warrior called Mwata Kazembe set up an Eastern Lundakingdom in the valley of the Luapula River. The Lunda's western expansion also saw claims of descent by the Yaka and the Pende. The Lunda linked middle Africa with the western coast trade. The kingdom of Lunda came to an end in the 19th century when it was invaded by the Chokwe, who were armed with guns.

Kingdom of Kongo

By the 15th century CE, the farming Bakongo people (*ba* being the plural prefix) were unified as the Kingdom of Kongo under a ruler called the *manikongo*, residing in the fertile Pool Malebo area on the lower Congo River. The capital was M'banza-Kongo. With superior organization, they were able to conquer their neighbours and extract tribute. They were experts in metalwork, pottery, and weaving raffia cloth. They stimulated interregional trade via a tribute system controlled by the *manikongo*. Later, maize (corn) and cassava (manioc) would be introduced to the region via trade with the Portuguese at their ports at Luanda and Benguela. The maize and cassava would result in population growth in the region and other parts of Africa, replacing millet as a main staple.

By the 16th century, the *manikongo* held authority from the Atlantic in the west to the Kwango River in the east. Each territory was assigned a *mani-mpembe* (provincial governor) by the*manikongo*. In 1506, Afonso I (1506–1542), a Christian, took over the throne. Slave trading increased with Afonso's wars of conquest. About 1568 to 1569, the Jaga invaded Kongo, laying waste to the kingdom and forcing the *manikongo* into exile. In 1574, Manikongo Álvaro I was reinstated with the help of Portuguese mercenaries. During the latter part of the 1660s, the Portuguese tried to gain control of Kongo. Manikongo António I (1661–1665), with a Kongolese army of 5,000, was destroyed by an army of Afro-Portuguese at the Battle of Mbwila. The empire dissolved into petty polities, fighting among each other for war captives to sell into slavery.

Kongo gained captives from the Kingdom of Ndongo in wars of conquest. Ndongo was ruled by the *ngola*. Ndongo would also engage in slave trading with the Portuguese, with São Tomé being a transit point to Brazil. The kingdom was not as welcoming as Kongo; it viewed the Portuguese with great suspicion and as an enemy. The Portuguese in the latter part of the 16th century tried to gain control of Ndongo but were defeated by the Mbundu. Ndongo experienced depopulation from slave raiding. The leaders established another state at Matamba, affiliated with Queen Nzinga, who put up a strong resistance to the Portuguese until coming to terms with them. The Portuguese settled along the coast as trade dealers, not venturing on conquest of the interior. Slavery wreaked havoc in the interior, with states initiating wars of conquest for captives. The Imbangala formed the slave-raiding state of Kasanje, a major source of slaves during the 17th and 18th centuries.

Horn of Africa

Somalia

The birth of Islam opposite Somalia's Red Sea coast meant that Somali merchants and sailors living on the Arabian Peninsula gradually came under the influence of the new religion through their converted Arab Muslim trading partners. With the migration of Muslim families from theIslamic world to Somalia in the early centuries of Islam, and the peaceful conversion of the Somali population by Somali Muslim scholars in the following centuries, the ancient city-states eventually transformed into Islamic Mogadishu, Berbera, Zeila, Barawa and Merka, which were part of the *Berber* (the medieval Arab term for the ancestors of the modern Somalis) civilization. The city of Mogadishu came to be known as the *City of Islam* and controlled the East African gold trade for several centuries.

During this period, sultanates such as the Ajuran Empire and the Sultanate of Mogadishu, andrepublics like Barawa, Merca and Hobyo and their respective ports flourished and had a lucrative foreign commerce with ships sailing to and coming from Arabia, India, Venice, Persia, Egypt, Portugal and as far away as China. Vasco da Gama, who passed by Mogadishu in the 15th century, noted that it was a large city with houses four or five stories high and big palaces in its centre, in addition to many mosques with cylindrical minarets.

In the 16th century, Duarte Barbosa noted that many ships from the Kingdom of Cambaya in modern-day India sailed to Mogadishu withcloth and spices, for which they in return received gold, wax, and ivory. Barbosa also highlighted the abundance of meat, wheat, barley, horses, and fruit in the coastal markets, which generated enormous wealth for the merchants. Mogadishu, the centre of a thriving weaving industry known as *toob benadir* (specialized for the markets in Egypt and Syria), together with Merca and Barawa, served as a transit stop for Swahili merchants from Mombasa and Malindi and for the gold trade from Kilwa. Jewish merchants from the Strait of Hormuz brought their Indian textiles and fruit to the Somali coast to exchange for grain and wood.

Trading relations were established with Malacca in the 15th century, with cloth, ambergris, and porcelain being the main commodities of the trade. Giraffes, zebras, and incense were exported to the Ming Empire of China, which established Somali merchants as leaders in the commerce between the Asia and Africa and influenced the Chinese language with borrowings from the Somali language in the process. Hindu merchants from Surat and southeast African merchants from Pate, seeking to bypass both the Portuguese blockade andOmani meddling, used the Somali ports of Merca and Barawa (which were out of the two powers' jurisdiction) to conduct their trade in safety and without any problems.

Ethiopia

The Zagwe dynasty ruled many parts of modern Ethiopia and Eritrea from approximately 1137 to 1270. The name of the dynasty comes from the Cushitic speaking Agaw of northern Ethiopia. From 1270 CE on for many centuries, the Solomonic dynasty ruled the Ethiopian Empire.

In the early 15th century Ethiopia sought to make diplomatic contact with European kingdoms for the first time since Aksumite times. A letter from King Henry IV of England to the Emperor of Abyssinia survives. In 1428, the Emperor Yeshaq sent two emissaries to Alfonso V of Aragon, who sent return emissaries who failed to complete the return trip.

The first continuous relations with a European country began in 1508 with Portugal under EmperorLebna Dengel, who had just inherited the throne from his father. This proved to be an important development, for when the empire was subjected to the attacks of the Adal general and imam,Ahmad ibn Ibrahim al-Ghazi (called

"*Grañ*", or "the Left-handed"), Portugal assisted the Ethiopian emperor by sending weapons and four hundred men, who helped his son Gelawdewos defeat Ahmad and re-establish his rule. This Abyssinian–Adal War was also one of the first proxy wars in the region as the Ottoman Empire, and Portugal took sides in the conflict.

When Emperor Susenyos converted to Roman Catholicism in 1624, years of revolt and civil unrest followed resulting in thousands of deaths. The Jesuit missionaries had offended the Orthodox faith of the local Ethiopians, and on June 25, 1632, Susenyos's son, Emperor Fasilides, declared the state religion to again be Ethiopian Orthodox Christianity and expelled the Jesuit missionaries and other Europeans.

North Africa

Maghreb

By 711 CE Arab Muslims had conquered all of North Africa. By the 10th century, the majority of the population of North Africa was Muslim.

By the 9th century CE, the unity brought about by the Islamic conquest of North Africa and the expansion of Islamic culture came to an end. Conflict arose as to who should be the successor of the prophet. The Umayyads had initially taken control of the Caliphate, with their capital at Damascus. Later, the Abbasids had taken control, moving the capital to Baghdad. The Berber people, being independent in spirit and hostile to outside interference in their affairs and to Arabexclusivity in orthodox Islam, adopted Shi'ite and Kharijite Islam, both considered unorthodox and hostile to the authority of the Abbasid Caliphate. Numerous Kharijite kingdoms came and fell during the 8th and 9th centuries, asserting their independence from Baghdad. In the early 10th century, Shi'ite groups from Syria, claiming descent from Muhammad's daughter Fatima, founded the Fatimid Dynasty in the Maghreb. By 950, they had conquered all of the Maghreb and by 969 all of Egypt. They had immediately broken away from Baghdad.

In an attempt to bring about a purer form of Islam among the Sanhaja Berbers, Abdallah ibn Yasin founded the Almoravid movement in present-day Mauritania and Western Sahara. The Sanhaja Berbers, like the Soninke, practiced an indigenous religion alongside Islam. Abdallah ibn Yasin found ready converts in the Lamtuna Sanhaja, who were dominated by the Soninke in the south and the Zenata Berbers in the north. By the 1040s, all of the Lamtuna was converted to the Almoravid movement. With the help of Yahya ibn Umar and his brother Abu Bakr ibn Umar, the sons of the Lamtuna chief, the Almoravids created an empire extending from the Sahel to the Mediterranean. After the death of Abdallah ibn Yassin and Yahya ibn Umar, Abu Bakr split the empire in half, between himself and Yusuf ibn Tashfin, because it was too big to be ruled by one individual. Abu Bakr took the south to continue fighting the Soninke, and Yusuf ibn Tashfin took the north, expanding it to southern Spain. The death of Abu Bakr in 1087 saw a breakdown of unity and increase military dissension in the south. This caused a re-expansion of the Soninke. The Almoravids were once held responsible for bringing down the Ghana Empire in 1076, but this view is no longer credited.

During the 10th through 13th centuries, there was a large-scale movement of bedouins out of the Arabian Peninsula. About 1050, a quarter of a million Arab nomads from Egypt moved into the Maghreb. Those following the northern coast were referred to as Banu Hilal. Those going south of the Atlas Mountains were the Banu Sulaym. This movement spread the use of the Arabic language and hastened the decline of the Berber language and the Arabisation of North Africa. Later an Arabised Berber group, the Hawwara, went south to Nubia via Egypt.

In the 1140s, Abd al-Mu'min declared jihad on the Almoravids, charging them with decadence and corruption. He united the northern Berbers against the Almoravids, overthrowing them and forming the Almohad Empire. During this period, the Maghreb became thoroughly Islamised and saw the spread of literacy, the development of algebra, and the use of the number zero and decimals. By the 13th century, the Almohad states had split into three rival states. Muslim states were largely extinguished in Spain by the Christian kingdoms of Castile, Aragon, andPortugal. Around 1415, Portugal engaged in a *reconquista* of North Africa by capturing Ceuta, and in later centuries Spain and Portugal acquired other ports on the North African coast. In 1492, Spain defeated Muslims in Granada, effectively ending eight centuries of Muslim domination in southern Iberia.

Portugal and Spain took the ports of Tangiers, Algiers, Tripoli, and Tunis. This put them in direct competition with the Ottoman Empire, which re-took the ports using Turkish corsairs (pirates and privateers). The Turkish corsairs would use the ports for raiding Christian ships, a major source of booty for the towns. Technically, North Africa was under the control of the Ottoman Empire, but only the coastal towns were fully under Istanbul's control. Tripoli benefited from trade with Borno. The pashas of Tripoli traded horses, firearms, and armor via Fez with the sultans of the Bornu Empire for slaves.

In the 16th century, an Arab nomad tribe that claimed descent from Muhammad's daughter, the Saadis, conquered and united Morocco. They prevented the Ottoman Empire from reaching to the Atlantic and expelled Portugal from Morocco's western coast. Ahmad al-Mansurbrought the state to the height of its power. He invaded Songhay in 1591, to control the gold trade, which had been diverted to the western coast of Africa for European ships and to the east, to Tunis. Morocco's hold on Songhay diminished in the 17th century. In 1603, after Ahmad's death, the kingdom split into the two sultanates of Fes and Marrakesh. Later it was reunited by Moulay al-Rashid, founder of theAlaouite Dynasty (1672–1727). His brother and successor, Ismail ibn Sharif(1672–1727), strengthen the unity of the country by importing slaves from the Sudan to build up the military.

Nile Valley

Egypt

In 642 CE, Arab Muslims conquered Byzantine Egypt.

Egypt under the Fatimid Caliphate was prosperous. Dams and canals were repaired, and wheat, barley, flax, and cotton production increased. Egypt became a major producer of linen and cotton cloth. Its Mediterranean and Red Sea trade increased. Egypt also minted a gold currency called the Fatimid dinar, which was used for international trade. The bulk of revenues came from taxing the fellahin (peasant farmers), and taxes were high. Tax collecting was leased to Berber overlords, who were soldiers who had taken part in the Fatimid conquest in 969 CE. The overlords paid a share to the caliphs and retained what was left. Eventually, they became landlords and constituted a settled land aristocracy.

To fill the military ranks, Mamluk Turkish slave cavalry and Sudanese slave infantry were used. Berber freemen were also recruited. In 1150s, tax revenues from farms diminished. The soldiers revolted and wreaked havoc in the countryside, slowed trade, and diminished the power and authority of the Fatimid caliphs.

During the 1160s, Fatimid Egypt came under threat from European crusaders. Out of this threat, a Kurdish general named balâ% ad-Dîn Yûsuf ibn Ayyûb (Saladin), with a small band of professional soldiers, emerged as an outstanding Muslim defender. Saladin defeated the Christian crusaders at Egypt's borders and recaptured Jerusalem in 1187. On the death of the Fatimid caliph in 1171, Saladin became the ruler of Egypt, ushering in the Ayyubid Dynasty. Under his rule, Egypt returned to Sunni Islam, Cairo became an important centre of Arab Islamic learning, and Mamluk slaves were increasingly recruited from Turkey and southern Russia for military service. Support for the military was tied to the *iqta*, a form of land taxation in which soldiers were given ownership in return for military service.

Over time, Mamluk slave soldiers became a very powerful landed aristocracy, to the point of getting rid of the Ayyubid dynasty in 1250 and establishing a Mamluk dynasty. The more powerful Mamluks were referred to as *amirs*. For 250 years, Mamluks controlled all of Egypt under a military dictatorship. Egypt extended her territories to Syria and Palestine, thwarted the crusaders, and halted a Mongol invasion in 1260 at the Battle of Ain Jalut. Mamluk Egypt came to be viewed as a protector of Islam, and of Medina and Mecca. Eventually the *iqta*system declined and proved unreliable for providing an adequate military. The Mamluks started viewing their *iqta* as hereditary and became attuned to urban living. Farm production declined, and dams and canals lapsed into disrepair. Mamluk military skill and technology did not keep pace with new technology of handguns and cannons.

With the rise of the Ottoman Empire, Egypt was easily defeated. In 1517, Egypt became part of the Ottoman Empire. Istanbul revived the *iqta* system. Trade was reestablished in the Red Sea, but it could not completely connect with Indian Ocean trade because of growing Portuguese presence. During the 17th and 18th centuries, hereditary Mamluks regained power. The leading Mamluks were referred to as*beys*. Pashas, or viceroys, represented the Istanbul government in name only, operating independently. During the 18th century, dynasties of pashas became established. The government was weak and corrupt.

In 1798, Napoleon invaded Egypt. The local forces had little ability to resist the French conquest. However, Britain and the Ottoman Empire were able to remove French occupation in 1801. These events marked the beginning of 19th-century Anglo-Franco rivalry over Egypt.

Sudan

Christian and Islamic Nubia

After Ezana of Aksum sacked Meroe, people associated with the site of Ballana moved into Nubia from the southwest and founded three kingdoms: Makuria, Nobatia, and Alodia. They would rule for 200 years. Makuria was above the third cataract, along the Dongola Reach with its capital at Dongola. Nobadia was to the north with its capital at Faras, and Alodia was to the south with its capital at Soba.

Makuria eventually absorbed Nobadia. The people of the region converted to Monophysite Christianity around 500 to 600 CE. The church initially started writing in Coptic, then in Greek, and finally in Old Nubian, a Nilo-Saharan language. The church was aligned with the Egyptian Coptic Church.

By 641, Egypt was conquered by Muslim Arabs. This effectively blocked Christian Nubia and Aksum from Mediterranean Christendom. In 651-652, Arabs from Egypt invaded Christian Nubia. Nubian archers soundly defeated the invaders. The Baqt (or Bakt) Treaty was drawn, recognizing Christian Nubia and regulating trade. The treaty controlled relations between Christian Nubia and Islamic Egypt for almost six hundred years.

By the 13th century, Christian Nubia began its decline. The authority of the monarchy was diminished by the church and nobility. Arab bedouin tribes began to infiltrate Nubia, causing further havoc.

Fakirs (holy men) practicing Sufism introduced Islam into Nubia. By 1366, Nubia had become divided into petty fiefdoms when she was invaded by Mamelukes. During the 15th century, Nubia was open to Arab immigration. Arab nomads intermingled with the population and introduced the Arabic culture and language. By the 16th century, Makuria and Nobadia had been Islamized. During the 16th century, Abdallah Jamma headed an Arab confederation that destroyed Soba, capital of Alodia, the last holdout of Christian Nubian. Later Alodia would fall under the Funj Sultanate.

During the 15th century, Funj herders migrated north to Alodia and occupied it. Between 1504 and 1505, the kingdom expanded, reaching its peak and establishing its capital at Sennar under Badi II Abu Daqn (c. 1644–1680). By end of the 16th century, the Funj had converted to Islam. They pushed their empire westward to Kordofan. They expanded eastward, but were halted by Ethiopia. They controlled Nubia down to the 3rd Cataract. The economy depended on captured enemies to fill the army and on merchants travelling through Sennar. UnderBadi IV (1724–1762), the army turned on the king, making him nothing but a figurehead. In 1821, the Funj were conquered by Muhammad Ali (1805–1849), Pasha of Egypt.

Southern Africa

Settlements of Bantu-speaking peoples who were iron-using agriculturists and herdsmen were present south of the Limpopo River by the 4th or 5th century CE, displacing and absorbing the original Khoisan speakers. They slowly moved south, and the earliest ironworks in modern-day Kwa Zulu-Natal Province are believed to date from around 1050. The southernmost group was the Xhosa people, whose language incorporates certain linguistic traits from the earlier Khoi-San people, reaching the Great Fish River in today's Eastern Cape Province.

Great Zimbabwe and Mapungubwe

The Kingdom of Mapungubwe was the first state in Southern Africa, with its capital at Mapungubwe. The state arose in the 12th century CE. Its wealth came from controlling the trade in ivory from the Limpopo Valley, copper from the mountains of northern Transvaal, and gold from the Zimbabwe Plateau between the Limpopo and Zambezi rivers, with the Swahilimerchants at Chibuene. By the mid-13th century, Mapungubwe was abandoned.

After the decline of Mapungubwe, Great Zimbabwe rose on the Zimbabwe Plateau. *Zimbabwe* means stone building. Great Zimbabwe was the first city in Southern Africa and was the centre of an empire, consolidating lesser Shona polities. Stone building was inherited from Mapungubwe. These building techniques were enhanced and came into maturity at Great Zimbabwe, represented by the wall of the Great Enclosure. The dry-stack stone masonry technology was also used to build smaller compounds in the area. Great Zimbabwe flourished by trading with Swahili Kilwa and Sofala. The rise of Great Zimbabwe parallels the rise of Kilwa. Great Zimbabwe was a major source of gold. Its royal court lived in luxury, wore Indian cotton, surrounded themselves with copper and gold ornaments, and ate on plates from as far away as Persia and China. Around the 1420s and 1430s, Great Zimbabwe was on the decline. The city was abandoned by 1450. Some have attributed the decline to the rise of the trading town Ingombe Ilede.

A new chapter of Shona history ensued. Nyatsimba Mutota, a northern Shona king of the Karanga, engaged in conquest. He and his son Mutope conquered the Zimbabwe Plateau, going through Mozambique to the east coast, linking the empire to the coastal trade. They called their empire *Wilayatu 'l Mu'anamutapah* or *mwanamutapa* (Lord of the Plundered Lands), or the Kingdom of Mutapa. *Monomotapa*was the Portuguese corruption. They did not build stone structures; the northern Shonas had no traditions of building in stone. After the death of Matope in 1480, the empire split into two small empires: Torwa in the south and Mutapa in the north. The split occurred over rivalry from two Shona lords, Changa and Togwa, with the *mwanamutapa* line. Changa was able to acquire the south, forming the Kingdom of Butua with its capital at Khami. The Mutapa Empire continued in the north under the *mwenemutapa* line. During the 16th century the Portuguese were able to establish permanent markets up the Zambezi River in an attempt to gain political and military control of Mutapa. They were partially successful. In 1628, a decisive battle allowed them to put a puppet *mwanamutapa* named Mavura, who signed treaties that gave favorable mineral export rights to the Portuguese. The Portuguese were successful in destroying the *mwanamutapa* system of government and undermining trade. By 1667, Mutapa was in decay. Chiefs would not allow digging for gold because of fear of Portuguese theft, and the population declined.

The Kingdom of Butua was ruled by a *changamire,* a title derived from the founder, Changa. Later it became the Rozwi Empire. The Portuguese tried to gain a foothold but were thrown out of the region in 1693, by Changamire Dombo. The 17th century was a period of peace and prosperity. The Rozwi Empire fell into ruins in the 1830s from invading Nguni from Natal.

Namibia

By 1500 CE, most of southern Africa had established states. In northwestern Namibia, theOvambo engaged in farming and the Herero engaged in herding. As cattle numbers increased, the Herero moved southward to central Namibia for grazing land. A related group, the Ovambanderu, expanded to Ghanzi in northwestern Botswana. The Nama, a Khoi-speaking, sheep-raising group, moved northward and came into contact with the Herero; this would set the stage for much conflict between the two groups. The expanding Lozi states pushed the Mbukushu, Subiya, and Yei to Botei, Okavango, and Chobe in northern Botswana.

South Africa and Botswana

Sotho–Tswana

The development of Sotho–Tswana states based on the highveld, south of the Limpopo River, began around 1000 CE. The chief's power rested on cattle and his connection to the ancestor. This can be seen in the Toutswemogala Hill settlements with stone foundations and stone walls, north of the highveld and south of the Vaal River. Northwest of the Vaal River developed early Tswana states centered on towns of thousands of people. When disagreements or rivalry arose, different groups moved to form their own states.

Nguni peoples

Southeast of the Drakensberg mountains lived Nguni-speaking peoples (Zulu, Xhosa, Swazi, and Ndebele). They too engaged in state building, with new states developing from rivalry, disagreements, and population pressure causing movement into new regions. This 19th-century process of warfare, state building and migration later became known as the Mfecane (Nguni) or Difaqane (Sotho). Its major catalyst was the consolidation of the Zulu state. They were metalworkers, cultivators of millet, and cattle herders.

Khoisan and Afrikaaner

The Khoisan lived in the southwestern Cape Province, where winter rainfall is plentiful. Earlier Khoisan populations were absorbed by Bantu peoples, such as the Sotho and Nguni, but theBantu expansion stopped at the region with winter rainfall. Some Bantu languages have incorporated the click characteristic of the Khoisan languages. The Khoisan traded with their Bantu neighbours, providing cattle, sheep, and hunted items. In return, their Bantu speaking neighbours traded copper, iron, and tobacco.

By the 16th century, the Dutch East India Company established a replenishing station at Table Bay for restocking water and purchasing meat from the Khoikhoi. The Khoikhoi received copper, iron, tobacco, and beads in exchange. In order to control the price of meat and stock and make service more consistent, the Dutch established a permanent settlement at Table Bay in 1652. They grew fresh fruit and vegetables and established a hospital for sick sailors. To increase produce, the Dutch decided to increase the number of farms at Table Bay by encouraging freeburgher *boers* (farmers) on lands worked initially by slaves from West Africa. The land was taken from Khoikhoi grazing land, triggering the first Khoikhoi-Dutch war in 1659. No victors emerged, but the

Dutch assumed a "right of conquest" by which they claimed all of the cape. In a series of wars pitting the Khoikhoi against each other, the Boers assumed all Khoikhoi land and claimed all their cattle. The second Khoikoi-Dutch war (1673–1677) was a cattle raid. The Khoikhoi also died in thousands from European diseases.

By the 18th century, the cape colony had grown, with slaves coming from Madagascar, Mozambique, and Indonesia. The settlement also started to expand northward, but Khoikhoi resistance, raids, and guerrilla warfare slowed the expansion during the 18th century. Boers who started to practice pastoralism were known as *trekboers*. A common source of *trekboer* labor was orphan children who were captured during raids and whose parents had to be been killed.

Southeast Africa

Prehistory

According to the theory of recent African origin of modern humans, the mainstream position held within the scientific community, all humans originate from either Southeast Africa or the Horn of Africa. During the first millennium AD, Nilotic and Bantu-speaking peoplesmoved into the region.

Swahili coast

Following the Bantu Migration, on the coastal section of Southeast Africa, a mixed Bantu community developed through contact with Muslim Arab and Persian traders, leading to the development of the mixed Arab, Persian and African Swahili City States. The Swahili culture that emerged from these exchanges evinces many Arab and Islamic influences not seen in traditional Bantu culture, as do the manyAfro-Arab members of the Bantu Swahili people. With its original speech community centered on the coastal parts of Tanzania (particularly Zanzibar) and Kenya—a seaboard referred to as the Swahili Coast—the Bantu Swahili language contains many Arabic loan-words as a consequence of these interactions.

The earliest Bantu inhabitants of the Southeast coast of Kenya and Tanzania encountered by these later Arab and Persian settlers have been variously identified with the trading settlements of Rhapta, Azania and Menouthias referenced in early Greek and Chinese writings from 50 CE to 500 CE, ultimately giving rise to the name for Tanzania. These early writings perhaps document the first wave of Bantu settlers to reach Southeast Africa during their migration.

Historically, the Swahili people could be found as far north as northern Kenya and as far south as the Ruvuma River in Mozambique. Arab geographers referred to the Swahili coast as the land of the *zanj* (blacks).

Although once believed to be the descendants of Persian colonists, the ancient Swahili are now recognized by most historians, historical linguists, and archaeologists as a Bantu people who had sustained important interactions with Muslim merchants, beginning in the late 7th and early 8th centuries CE.

Medieval Swahili kingdoms are known to have had island trade ports, described by Greek historians as "metropolises", and to have established regular trade routes with the Islamic world and Asia. Ports such as Mombasa, Zanzibar, and Kilwa were known to Chinese sailors under Zheng He and medieval Islamic geographers such as the Berber traveller Abu Abdullah ibn Battuta. The main Swahili exports were ivory, slaves, and gold. They traded with Arabia, India, Persia, and China.

The Portuguese arrived in 1498. On a mission to economically control and Christianize the Swahili coast, the Portuguese attacked Kilwa first in 1505 and other cities later. Because of Swahili resistance, the Portuguese attempt at establishing commercial control was never successful. By the late 17th century, Portuguese authority on the Swahili coast began to diminish. With the help of Omani Arabs, by 1729 the Portuguese presence had been removed. The Swahili coast eventually became part of the Sultanate of Oman. Trade recovered, but it did not regain the levels of the past.

Urewe

The Urewe culture developed and spread in and around the Lake Victoria region of Africa during the African Iron Age. The culture's earliest dated artifacts are located in the Kagera Region of Tanzania, and it extended as far west as the Kivu region of the Democratic Republic of the Congo, as far east as the Nyanza and Western provinces of Kenya, and north into Uganda, Rwanda and Burundi. Sites from the Urewe culture date from the Early Iron Age, from the 5th century BC. to the 6th century AD.

The origins of the Urewe culture are ultimately in the Bantu expansion originating in Cameroon. Research into early Iron Age civilizations in sub-Saharan Africa has been undertaken concurrently with studies on African linguistics on Bantu expansion. The Urewe culture may correspond to the Eastern subfamily of Bantu languages, spoken by the descendants of the first wave of Bantu peoples to settle East Africa. At first sight, Urewe seems to be a fully developed civilization recognizable through its distinctive, stylish earthenware and highly technical and sophisticated iron working techniques. Given our current level of knowledge, neither seems to have developed or altered for nearly 2000 years. However, minor local variations in the ceramic ware can be observed.

Urewe is the name of the site in Kenya brought to prominence through the publication in 1948 of Mary Leakey's archaeological findings. She describes the early Iron Age period in the Great Lakes region in Central East Africa around Lake Victoria.

Madagascar and Merina

Madagascar was apparently first settled by Austronesian speakers from southeast Asia before the 6th century CE and subsequently byBantu speakers from the east African mainland in the 6th or 7th century, according to archaeological and linguistic data. The Austronesians introduced banana and rice cultivation, and the Bantu speakers introduced cattle and other farming practices. About 1000, Arab and Indian trade settlement were started in northern Madagascar to exploit the Indian Ocean trade. By the 14th century, Islam was introduced on the island by traders. Madagascar functioned in the East African medieval period as a contact port for the other Swahili seaport city-states such as Sofala, Kilwa, Mombasa, and Zanzibar.

Several kingdoms emerged after the 15th century: the Sakalava Kingdom (16th century) on the west coast, Tsitambala Kingdom (17th century) on the east coast, and Merina (15th century) in the central highlands. By the 19th century, Merina controlled the whole island. In 1500, the Portuguese were the first Europeans on the island, raiding the trading settlements.

The British and later the French arrived. During the latter part of the 17th century, Madagascar was a popular transit point for pirates. Radama I (1810–1828) invited Christian missionaries in the early 19th century. Queen Ranavalona I "the Cruel" (1828–61) banned the practice of Christianity in the kingdom, and an estimated 150,000 Christians perished. Under Radama II (1861–1863), Madagascar took a French orientation, with great commercial concession given to the French. In 1895, in the second Franco-Hova War, the French invaded Madagascar, taking over Antsiranana (Diego Suarez) and declaring Madagascar a protectorate.

Lake Plateau states and empires

Between the 14th and 15th centuries, large Southeast African kingdoms and states emerged, such as the Buganda and Karagwe Kingdoms of Uganda and Tanzania.

Kitara and Bunyoro

By 1000 CE, numerous states had arisen on the Lake Plateau among the Great Lakes of East Africa. Cattle herding, cereal growing, and banana cultivation were the economic mainstays of these states. The Ntusi and Bigo earthworks are representative of one of the first states, the Bunyoro kingdom, which oral tradition stipulates was part of the Empire of Kitara that dominated the whole lakes region. A Luo ethnic elite, from the Bito clan, ruled over the Bantu-speaking Nyoro people. The society was essentially Nyoro in its culture, based on the evidence from pottery, settlement patterns, and economic specialization.

The Bito clan claimed legitimacy by being descended from the Bachwezi clan, who were said to have ruled the Empire of Kitara. However, very little is known about Kitara; some scholars even question its historical existence. Most founding leaders of the various polities in the lake region seem to have claimed descent from the Bachwezi. There are now 13 million Tara who are part of the second African loss,(Nafi and Uma are two losses).

Buganda

The Buganda kingdom was founded by the Ganda or Baganda people around the 14th century CE. The ancestors of the Ganda may have migrated to the northwest of Lake Victoria as early as 1000 BCE. Buganda was ruled by the *kabaka* with a *bataka* composed of the clan heads. Over time, the *kabakas* diluted the authority of the *bataka*, with Buganda becoming a centralized monarchy. By the 16th century, Buganda was engaged in expansion but had a serious rival in Bunyoro. By the 1870s, Buganda was a wealthy nation-state. The *kabaka*ruled with his *Lukiko* (council of minister). Buganda had a naval fleet of a hundred vessels, each manned by thirty men. Buganda supplanted Bunyoro as the most important state in the region. However, by the early 20th century, Buganda became a province of the British Uganda Protectorate.

Rwanda

Southeast of Bunyoro, near Lake Kivu at the bottom of the western rift, the Kingdom of Rwanda was founded, perhaps during the 17th century. Tutsi (BaTutsi) pastoralists formed the elite, with a king called the *mwami*. The Hutu (BaHutu) were farmers. Both groups spoke the same language, but there were strict social norms against marrying each other and interaction. According to oral tradition, the Kingdom of Rwanda was founded by Mwami Ruganzu II (Ruganzu Ndori) (c. 1600–1624), with his capital near Kigali. It took 200 years to attain a truly centralized kingdom under Mwami Kigeli IV (Kigeri Rwabugiri) (1840–1895). Subjugation of the Hutu proved more difficult than subduing the Tutsi. The last Tutsi chief gave up to Mwami Mutara II (Mutara Rwogera) (1802–1853) in 1852, but the last Hutu holdout was conquered in the 1920s by Mwami Yuhi V (Yuli Musinga) (1896–1931).

Burundi

South of the Kingdom of Rwanda was the Kingdom of Burundi. It was founded by the Tutsi chief Ntare Rushatsi (c. 1657–1705).

Like Rwanda, Burundi was built on cattle raised by Tutsi pastoralists, crops from Hutu farmers, conquest, and political innovations. Under Mwami Ntari Rugaamba (c. 1795–1852), Burundi pursued an aggressive expansionist policy, one based more on diplomacy than force.

Maravi (Malawi)

The Maravi claimed descent from Karonga (*kalonga*), who took that title as king. The Maravi connected middle Africa to the east coastal trade, with Swahili Kilwa. By the 17th century, the Maravi Empire encompassed all the area between Lake Malawi and the mouth of the Zambezi River. The *karonga* was Mzura, who did much to extend the empire. Mzura made a pact with the Portuguese to establish a 4,000-man army to attack the Shona in return for aid in defeating his rival Lundi, a chief of the Zimba. In 1623, he turned on the Portuguese and assisted the Shona. In 1640, he welcome back the Portuguese for trade. The Maravi Empire did not long survive the death of Mzura. By the 18th century, it had broken into its previous polities.

West Africa

Sahelian empires & states

Ghana

The Ghana Empire may have been an established kingdom as early as the 4th century CE, founded among the Soninke by Dinge Cisse. Ghana was first mentioned by Arab geographer Al-Farazi in the late 8th century. Ghana was inhabited by urban dwellers and rural farmers. The urban dwellers were the administrators of the empire, who were Muslims, and the *Ghana* (king), who practiced traditional religion. Two towns existed, one where the Muslim administrators and Berber-Arabs lived, which was connected by a stone-paved road to the king's residence. The rural dwellers lived in villages, which joined together into broader polities that pledged loyalty to the *Ghana*. The *Ghana* was viewed as divine, and his physical well-being reflected on the whole society. Ghana converted to Islam around 1050, after conquering Aoudaghost.

The Ghana Empire grew wealthy by taxing the trans-Saharan trade that linked Tiaret and Sijilmasa to Aoudaghost. Ghana controlled access to the goldfields of Bambouk, southeast of Koumbi Saleh. A percentage of salt and gold going through its territory was taken. The empire was not involved in production.

By the 11th century, Ghana was in decline. It was once thought that the sacking of Koumbi Saleh by Berbers under the Almoravid dynastyin 1076 was the cause. This is no longer accepted. Several alternative explanations are cited. One important reason is the transfer of the gold trade east to the Niger River and the Taghaza Trail, and Ghana's consequent economic decline. Another reason cited is political instability through rivalry among the different hereditary polities. The empire came to an end in 1230, when Takrur in northern Senegaltook over the capital.

Mali

The Mali Empire began in the 13th century CE, when a Mande (Mandingo) leader, Sundiata (Lord Lion) of the Keita clan, defeated Soumaoro Kanté, king of the Sosso or southern Soninke, at the Battle of Kirina in c. 1235. Sundiata continued his conquest from the fertile forests and Niger Valley, east to the Niger Bend, north into the Sahara, and west to the Atlantic Ocean, absorbing the remains of the Ghana Empire. Sundiata took on the title of *mansa*. He established the capital of his empire at Niani.

Although the salt and gold trade continued to be important to the Mali Empire, agriculture and pastoralism was also critical. The growing of sorghum, millet, and rice was a vital function. On the northern borders of the Sahel, grazing cattle, sheep, goats, and camels were major activities. Mande society was organize around the village and land. A cluster of villages was called a *kafu*, ruled by a *farma*. The *farma* paid tribute to the *mansa*. A dedicated army of elite cavalry and infantry maintained order, commanded by the royal court. A formidable force could be raised from tributary regions, if necessary.

Conversion to Islam was a gradual process. The power of the *mansa* depended on upholding traditional beliefs and a spiritual foundation of power. Sundiata initially kept Islam at bay. Later *mansas* were devout Muslims but still acknowledged traditional deities and took part in traditional rituals and festivals, which were important to the Mande. Islam became a court religion under Sundiata's son Uli I (1225–1270).*Mansa* Uli made a pilgrimage to Mecca, becoming recognized within the Muslim world. The court was staffed with literate Muslims as secretaries and accountants. Muslim traveller Ibn Battuta left vivid descriptions of the empire.

Mali reached the peak of its power and extent in the 14th century, when *Mansa* Musa (1312–1337) made his famous *hajj* to Mecca with 500 slaves, each holding a bar of gold worth 500 mitqals. *Mansa* Musa's *hajj* devalued gold in Mamluk Egypt for a decade. He made a great impression on the minds of the Muslim and European world. He invited scholars and architects like Ishal al-Tuedjin (al-Sahili) to further integrate Mali into the Islamic world.

The Mali Empire saw an expansion of learning and literacy. In 1285, Sakura, a freed slave, usurped the throne. This *mansa* drove theTuareg out of Timbuktu and established it as a centre of learning and commerce. The book trade increased, and book copying became a very respectable and profitable profession. Timbuktu and Djenné became important centers of learning within the Muslim world.

After the reign of Mansa Suleyman (1341–1360), Mali began its spiral downward. Mossi cavalry raided the exposed southern border. Tuareg harassed the northern border in order to retake Timbuktu. Fulani (Fulbe) eroded Mali's authority in the west by establishing the independent Imamate of Futa Toro, a successor to the kingdom of Takrur. Serer and Wolof alliances were broken. In 1545 to 1546, the Songhai Empiretook Niani. After 1599, the empire lost the Bambouk goldfields and disintegrated into petty polities.

Songhai

The Songhai people are descended from fishermen on the Middle Niger River. They established their capital at Kukiya in the 9th century CE and at Gao in the 12th century. The Songhai speak a Nilo-Saharan language.

Sonni Ali, a Songhai, began his conquest by capturing Timbuktu in 1468 from the Tuareg. He extended the empire to the north, deep into the desert, pushed the Mossi further south of the Niger, and expanded southwest to Djenne. His army consisted of cavalry and a fleet of canoes. Sonni Ali was not a Muslim, and he was portrayed negatively by Berber-Arab scholars, especially for attacking Muslim Timbuktu. After his death in 1492, his heirs were deposed by General Muhammad Ture, a Muslim of Soninke origins.

Muhammad Ture (1493–1528) founded the Askiya Dynasty, *askiya* being the title of the king. He consolidated the conquests of Sonni Ali. Islam was used to extend his authority by declaring jihad on the Mossi, reviving the trans-Saharan trade, and having the Abbasid "shadow" caliph in Cairo declare him as caliph of Sudan. He established Timbuktu as a great centre of Islamic learning. Muhammad Ture expanded the empire by pushing the Tuareg north, capturing Aïr in the east, and capturing salt-producing Taghaza. He brought the Hausa states into the Songhay trading network. He further centralized the administration of the empire by selecting administrators from loyal servants and families and assigning them to conquered territories. They were responsible for raising local militias. Centralization made Songhay very stable, even during dynastic disputes. Leo Africanus left vivid descriptions of the empire under Askiya Muhammad. Askiya Muhammad was deposed by his son in 1528. After much rivalry, Muhammad Ture's last son Askiya Daoud (1529–1582) assumed the throne.

In 1591, Morocco invaded the Songhai Empire under Ahmad al-Mansur of the Saadi Dynasty in order to secure the goldfields of the Sahel. At the Battle of Tondibi, the Songhai army was defeated. The Moroccans captured Djenne, Gao, and Timbuktu, but they were unable to secure the whole region. Askiya Nuhu and the Songhay army regrouped at Dendi in the heart of Songhai territory where a spirited guerrilla resistance sapped the resources of the Moroccans, who were dependent upon constant resupply from Morocco. Songhai split into several states during the 17th century.

Morocco found its venture unprofitable. The gold trade had been diverted to Europeans on the coast. Most of the trans-Saharan trade was now diverted east to Bornu. Expensive equipment purchased with gold had to be sent across the Sahara, an unsustainable scenario. The Moroccans who remained married into the population and were referred to as *Arma* or *Ruma*. They established themselves at Timbuktu as a military caste with various fiefs, independent from Morocco. Amid the chaos, other groups began to assert themselves, including the Fulani of Futa Tooro who encroached from the west. The Bambara Empire, one of the states that broke from Songhai, sacked Gao. In 1737, the Tuareg massacred the *Arma*.

Sokoto Caliphate

The Fulani were migratory people. They moved from Mauritania and settled in Futa Tooro, Futa Djallon, and subsequently throughout the rest of West Africa. By the 14th century CE, they had converted to Islam. During the 16th century, they established themselves at Macinain southern Mali. During the 1670s, they declared jihads on non-Muslims. Several states were formed from these jihadist wars, at Futa Toro, Futa Djallon, Macina, Oualia, and Bundu. The most important of these states was the Sokoto Caliphate or Fulani Empire.

In the city of Gobir, Usman dan Fodio (1754–1817) accused the Hausa leadership of practicing an impure version of Islam and of being morally corrupt. In 1804, he launched the Fulani War as a jihad among a population that was restless about high taxes and discontented with its leaders. Jihad fever swept northern Nigeria, with strong support among both the Fulani and the Hausa. Usman created an empire that included parts of northern Nigeria, Benin, and Cameroon, with Sokoto as its capital. He retired to teach and write and handed the empire to his son Muhammed Bello. The Sokoto Caliphate lasted until 1903 when the British conquered northern Nigeria.

Forest empires and states

Akan kingdoms and emergence of Asante Empire

The Akan speak a Kwa Language. The speakers of Kwa languages are believed to have come from East/Central Africa, before settling in the Sahel. By the 12th century, the Akan Kingdom of Bonoman (Bono State) was established. During the 13th century, when the gold mines in modern-day Mali started to dry up, Bonoman and later other Akan states began to rise to promince as the major players in the Gold trade. It was Bonoman and other Akan kingdoms like Denkyira, Akyem, Akwamu which were the predecessors to what became the all-powerful Empire of Ashanti. When and how the Ashante got to their present location is debatable. What is known is that by the 17th century an Akan people were identified as living in a state called Kwaaman. The location of the state was north of Lake Bosomtwe. The state's revenue was mainly derived from trading in gold and kola nuts and clearing forest to plant yams. They built towns between the Pra and Ofin rivers. They formed alliances for defense and paid tribute toDenkyira one of the more powerful Akan states at that time along with Adansi and Akwamu. During the 16th century, Ashante society experienced sudden changes, including population growth because of cultivation of New World plants such as cassava and maize and an increase in the gold trade between the coast and the north.

By the 17th century, Osei Kofi Tutu I (c. 1695–1717), with help of Okomfo Anokye, unified what became the Ashante into a confederation with the Golden Stool as a symbol of their unity and spirit. Osei Tutu engaged in a massive territorial expansion. He built up the Ashante army based on the Akan state of Akwamu, introducing new organization and turning a disciplined militia into an effective fighting machine. In 1701, the Ashante conquered Denkyira, giving them access to the coastal trade with Europeans, especially the Dutch. Opoku Ware I(1720–1745) engaged in further expansion, adding other southern Akan states to the growing empire. He turned north adding Techiman, Banda, Gyaaman, and Gonja, states on the Black Volta. Between 1744 and 1745, *Asantehene* Opoku attacked the powerful northern state of Dagomba, gaining control of the important middle Niger trade routes. Kusi Obodom (1750–1764) succeeded Opoku. He solidified all the newly won territories. Osei Kwadwo (1777–1803) imposed administrative reforms that allowed the empire to be governed effectively and to continue its military expansion. Osei Kwame Panyin (1777–

1803), Osei Tutu Kwame (1804–1807), and Osei Bonsu (1807–1824) continued territorial comsolidation and expansion. The Ashante Empire included all of present-day Ghana and large parts of Ivory Coast.

The *ashantehene* inherited his position from his mother. He was assisted at the capital, Kumasi, by a civil service of men talented in trade, diplomacy, and the military, with a head called the *Gyaasehene*. Men from Arabia, Sudan, and Europe were employed in the civil service, all of them appointed by the *ashantehene*. At the capital and in other towns, the *ankobia* or special police were used as bodyguards to the*ashantehene*, as sources of intelligence, and to suppress rebellion. Communication throughout the empire was maintained via a network of well-kept roads from the coast to the middle Niger and linking together other trade cities.

For most of the 19th century, the Ashante Empire remained powerful. It was later destroyed in 1900 by British superior weaponry and organization following the four Anglo-Ashanti wars.

Dahomey

The Dahomey Kingdom was founded in the early 17th century CE when the Aja peopleof the Allada kingdom moved northward and settled among the Fon. They began to assert their power a few years later. In so doing they established the Kingdom of Dahomey, with its capital at Agbome. King Houegbadja (c. 1645–1685) organized Dahomey into a powerful centralized state. He declared all lands to be owned of the king and subject to taxation. Primogeniture in the kingship was established, neutralizing all input from village chiefs. A "cult of kingship" was established. A captive slave would be sacrificed annually to honor the royal ancestors. During the 1720s, the slave-trading states of Whydah and Allada were taken, giving Dahomey direct access to the slave coast and trade with Europeans. King Agadja (1708–1740) attempted to end the slave trade by keeping the slaves on plantations producing palm oil, but the European profits on slaves and Dahomey's dependency on firearms were too great. In 1730, under king Agaja, Dahomey was conquered by the Oyo Empire, and Dahomey had to pay tribute. Taxes on slaves were mostly paid in cowrie shells. During the 19th century, palm oil was the main trading commodity. France conquered Dahomey during the Second Franco-Dahomean War (1892–1894) and established a colonial government there. Most of the troops who fought against Dahomey were native Africans.

Yoruba

Traditionally, the Yoruba people viewed themselves as the inhabitants of a united empire, in contrast to the situation today, in which "Yoruba" is the cultural-linguistic designation for speakers of a language in the Niger–Congo family. The name comes from a Hausa word to refer to the Oyo Empire. The first Yoruba state was Ile-Ife, said to have been founded around 1000 CE by a supernatural figure, the first *oni* Oduduwa. Oduduwa's sons would be the founders of the different city-states of the Yoruba, and his daughters would become the mothers of the various Yoruba *obas*, or kings. Yoruba city-states were usually governed by an *oba* and a*iwarefa*, a council of chiefs who advised the *oba*. By the 18th century, the Yoruba city-states formed a loose confederation, with the *Oni* of Ife as the head and Ife as the capital. As time went on, the individual city-states became more powerful with their *obas* assuming more powerful spiritual positions and diluting the authority of the *Oni* of Ife. Rivalry became intense among the city-states.

The Oyo Empire rose in the 16th century. The Oyo state had been conquered in 1550 by the kingdom of Nupe, which was in possession of cavalry, an important tactical advantage. The *alafin* (king) of Oyo was sent into exile. After returning, *Alafin* Orompoto (c. 1560–1580) built up an army based on heavily armed cavalry and long-service troops. This made them invincible in combat on the northern grasslands and in the thinly wooded forests. By the end of the 16th century, Oyo had added the western region of the Niger to the hills of Togo, the Yoruba ofKetu, Dahomey, and the Fon nation.

A governing council served the empire, with clear executive divisions. Each acquired region was assigned a local administrator. Families served in king-making capacities. Oyo, as a northern Yoruba kingdom, served as middle-man in the north-south trade and connecting the eastern forest of Guinea with the western and central Sudan, the Sahara, and North Africa. The Yoruba manufactured cloth, ironware, and pottery, which were exchanged for salt, leather, and most importantly horses from the Sudan to maintain the cavalry. Oyo remained strong for two hundred years. It became a protectorate of Great Britain in 1888, before further fragmenting into warring factions. The Oyo state ceased to exist as any sort of power in 1896.

Benin

The Kwa Niger–Congo speaking Edo people. By the mid-15th century, the Benin Empire was engaged in political expansion and consolidation. Under *Oba* (king) Ewuare (c. 1450–1480 CE), the state was organized for conquest. He solidified central authority and initiated 30 years of war with his neighbours. At his death, the Benin Empire extended to Dahomey in the west, to the Niger Delta in the east, along the west African coast, and to the Yoruba towns in the north. Ewuare's grandson *Oba* Esigie (1504–1550) eroded the power of the *uzama* (state council) and increase contact and trade with Europeans, especially with the Portuguese who provided a new source of copper for court art. The *oba* ruled with the advice from the *uzama,* a council consisting of chiefs of powerful families and town chiefs of different guilds. Later its authority was diminished by the establishment of administrative dignitaries. Women wielded power. The queen mother who produced the future *oba* wielded immense influence.

Benin was never a significant exporter of slaves, as Alan Ryder's book Benin and the Europeans showed. By the early 1700s, it was wrecked with dynastic disputes and civil wars. However, it regained much of its former power in the reigns of Oba Eresoyen and Oba Akengbuda. After the 16th century, Benin mainly exported pepper, ivory, gum, and cotton cloth to the Portuguese and Dutch who resold it to other African societies on the coast. In 1897, the British sacked the city.

Niger Delta and Igbo

The Niger Delta comprised numerous city-states with numerous forms of government. These city-states were protected by the waterways and thick vegetation of the delta. The region was transformed by trade in the 17th century CE. The delta's city-states were comparable to those of the Swahili people in East Africa. Some, like Bonny, Kalabari, and Warri, had kings. Others, like Brass, were republics with small senates, and those at Cross River and Old Calabar were ruled by merchants of the *ekpe* society. The*ekpe* society regulated trade and made rules for members known as house systems. Some of these houses, like the Pepples of Bonny, were well known in the Americas and Europe.

The Igbo lived east of the delta (but with the Anioma on the west of the Niger River). The Kingdom of Nri rose in the 9th century CE, with the *Eze* Nri being its leader. It was a political entity composed of villages, and each village was autonomous and independent with its own territory and name, each recognized by its neighbours. Villages were democratic with all males and sometimes females a part of the decision-making process. Graves at Igbo-Ukwu (800 CE) contained brass artifacts of local manufacture and glass beads from Egypt or India, indicative of extraregional trade.

19TH CENTURY

Southern Africa

By the 1850s, British and German missionaries and traders had penetrated present-day Namibia. Herero and Nama competed for guns and ammunition, providing cattle, ivory, and ostrich feathers. The Germans were more firmly established than the British in the region. By 1884, the Germans declared the coastal region from the Orange River to the Kunene River a German protectorate. They pursued an aggressive policy of land expansion for white settlements. They exploited rivalry between the Nama and Herero.

The Herero entered into an alliance with the Germans, thinking they could get an upper hand on the Nama. The Germans set up a garrison at the Herero capital and started allocating Herero land for white settlements, including the best grazing land in the central plateau, and made tax and labor demands. The Herero and

Ovambanderu rebelled, but the rebellion was crushed and leaders were executed. Between 1896 and 1897, rinderpest crippled the economic backbone of the Herero and Nama economy and slowed white expansion. The Germans continued the policy of making Namibia a white settlement by seizing land and cattle, and even trying to export Herero labor to South Africa.

In 1904, the Herero rebelled. German General Lothar von Trotha implemented an extermination policy at the Battle of Waterberg, which drove the Herero west of the Kalahari Desert. At the end of 1905, only 16,000 Herero were alive, out of a previous population of 80,000. Nama resistance was crushed in 1907. All Nama and Herero cattle and land were confiscated from the very diminished population, with remaining Nama and Herero assuming a subordinate position. Labor had to be imported from among the Ovambo.

Nguniland

A moment of great disorder in southern Africa was the *Mfecane*, "the crushing." It was started by the northern Nguni kingdoms ofMthethwa, Ndwandwe, and Swaziland over scarce resource and famine. When Dingiswayo of Mthethwa died, Shaka of the Zulu people took over. He established the Zulu Kingdom, asserting authority over the Ndwandwe and pushing the Swazi north. The scattering Ndwandwe and Swazi caused the Mfecane to spread. During the 1820s, Shaka expanded the empire all along the Drakensberg foothills, with tribute being paid as far south as the Tugela and Umzimkulu rivers. He replaced the chiefs of conquered polities with *indunas*, responsible to him. He introduced a centralized, dedicated, and disciplined military force not seen in the region, with a new weapon in the short stabbing-spear.

In 1828, Shaka was assassinated by his half brother Dingane, who lacked the military genius and leadership skills of Shaka. Voortrekkerstried to occupy Zulu land in 1838. In the early months they were defeated, but the survivors regrouped at the Ncome River and soundly defeated the Zulu. However, the Voortrekkers dared not settle Zulu land. Dingane was killed in 1840 during a civil war. His brother Mpandetook over and strengthened Zulu territories to the north. In 1879 the Zulu Kingdom was invaded by Britain in a quest to control all of South Africa. The Zulu Kingdom was victorious at the Battle of Isandlwana but was defeated at the Battle of Ulundi.

One of the major states to emerge from the Mfecane was the Sotho Kingdom founded at Thaba Bosiu by Moshoeshoe I around 1821 to 1822. It was a confederation different polities that accepted the absolute authority of Moshoeshoe. During the 1830s, the kingdom invited missionaries as a strategic means of acquiring guns and horses from the Cape. Orange Free State slowly diminished the kingdom but never completely defeated it. In 1868, Moshoeshoe asked that the Sotho Kingdom be annexed by Britain, to save the remnant. It became the British protectorate of Basutoland.

Voortrekkers

By the 19th century, most Khoikhoi territory was under Boer control. The Khoikhoi had lost economic and political independence and had been absorbed into Boer society. The Boers spoke Afrikaans, a language or dialect derived from Dutch, and no longer called themselves Boers but Afrikaner. Some Khoikhoi were used as commandos in raids against other Khoikhoi and later Xhosa. A mixed Khoi, slave, and European population called the Cape Coloureds, who were outcasts within colonial society, also arose. Khoikhoi who lived far on the frontier included the Kora, Oorlams, and Griqua. In 1795, the British took over the cape colony from the Dutch.

In the 1830s, Boers embarked on a journey of expansion, east of the Great Fish River into the Zuurveld. They were referred to as*Voortrekkers*. They founded republics of the Transvaal and Orange Free State, mostly in areas of sparse population that had been diminished by the *Mfecane/Difaqane*. Unlike the Khoisan, the Bantu states were not conquered by the Afrikaners, because of population density and greater unity. Additionally, they began to arm themselves with guns acquired through trade at the cape. In some cases, as in the Xhosa/Boer Wars, Boers were removed from Xhosa lands. It required a dedicated imperial military force to subdue the Bantu-speaking states. In 1901, the Boer republics were defeated by Britain in the Second Boer War. The defeat however consummated many Afrikaners' ambition: South Africa would be under white rule. The British placed all power—legislative, executive, administrative—in English and Afrikaner hands.

European trade, exploration and conquest

Between 1878 and 1898, European states partitioned and conquered most of Africa. For 400 years, European nations had mainly limited their involvement to trading stations on the African coast. Few dared venture inland from the coast; those that did, like the Portuguese, often met defeats and had to retreat to the coast. Several technological innovations helped to overcome this 400-year pattern. One was the development of repeating rifles, which were easier and quicker to load than muskets. Artillery was being used increasingly. In 1885, Hiram S. Maximdeveloped the maxim gun, the model of the modern-day machine gun. European states kept these weapons largely among themselves by refusing to sell these weapons to African leaders.

African germs took numerous European lives and deterred permanent settlements. Diseases such as yellow fever, sleeping sickness, yaws, and leprosy made Africa a very inhospitable place for Europeans. The deadliest disease was malaria, endemic throughout tropical Africa. In 1854, the discovery of quinine and other medical innovations helped to make conquest and colonization in Africa possible.

Strong motives for conquest of Africa were at play. Raw materials were needed for European factories. Europe in the early part of the 19th century was undergoing its Industrial Revolution. Nationalist rivalries and prestige were at play. Acquiring African colonies would show rivals that a nation was powerful and significant. These factors culminated in the Scramble for Africa.

Knowledge of Africa increased. Numerous European explorers began to explore the continent.Mungo Park traversed the Niger River. James Bruce travelled through Ethiopia and located the source of the Blue Nile. Richard Francis Burton was the first European at Lake Tanganyika. Samuel White Baker explored the Upper Nile. John Hanning Speke located a source of the Nileat Lake Victoria. Other significant European explorers included Heinrich Barth, Henry Morton Stanley, Silva Porto, Alexandre de

Serpa Pinto, Rene Caille, Friedrich Gerhard Rohlfs, Gustav Nachtigal, George Schweinfurth, and Joseph Thomson. The most famous of the explorers wasDavid Livingstone, who explored southern Africa and traversed the continent from the Atlantic atLuanda to the Indian Ocean at Quelimane. European explorers made use of African guides and servants, and established long-distance trading routes were used.

Missionaries attempting to spread Christianity also increased European knowledge of Africa. Between 1884 and 1885, European nations met at the Berlin West Africa Conference to discuss the partitioning of Africa. It was agreed that European claims to parts of Africa would only be recognised if Europeans provided effective occupation. In a series of treaties in 1890–1891, colonial boundaries were completely drawn. All of sub saharan Africa was claimed by European powers, except for Ethiopia (Abyssinia) and Liberia.

The European powers set up a variety of different administrations in Africa, reflecting different ambitions and degrees of power. In some areas, such as parts of British West Africa, colonial control was tenuous and intended for simple economic extraction, strategic power, or as part of a long term development plan. In other areas, Europeans were encouraged to settle, creating settler states in which a European minority dominated. Settlers only came to a few colonies in sufficient numbers to have a strong impact. British settler colonies included British East Africa (now Kenya), Northern and Southern Rhodesia, (Zambia and Zimbabwe, respectively), and South Africa, which already had a significant population of European settlers, the Boers. France planned to settle Algeria and eventually incorporate it into the French state on an equal basis with the European provinces. Algeria's proximity across the Mediterranean allowed plans of this scale.

In most areas colonial administrations did not have the manpower or resources to fully administer the territory and had to rely on local power structures to help them. Various factions and groups within the societies exploited this European requirement for their own purposes, attempting to gain positions of power within their own communities by cooperating with Europeans. One aspect of this struggle included what Terence Ranger has termed the "invention of tradition." In order to legitimize their own claims to power in the eyes of both the colonial administrators and their own people, native elites would essentially manufacture "traditional" claims to power, or ceremonies. As a result, many societies were thrown into disarray by the new order.

Following the Scramble for Africa, an early but secondary focus for most colonial regimes was the suppression of slavery and the slave trade. By the end of the colonial period they were mostly successful in this aim, though slavery is still very active in Africa.

European colonial territories

Belgium

- Congo Free State and Belgian Congo (today's Democratic Republic of the Congo)
- Ruanda-Urundi (comprising modern Rwanda and Burundi, between 1916 and 1960)

Germany

- German Kamerun (now Cameroon and part of Nigeria)
- German East Africa (now Rwanda, Burundi and most of Tanzania)
- German South-West Africa (now Namibia)
- German Togoland (now Togo and eastern part of Ghana)

Italy

- Italian North Africa (now Libya)
- Eritrea
- Italian Somaliland (now part of Somalia)

Independent states

- Liberia, founded by the American Colonization Society of the United States in 1821; declared independence in 1847
- Ethiopian Empire (Abyssinia) had its borders re-drawn with Italian Eritrea and French Somaliland (modern Djibouti), briefly occupied byItaly from 1936 to 1941 during the Abyssinia Crisis;
- Sudan, independent under Mahdi rule between 1885 and 1899. It was then under British rule from 1899 to 1956.

20th century

During this era a sense of local patriotism or nationalism took deeper root among African intellectuals and politicians. Some of the inspiration for this movement came from the First World War in which European countries had relied on colonial troops for their own defense. Many in Africa realized their own strength with regard to the colonizer for the first time. At the same time, some of the mystique of the "invincible" European was shattered by the barbarities of the war. However, in most areas European control remained relatively strong during this period.

After World War I, former German colonies in Africa were taken over by France, Belgium, and the United Kingdom. Ethiopia, the last independent African nation, was invaded in 1935 under the government of Benito Mussolini, maintaining control until 1941.

Second half of 20th century: decolonization

The decolonization of Africa started with Libya in 1951. (Although Liberia, South Africa, Egypt and Ethiopia were already independent.) Many countries followed in the 1950s and 1960s, with a peak in 1960 with independence of a large part of French West Africa. Most of the remaining countries gained independence throughout the 1960s, although some colonizers (Portugal in particular) were reluctant to relinquish sovereignty, resulting in bitter wars of independence which lasted for a decade or more. The last African countries to gain formal independence wereGuinea-Bissau (1974), Mozambique (1975) and Angola (1975) from Portugal; Djibouti fromFrance in 1977; Zimbabwe from United Kingdom in 1980; and Namibia from South Africa in 1990. Eritrea later split off from Ethiopia in 1993. Because many cities were founded, enlarged and renamed by the Europeans, after independence many place names were renamed.

East Africa

The Mau Mau Rebellion took place in Kenya from 1952 until 1956 but was put down by British and local forces. A State of Emergency remained in place until 1960. Kenya became independent in 1963, and Jomo Kenyatta served as its first president.

The early 1960s also signaled the start of major clashes between the Hutus and the Tutsis in Rwanda and Burundi. In 1994 this culminated in the Rwandan Genocide, a conflict in which over 800,000 people were murdered.

North Africa

Moroccan nationalism developed during the 1930s; the Istiqlal Party was formed, pushing for independence. In 1953 sultan Muhammad Vcalled for independence. On March 2, 1956, Morocco became independent of France. Muhammad V became ruler of independent Morocco.

In 1954, Algeria formed the National Liberation Front (FLN) as it split from France. This resulted in the Algerian War, which lasted until independence negotiations in 1962. Muhammad Ahmed Ben Bella was elected president. Over a million French nationals, predominantlyPied-Noirs, left the country, crippling the economy.

In 1934, the "Neo-Destour" (New Constitution) party was founded by Habib Bourguiba pushing for independence in Tunisia. Tunisia became independent in 1955. Its *bey* was disposed and Habib Bourguiba elected.

In 1954, Gamal Abdel Nasser deposed the monarchy of Egypt and came to power. Muammar Gaddafi led a coup in Libya in 1969 and remained in power until he was killed in 2011.

Egypt was involved in several wars against Israel and was allied with other Arab countries. The first was right after the state of Israel was founded, in 1948. Egypt went to war again in 1967 and lost the Sinai Peninsula to Israel. They went to war yet again in 1973. In 1979,Anwar Sadat and Menachem Begin signed the Camp David Accords, which gave back the Sinai Peninsula to Egypt in exchange for the recognition of Israel. The accords are still in effect today. In 1981, Sadat was assassinated by an Islamist for signing the accords.

Southern Africa

In 1948 the apartheid laws were started in South Africa by the dominant National Party. These were largely a continuation of existing policies; the difference was the policy of "separate development." Where previous policies had only been disparate efforts to economically exploit the African majority, apartheid represented an entire philosophy of separate racial goals, leading to both the divisive laws of 'petty apartheid,' and the grander scheme of African homelands.

In 1994, the South African government abolished apartheid. South Africans elected Nelson Mandela of the African National Congress in the country's first multiracial presidential election.

West Africa

Following World War II, nationalist movements arose across West Africa, most notably in Ghana under Kwame Nkrumah. In 1957, Ghana became the first sub-Saharan colony to achieve its independence, followed the next year by France's colonies; by 1974, West Africa's nations were entirely autonomous. Since independence, many West African nations have been plagued by corruption and instability, with notable civil wars in Nigeria, Sierra Leone, Liberia, and Ivory Coast, and a succession of military coups in Ghana and Burkina Faso. Many states have failed to develop their economies despite enviable natural resources, and political instability is often accompanied by undemocratic government.

3

Culture of Africa

The culture of Africa is varied and manifold. It is a product of the diverse populations that today inhabit the continent of Africa and the African Diaspora. It has been affected by both internal and external forces.

Historical overview

Africa is divided into a great number of ethnic cultures. The continent's cultural regeneration has also been an integral aspect of post-independence nation-building on the continent, with a recognition of the need to harness the cultural resources of Africa to enrich the process of education, requiring the creation of an enabling environment in a number of ways. In recent times, the call for a much greater emphasis on the cultural dimension in all aspects of development has become increasingly vocal. During colonialism in Africa, Europeans possessed attitudes of superiority and a sense of mission. The French were able to accept an African as French if that person gave up their African culture and adopted French ways. Knowledge of the Portuguese language and culture and abandonment of traditional African ways defined one as civilized. Kenyan social commentator Mwiti Mugambi argues that the future of Africa can only be forged from accepting and mending the sociocultural present. For Mugambi, colonial cultural hangovers, pervasive Western cultural inundation, and aid-giving arm-twisting donors are, he argues, here to stay and no amount of looking into Africa's past will make them go away. However, Maulana Karenga states:

Our culture provides us with an ethos we must honor in both thought and practice. By ethos, we mean a people's self-understanding as well as its self-presentation in the world through its thought and practice in the other six areas of culture. It is above all a cultural challenge. For culture is here defined as the totality of thought and practice by which a people creates itself, celebrates, sustains and develops itself and introduces itself to history and humanity.

— *Maulana Karenga , African Culture and the Ongoing Quest for Excellence*

African arts and crafts

Africa has a rich tradition of arts and crafts. African arts and crafts find expression in a variety of wood carvings,brass and leather art works. African arts and crafts also include sculpture, paintings, pottery, ceremonial and religious headgear and dress. Maulana Karenga states that in African art, the object was not as important as the soul force behind the creation of the object. He also states that All art must be revolutionary and in being revolutionary it must be collective, committing, and functional.

Certain African cultures has always placed emphasis on personal appearance and jewelry has remained an important personal accessory. Many pieces of such jewelry are made of cowry shells and similar materials. Similarly, masks are made with elaborate designs and are an important part of some cultures in Africa. Masks are used in various ceremonies depicting ancestors and spirits, mythological characters and deities.

In many traditional arts and craft traditions in Africa, certain themes significant to those particular cultures recur, including a couple, a woman with a child, a male with a weapon or animal, and an outsider or a stranger. Couples may represent ancestors, community founder, married couple or twins. The couple theme rarely exhibit intimacy of men and women. The mother with the child or children reveals intense desire of the women to have children. The theme is also representative of mother mars and the people as her children. The man with the weapon or animal theme symbolizes honour and power. A stranger may be from some other tribe or someone from a different country, and more distorted portrayal of the stranger indicates proportionately greater gap from the stranger.

Folklore and religion

Like all human cultures, African folklore and religion represents a variety of social facets of the various cultures in Africa. Like almost all civilizations and cultures, flood myths have been circulating in different parts of Africa. Culture and religion share space and are deeply intertwined in African cultures. In Ethiopia, Christianity and Islam form the core aspects of Ethiopian culture and inform dietary customs as well as rituals and rites. According to a Pygmy myth, Chameleon, hearing a strange noise in a tree, cut open its trunk and water came out in a great flood that spread all over the land.

Folktales also play an important role in many African cultures. Stories reflect a group cultural identity and preserving the stories of Africa will help preserve an entire culture. Storytelling affirms pride and identity in a culture. In Africa, stories are created by and for the ethnic group telling them. Different ethnic groups in Africa have different rituals or ceremonies for storytelling, which creates a sense of belonging to a cultural group. To outsiders hearing an ethnic group's stories, it provides an insight into the community's beliefs, views, and customs. For people within the community, it allows them to encompass their group's uniqueness. They show the human desires and fears of a group, such as love, marriage, and death. Folktales are also seen as a tool for education and entertainment. They provide a way for children to understand the material and social environment. Every story has a moral to teach people, such as good will prevail over evil. For entertainment, stories are set in fantastic, non-human worlds. Often, the main character of the story would be a talking animal or something unnatural would happen to human character. Even though folktales are for entertainment, they bring a sense of belonging and pride to communities in Africa.

There are different types of African stories: animal tales and day-to-day tales. Animal tales more oriented towards entertainment, but still have morals and lessons to them. Animal tales are normally divided into trickster tales and ogre tales. In the animal tales, a certain animal would always have the same character or role in each story so the audience does not have to worry about characterization. The Hare was always the trickster, clever and cunning, while the Hyena was always being tricked by the Hare. Ogres are always cruel, greedy monsters. The messengers in all the stories were the Birds. Day-to-Day tales are the most serious tales, never including humour, that explained the everyday life and struggles of an African community. These tales take on matters such as famine, escape from death, courtship, and family matters, using a song form when the climax of the story was being told.

African stories all have a certain structure to them. Villagers would gather around a common meeting place at the end of the day to listen and tell their stories. Storytellers had certain commands to start and end the stories, "Ugai Itha" to get the audience's attention and begin the story, and "Rukirika" to signal the end of a tale. Each scene of a story is depicted with two characters at a time, so the audience does not get overwhelmed. In each story, victims are able to overcome their predators and take justice out on the culprit. Certain tools were used in African folktales. For example, idiophones, such as drums, were used to make the sounds of different animals. Repetition and call-back techniques in the form of prose or poem were also used to get the audience involved in the stories.

Clothing

Women's traditional clothes in Ethiopia are made from cloth called *shemma* and are used to make *habesha kemis*. The latter garment is basically cotton cloth, about 90 cm wide, woven in long strips which are then sewn together. Sometimes shiny threads are woven into the fabricfor an elegant effect. Men wear pants and a knee-length shirt with a white collar, and perhaps a sweater. Men often wear knee-high socks, while women might not wear socks at all. Men as well as women wear shawls, the *netela*.

Zulus wear a variety of attire, both traditional for ceremonial or culturally celebratory occasions, and modern westernised clothing for everyday use. Traditional male clothing is usually light, consisting of a two-part apron (similar to a loincloth) used to cover the genitals and buttocks. The front piece is called the *umutsha* (pronounced Zulu pronunciation: [umtifash]), and is usually made of springbok or other animal hide twisted into different bands which cover the genitals. The rear piece, called the *ibheshu,* is made of a single piece of springbok or cattle hide, and its length is usually used as an indicator of age and social position; longer amabheshu (plural of ibheshu) are worn by older men. Married men will usually also wear a headband, called the *umqhele,* which is usually also made of springbok hide, orleopard hide by men of higher social status, such as chiefs. Zulu men will also wear cow tails as bracelets and anklets called *imishokobezi* during ceremonies and rituals, such as weddings or dances.

In the Muslim parts of Africa, daily attire also often reflects Islamic tradition.

Cuisine

The various cuisines of Africa use a combination of locally available fruits, cereal grains andvegetables, as well as milk and meat products. In some parts of the continent, the traditional diet features a preponderance of milk, curd and whey products. In much of tropical Africa, however, cow's milk is rare and cannot be produced locally (owing to various diseases that affect livestock). The continent's diverse demographic makeup is reflected in the many different eating and drinking habits, dishes, and preparation techniques of its manifold populations.

In Central Africa, the basic ingredients are plantains and cassava. Fufu-like starchy foods (usually made from fermented cassava roots) are served with grilled meat and sauces. A variety of local ingredients are used while preparing other dishes like spinach stew, cooked with tomato, peppers, chillis, onions, and peanut butter. Cassava plants are also consumed as cooked greens. Groundnut (peanut) stew is also prepared, containing chicken, okra, ginger, and other spices. Another favorite is Bambara, a porridge of rice, peanut butter and sugar. Beef and chicken are favorite meat dishes, but game meat preparations containing crocodile, monkey, antelope and warthog are also served occasionally.

The cuisine of the African Great Lakes region varies from area to area. In the inland savannah, the traditional cuisine of cattle-keeping peoples is distinctive in that meat products are generally absent.Cattle, sheep and goats were regarded as a form of currency and a store of wealth, and are not generally consumed as food. In some areas, traditional peoples consume the milk and blood of cattle, but rarely the meat. Elsewhere, other peoples are farmers who grow a variety of grains and vegetables. Maize (corn) is the basis of ugali, the East African version of West Africa's fufu. Ugali is a starch dish eaten with meats or stews. In Uganda, steamed, green bananas called matoke provide the starch filler of many meals.

In the Horn of Africa, the main traditional dishes in Ethiopian cuisine and Eritrean cuisine are *tsebhis* (stews) served with *injera* (flatbread made from teff, wheat, or sorghum), and hilbet (paste made from legumes, mainly lentil, faba beans). Eritrean and Ethiopian cuisine (especially in the northern half) are very similar, given the shared history of the two countries. The related Somalian cuisine consists of an exotic fusion of diverse culinary influences. Varieties of *bariis* (rice), the most popular probably being basmati, usually serve as the main dish. *Xalwo* (halwo) or halvą is a popular confection served during special occasions such as Eid celebrations or wedding receptions. After meals, homes are traditionally perfumed usingfrankincense (*lubaan*) or incense (*cuunsi*), which is prepared inside an incense burner referred to as a *dabqaad*. All food is served halal.

The roots of North African cuisine can be traced back to the ancient empires of North Africa, particularly in Egypt where many of the country's dishes and culinary traditions date back to ancient Egypt. Over several centuries traders, travelers, invaders, migrants and immigrants all have influenced the cuisine of North Africa. Most of the North African countries today have several similar dishes, sometimes almost the same dish with a different name (the Moroccan *tangia* and the Tunisian *coucha* are both essentially the same dish: a meat stew prepared in an urn and cooked overnight in a public oven), sometimes with a slight change in ingredients and cooking style. To add to the confusion, two completely different dishes may also share the same name (for example, a "tajine" dish is a slow-cooked stew in Morocco, whereas the Tunisian "tajine" is a baked omelette/quiche-like dish). There are noticeable differences between the cooking styles of different nations – there's the sophisticated, full-bodied flavours of Moroccan palace cookery, the fiery dishes of Tunisian cuisine, and the humbler, simpler cuisines of Egypt and Algeria.

The cooking of Southern Africa is sometimes called 'rainbow cuisine', as the food in this region is a blend of many culinary traditions, including those of the Khoisan, Bantu, European and Asian populations. Basic ingredients include seafood, meat products (including wild game), poultry, as well as grains, fresh fruits and vegetables. Fruits include apples, grapes, mangoes, bananas and papayas, avocado, oranges,peaches and apricots. Desserts may simply be fruit. However, there are some more western style puddings, such as the Angolan Cocada amarela, which was inspired by Portuguese cuisine. Meat products include lamb, as well as game like venison, ostrich, and impala. The seafood includes a wide variety such as crayfish, prawns, tuna, mussels, oysters, calamari, mackerel, and lobster. There are also several types of traditional and modern alcoholic beverages including many European-style beers.

A typical West African meal is heavy with starchy items, meat, spices and flavors. A wide array of staples are eaten across the region, including those of Fufu, Banku and Kenkey (originating from Ghana), Foutou, Couscous, Tô, and Garri, which are served alongside soups and stews. Fufu is often made from starchy root vegetables such as yams, cocoyams, or cassava, but also from cereal grains like millet, sorghum or plantains. The staple grain or starch varies region to region and ethnic group to ethnic group, although corn has gained significant ground as it is cheap, swells to greater volumes and creates a beautiful white final product that is greatly desired. Banku and Kenkey are maize dough staples, and Gari is made from dried grated cassavas. Rice-dishes are also widely eaten in the region, especially in the dry Sahel belt inland. Examples of these include Benachin from The Gambia and Jollof rice, a pan-West African rice dish similar to Arab kabsah.

African music

Traditional Sub-Saharan African music is as diverse as the region's various populations. The common perception of Sub-Saharan African music is that it is rhythmic music centered on the drums, and indeed, a large part of Sub-Saharan music, mainly among speakers of Niger–Congo andNilo-Saharan languages, is rhythmic and centered on the drum. Sub-Saharan music is polyrhythmic, usually consisting of multiple rhythms in one composition. Dance involves moving multiple body parts. These aspects of Sub-Saharan music were transferred to the new world by enslaved Sub-Saharan Africans and can be seen in its influence on music forms as Samba, Jazz, Rhythm and Blues, Rock & Roll, Salsa, and Rap music.

Other African musical traditions also involve strings, horns, and very little poly-rhythms. Music from the eastern Sahel and along the Nile, among the Nilo-Saharan, made extensive use of strings and horns in ancient times. Dancing involve swaying body movements and footwork.Among the Khoisansextensive use of string instruments with emphasis on footwork.

Modern Sub-Saharan African music has been influenced by music from the New World (Jazz, Salsa, Rhythm and Blues etc.). Popular styles include Mbalax in Senegal and Gambia, Highlife in Ghana, Zoblazo in Côte d'Ivoire, Makossa in Cameroon, Soukous in the Democratic Republic of Congo, Kizomba in Angola, and Mbaqanga in South Africa. New World styles like Salsa, R&B/Rap, Reggae, and Zouk also have widespread popularity.

Like the musical genres of the Nile Valley and the Horn of Africa, North African music has close ties with Middle Eastern music and utilizes similar melodic modes (*maqamat*). It has a considerable range, from the music of ancient Egypt to the Berber and the Tuareg music of the desert nomads. The region's art music has for centuries followed the outline of Arabic and Andalusian classical music. Its popular contemporary genres include the Algerian Raï. Somali music is typically pentatonic, using five pitches per octave in contrast to aheptatonic (seven note) scale such as the major scale. In Ethiopia, the music of the highlands uses a fundamental modal system called *qenet*, of which there are four main modes: *tezeta, bati, ambassel,* and *anchihoy*. Three additional modes are variations on the above: tezeta minor, bati major, and bati minor. Some songs take the name of their qenet, such as tizita, a song of reminiscence.

Languages

The main ethno-linguistic divisions in Africa are Afro-Asiatic (North Africa, Horn of Africa), Niger–Congo (including speakers from the Bantubranch) in most of Sub-Saharan Africa, Nilo-Saharan in parts of the Sahara and the Sahel and parts of Eastern Africa, and Khoisan (indigenous minorities of Southern Africa). The continent of Africa speaks hundreds of languages, and if dialects spoken by various ethnic groups are also included, the number is much higher. These languages and dialects do not have the same importance: some are spoken by only few hundred persons, others are spoken by millions. Among the most prominent languages spoken are Arabic, Swahili and Hausa. Very few countries of Africa use any single language and for this reason several official languages coexist, African and European. Some Africans speak various European languages such as English, Spanish, French, and Dutch.

AFRICAN ART

African art is a term typically used for the art of Sub-Saharan Africa. Often, casual, amateur observers tend to generalize "traditional" African art, but the continent is full of people, societies and civilizations, each with a unique visual culture. The definition may also include the art of the African Diasporas, such as the art of African Americans. Despite this diversity, there are some unifying artistic themes when considering the totality of the visual culture from the continent of Africa.

The term African art does not usually include the art of the North African areas along the Mediterranean coast, as such areas had long been part of different traditions. For more than a millennium, the art of such areas had formed part of Islamic art, although with many particular characteristics. The Art of Ethiopia, with a long Christian tradition, is also different from that of most of Africa, where Traditional African religion (with Islam in the north) was dominant until relatively recently.

Most African sculpture was historically in wood and other natural materials that have not survived from earlier than, at most, a few centuries ago; older pottery figures can be found from a number of areas. Masks are important elements in the art of many peoples, along with human figures, often highly stylized. There is a vast variety of styles, often varying within the same context of origin depending on the use of the object, but wide regional trends are apparent; sculpture is most common among "groups of settled cultivators in the areas drained by the Niger and Congo rivers" in West Africa. Direct images of deities are relatively infrequent, but masks in particular are or were often made for religious ceremonies; today many are made for tourists as "airport art". African masks were an influence on European Modernist art, which was inspired by their lack of concern for naturalistic depiction. Since the late 19th century there has been an increasing amount of African art in Western collections, the finest pieces of which are now prominently displayed.

Later West African cultures developed bronze casting for reliefs, like the famous Benin Bronzes, to decorate palaces and for highly naturalistic royal heads from around the Yoruba town of Ife, in terracotta as well as metal, from the 12th–14th centuries. Akan goldweights are a form of small metal sculptures produced over the period 1400–1900; some apparently represent proverbs, contributing a narrative element rare in African sculpture; and royal regalia included impressive gold sculptured elements. Many West African figures are used in religious rituals and are often coated with materials placed on them for ceremonial offerings. The Mande-speaking peoples of the same region make pieces from wood with broad, flat surfaces and arms and legs shaped like cylinders. In Central Africa, however, the main distinguishing characteristics include heart-shaped faces that are curved inward and display patterns of circles and dots.

Eastern Africans, in many areas shorter of large timber to carve, are known for Tinga Tinga paintings and Makonde sculptures. There is also tradition of producing textile art, . The culture from Great Zimbabwe left more impressive buildings than sculpture, but the eight soapstone Zimbabwe Birds appear to have had a special significance and were presumably mounted on monoliths. Modern Zimbabwean sculptors in soapstone have achieved considerable international success. Southern Africa's oldest known clay figures date from 400 to 600 AD and have cylindrical heads with a mixture of human and animal features.

Thematic elements

- Artistic creativity or Expressive individualism: In Western African art in particular, there is a widespread emphasis on expressive individualism while simultaneously being influenced by the work of predecessors. An example would be Dan artistry as well as its presence in the Western African diaspora.
- Emphasis on the human figure: The human figure has always been the primary subject matter for most African art, and this emphasis even influenced certain European traditions. For example, in the fifteenth century Portugal traded with the Sapi culture near Ivory Coastin West Africa, who created elaborate ivory saltcellars that were hybrids of African and European designs, most notably in the addition of the human figure (the human figure typically did not appear in Portuguese saltcellars). The human figure may symbolize the living or the dead, may reference chiefs, dancers, or various trades such as drummers or hunters, or even may be an anthropomorphic representation of a god or have other votive function. Another common theme is the inter-morphosis of human and animal.
- Visual abstraction: African artworks tend to favor visual abstraction over naturalistic representation. This is because many African artworks generalize stylistic norms. Ancient Egyptian art, also usually thought of as naturalistically depictive, makes use of highly abstracted and regimented visual canons, especially in painting, as well as the use of different colours to represent the qualities and characteristics of an individual being depicted.

- Emphasis on sculpture: African artists tend to favour three-dimensional artworks over two-dimensional works. Even many African paintings or cloth works were meant to be experienced three-dimensionally. House paintings are often seen as a continuous design wrapped around a house, forcing the viewer to walk around the work to experience it fully; while decorated cloths are worn as decorative or ceremonial garments, transforming the wearer into a living sculpture. Distinct from the static form of traditional Western sculpture African art displays animation, a readiness to move.
- Emphasis on performance art: An extension of the utilitarianism and three-dimensionality of traditional African art is the fact that much of it is crafted for use in performance contexts, rather than in static ones. For example, traditional African masks and costumes very often are used in communal, ceremonial contexts, where they are "danced." Most societies in Africa have names for their masks, but this single name incorporates not only the sculpture, but also the meanings of the mask, the dance associated with it, and the spirits that reside within. In African thought, the three cannot be differentiated.
- Nonlinear scaling: Often a small part of an African design will look similar to a larger part, such as the diamonds at different scales in the Kasai pattern at right. Louis Senghor, Senegal's first president, referred to this as "dynamic symmetry." William Fagg, the British art historian, compared it to the logarithmic mapping of natural growth by biologist D'Arcy Thompson. More recently it has been described in terms of fractal geometry.

Scope

Until recently, the designation "African" was usually only bestowed on the arts of "Black Africa", the peoples living in Sub-Saharan Africa. The non-black peoples of North Africa, the people of the Horn of Africa, as well as the art of ancient Egypt, generally were not included under the rubric of African art. Recently, however, there has been a movement among African art historians and other scholars to include the visual culture of these areas, since all the cultures that produced them, in fact, are located within the geographic boundaries of the African continent. The notion is that by including all African cultures and their visual culture in *African art*, laypersons will gain a greater understanding of the continent's cultural diversity. Since there was often a confluence of traditional African, Islamic and Mediterranean cultures, scholars have found that drawing distinct divisions between Muslim areas, ancient Egypt, the Mediterranean and indigenous black African societies makes little sense. Finally, the arts of the people of the African diaspora, in Brazil, the Caribbean and the southeastern United States, have also begun to be included in the study of African art. The inclusion of art attributed to non-native influences serves to obfuscate the absence of indigenous artistic merit, in particular the period prior to civilization brought to the continent from cultures with a longer history of development.

Materials

African art takes many forms and is made from many different materials. Jewellery is a popular art form and is used to indicate rank, affiliation with a group, or purely for aesthetics. African jewelry is made from such diverse materials as Tiger's eye stone, haematite, sisal, coconut shell, beads and ebony wood. Sculptures can be wooden, ceramic or carved out of stone like the famous Shona sculptures, and decorated or sculpted pottery comes from many regions. Various forms of textiles are made including chitenge, mud cloth and kente cloth. Mosaics made of butterfly wings or coloured sand are popular in west Africa.

History

The origins of African art lie long before recorded history. African rock art in the Sahara in Niger preserves 6000-year-old carvings. Along with sub-Saharan Africa, the western cultural arts, ancient Egyptian paintings and artifacts, and indigenous southern crafts also contributed greatly to African art. Often depicting the abundance of surrounding nature, the art was often abstract interpretations of animals, plant life, or natural designs and shapes. The Nubian Kingdom of Kush in modern Sudan was in close and often hostile contact with Egypt, and produced monumental sculpture mostly derivative of styles that did not lead to the north. In West Africa, the earliest known sculptures are from the Nok culture which thrived between 500 BC and 500 AD in modern Nigeria, with clay figures typically with elongated bodies and angular shapes.

More complex methods of producing art were developed in sub-Saharan Africa around the 10th century, some of the most notable advancements include the bronzework of Igbo Ukwu and the terracottas and metalworks of Ile Ife Bronze and brass castings, often ornamented with ivory and precious stones, became highly prestigious in much of West Africa, sometimes being limited to the work of court artisans and identified with royalty, as with the Benin Bronzes.

Influence on Western art

Westerners had long misunderstood African art as "primitive." The term carries with it negative connotations of underdevelopment and poverty. Colonization and the slave trade in Africa during the nineteenth century set up a Western understanding hinged on the belief that African art lacked technical ability due to its low socioeconomic status.

At the start of the twentieth century, artists like Picasso, Matisse, Vincent van Gogh, Paul Gauguin and Modigliani became aware of, and inspired by, African art. In a situation where the established avant garde was straining against the constraints imposed by serving the world of appearances, African art demonstrated the power of supremely well organised forms; produced not only by responding to the faculty of sight, but also and often primarily, the faculty of imagination, emotion and mystical and religious experience. These artists saw in African Art a formal perfection and sophistication unified with phenomenal expressive power. The study of and response to African Art, by artists at the beginning of the twentieth century facilitated an explosion of interest in the abstraction, organisation and reorganisation of forms, and the exploration of emotional and psychological areas hitherto unseen in Western art. By these means, the status of visual art was changed. Art ceased to be merely and primarily aesthetic, but became also a true medium for philosophic and intellectual discourse, and hence more truly and profoundly aesthetic than ever before.

Influence on Western architecture

European architecture was strongly influenced by African art. Pioneers like Antonio Sant'Elia, Le Corbusier, Pier Luigi Nervi, Theo van Doesburg and Erich Mendelsohn were also sculptures and painters; Futurist, Rationalist and Expressionist architecture discovered in Africa a new repertoire of proto-symbols; in a formal level, the space is now composed by single forms that do not only refer to human proportions and scale, but to its psychology; surfaces are modelled by geometric patterns. During the 50's, European architects transformed buildings into big-scale sculptures, replacing unnecessary decoration (so criticized by Adolf Loos), by integrating textured murals and large bas-reliefs in walls. During the 60's, African Art influenced Brutalism, both in language and symbolism, particularly in the late Le Corbusier,Oscar Niemeyer and Paul Rudolph. The powerful work of John Lautner reminds of artifacts from the Yoruba; the sensual projects of Patricio Pouchulu honour the bare wooden sculptures of the Dogon and Baoulé. Unlike Europe, African art never established boundaries between body art, painting, sculpture and architecture; thanks to this, Western architects can now extend towards different art expressions.

Traditional art

Traditional art describes the most popular and studied forms of African art which are typically found in museum collections.

Wooden masks, which might either be of human, animal or mythical creatures, are one of the most commonly found forms of art in western Africa. In their original contexts, ceremonial masks are used for celebrations, initiations, crop harvesting, and war preparation. The masks are worn by a chosen or initiated dancer. During the mask ceremony the dancer goes into deep trance, and during this state of mind he "communicates" with his ancestors. The masks can be worn in three different ways: vertically covering the face: as helmets, encasing the entire head, and as crest, resting upon the head, which was commonly covered by material as part of the disguise. African masks often represent a spirit and it is strongly believed that the spirit of the ancestors possesses the wearer. Most African masks are made with wood, and can be decorated with: Ivory, animal hair, plant fibers (such as raffia), pigments (like kaolin), stones, and semi-precious gems also are included in the masks.

Statues, usually of wood or ivory, are often inlaid with cowrie shells, metal studs and nails. Decorative clothing is also commonplace and comprises another large part of African art. Among the most complex of African textiles is the colorful, strip-woven Kente cloth of Ghana. Boldly patterned mudcloth is another well known technique.

Contemporary African art

Africa is home to a thriving contemporary art fine art culture. This has been sadly understudied until recently, due to scholars' and art collectors' emphasis on traditional art. Notable modern artists include El Anatsui, Marlene Dumas, William Kentridge, Karel Nel, Kendell Geers, Yinka Shonibare, Zerihun Yetmgeta, Odhiambo Siangla, Elias Jengo, Olu Oguibe, Lubaina Himid, and Bili Bidjocka, Henry Tayali. Art bienniales are held in Dakar, Senegal, and Johannesburg, South Africa. Many contemporary African artists are represented in museum collections, and their art may sell for high prices at art auctions. Despite this, many contemporary African artists tend to have difficult times finding a market for their work. Many contemporary African arts borrow heavily from traditional predecessors. Ironically, this emphasis on abstraction is seen by Westerners as an imitation of European and American cubist and totemic artists, such as Pablo Picasso, Amedeo Modigliani and Henri Matisse, who, in the early twentieth century, were heavily influenced by traditional African art. This period was critical to the evolution of Western modernism in visual arts, symbolized by Picasso's breakthrough painting "Les Demoiselles d'Avignon."

Contemporary African art was pioneered in the 1950s and 1960s in South Africa by artists like Irma Stern, Cyril Fradan, Walter Battiss and through galleries like the Goodman Gallery in Johannesburg. More recently European galleries like the October Gallery in London and collectors such as Jean Pigozzi, Artur

Walther and Gianni Baiocchi in Rome have helped expand the interest in the subject. Numerous exhibitions at the Museum for African Art in New York and the African Pavilion at the 2007 Venice Biennale, which showcased the Sindika Dokolo African Collection of Contemporary Art, have gone a long way to countering many of the myths and prejudices that haunt Contemporary African Art. The appointment of Nigerian Okwui Enwezor as artistic director of Documenta 11 and his African centred vision of art propelled the careers of countless African artists onto the international stage.

A wide range of more-or-less traditional forms of art, or adaptations of traditional style to contemporary taste are made for sale to tourists and others, including so-called "airport art". A number of vigorous popular traditions assimilate Western influences into African styles such as the elaborate fantasy coffins in shapes such as airplanes, cars or animals of West African cities, and the banners of clubs.

By country or people

Zambia

While the world is looking in another direction art flourishes in Zambia on a shoestring. Zambia is arguably home to some of the world's most creative and talented artists. The desire of artists in Zambia to create is so strong that they will use anything. From burlap sacks to car paint, even old bed sheets are often used in the place of canvases as the materials for art. Garbage and detritus are turned in works of art that are often staggering in their scope. The tradition of fine art, in the Western concept of the term, in Zambia goes back to colonial times and has been steadily growing ever since. Thanks to the Lechwe Trust, the Zambia's body of art is assured a home in the country it was created.

The Lechwe Trust was founded by Cynthia Zukas. An artist herself, in the early 1980s Zukas was a friend to many artists in Zambia including William Bwalya Miko, who remembers with fondness how Zukas would return from trips abroad with cases full of art materials to pass on to local artists who had no access to such tools. In 1986, she came into an inheritance and decided it was time to support artists more substantially, and the Lechwe Trust was born. Their aim was to provide bursaries for artists who wished to study formally or attend art workshops and residencies. In addition, they decided to start a collection, ensuring an art legacy for Zambia. The collection houses works predominantly by Zambians, however there are works by those who have lived in Zambia or have a connection with the country. Now numbering over 200 pieces of art from paintings to sculpture, from etchings to sketches the legacy is one of which Zambians should be proud, and yet few know of its existence. Or at least that was the case until the recent exhibition. A lack of promotion of the art scene in Zambia is only one issue artists have to address.

The Lechwe Trust Exhibition

"Destiny" is a prime example of the importance of the Lechwe Trust's work. With Henry Tayali's seminal painting "Destiny" (1975–1980), writ large is the struggle for identity in a time of progress. In the foreground a myriad of figures scramble and work, carrying iron girders, spades, while they are seemingly penned in by a huge, steam obscured modern city. The city itself is painted in muted greys, browns, mauves however the crowd is dressed in bright colours. According to the catalogue for the exhibition and an article by local magazine The Lowdown, this painting has had a long and well-travelled life. In 1966, the painting was sold to Tim Gibbs, son of then Southern Rhodesian governor, Sir Humphrey Gibbs. In 1980, Tayali went to the now independent Zimbabwe to but his painting back. Unsurprisingly, he was turned down but was granted allowance to borrow the painting for exhibitions. "Destiny" did its rounds in London, Zambia and Paris before returning to the Gibbs. By 1989 Henry Tayali had died and "Destiny" was exhibited again in London — enter the Lechwe Trust. It took two years but the trust now owns the painting, a linchpin of their impressive collection.

Artists in Zambia are faced with particular, though assuredly not unique, challenges. Even today, materials such as oil paints, brushes, canvas still have to be imported from South Africa and this makes them prohibitively expensive. A lack of public library facilities and subject specific magazines means artists are deprived of learning from more established artists or feeling part of a wider international community. Until a year ago, if you wished to study art within Zambia there was only one course available in the country — a certificate in art education, which prepares its candidates to teach, rather than make art.

Two paintings from artists of two different generations: Henry Tayali (1943–1987) on the left and living artist Stary Mwaba on the right. Then of course there is the business of trying to sell one's work. In economically more stable countries only a handful of artists can truly claim they make a living by their art alone, this handful becomes considerably smaller in Zambia. This is not merely due to fewer people with disposable income wishing to buy paintings, but also because of an unfortunate preconception by some tourists and ex-pats who look into buying work expecting a bargain basement souvenir only to find the prices higher than they planned to pay. The complaint that artwork is overpriced is a bone of contention. Lusaka is one of the more expensive cities in sub-Saharan Africa in terms of rents and product prices, plus as mentioned before, art materials are particularly expensive. Artists argue that the prices of their pieces fairly reflect their economic realities, plus some artists have shown internationally and feel they are justified in asking for more money. The low numbers of sales reveals how many may sadly disagree. Low sales may also be the result of something else. Very few people outside of the very small Zambian art world are aware of how active the art scene currently is. A look through international art magazines reveals a dearth of coverage of sub-Saharan Africa, only a few artists of sub-Saharan African heritage, such as Chris Ofili and Yinka Shonibare, have managed to break through. Many contemporary Zambian artists like Zenzele Chulu and Stary Mwaba, both of whom have exhibited internationally, feel this is because the art world wishes to see art from Africa in a very specific, ethnocentric stereotype. As result, they are often asked to participate in African-themed exhibitions, which limits their platform and frustrates them. As Mwaba asks, "Am I an African artist or an artist from Africa?" And more importantly, why does this question still matter?

And yet Lusaka is bursting at the seams with artists and The Henry Tayali gallery — Lusaka's main fine art gallery — is filled almost from floor to ceiling with works of art, and although they only get a small trickle of visitors (some days, I was told, none at all) the gallery is a hub of activity. Why? Well, in a country where opportunities for work are limited, it is better to be an artist and working, than to wait for a job that may never come. School is not possible for a large number of children who cannot afford the fees or the time, which is often spent helping at home. But through art, one can express oneself without the ability to read or write. The community of artists is a warm and friendly one full of people who understand that their richest resource is one another; new members are welcomed into the fold with open arms. There is a more abstract and perhaps rarely articulated motivation also, a pride and desire to depict and explore Zambia using the visual medium. Through their work, Zambian artists exude a dignity and an understanding of the good and bad of their society. They question, they examine and sometimes judge; the conversation shows no signs of abating. Artists here just love art, they thirst after it and it is a crucial contribution to their sense of identity, their sense of purpose.

Zambia's history is full of talent and characters even if their exploits and accomplishments are not always well documented. Take Akwila Simpasa. In his time, Simpasa was an internationally renowned artist, and sculpture and drawing were his favourite media, but it has been reported that art was so deeply ingrained in him that he painted and created music as well. He was friends with Eddy Grant and rubbed shoulders with Jimi Hendrix and Mick Jagger. Simpasa was a major pioneer. Sadly, he also had mental health problems and died relatively young in the 1980s and has since sunk into virtual obscurity. Those of his contemporaries that are still living remember him well. When asked to comment on his friend Simpasa, artist Patrick Mweemba offered the following remark: "he was the best Zambian artist." Stories of him exist through oral history, which is just as well, as little of the artist and his life seems to have been documented. William Miko and Zenzele Chulu both mentioned how some believe he is still alive, like Elvis he has become legend, and now thanks to the Lechwe Trust, the legend is able to speak through his work.

It cannot be denied that the Lechwe Trust, has gone a great way to tackling many of the problems facing Zambian artists. By buying art at a fair price, some artists are able to stay in Zambia and work rather than leaving the country as many like Henry Tayali did. William Miko was himself helped to develop as an artist by the trust and taught abroad in Europe. He eventually returned to work and to help the trust. Lechwe is the only trust of its kind in Zambia. A country that is full of NGOs, few if any of which are interested in the art scene. Yet, "You cannot have development without also the development of art and culture," argues William Miko. He cites the example of Japan that has a centuries-old and highly respected art tradition. He feels this tradition of inspiration, creativity and hard work has helped turn Japan into the technological powerhouse it has become in modern times. The Lechwe Trust's tireless support of the Zambian art scene could be key to bringing recognition, especially now they have decided to build their own gallery.

Mali

The primary ethnic groups in Mali are the Bambara (also known as Bamana) and the Dogon. Smaller ethnic groups consist of the Marka, and the Bozo fisherman of the Niger River. Ancient civilizations flourished in areas like Djene and Timbuktu, where a great variety of ancient bronze and terra-cotta figures have been unearthed.

Bambara

The Bambara people (Bambara: *Bamananankaw*) adapted many artistic traditions and began to create display pieces. Before money was the main drive of creation of their artworks they used their abilities solely as a sacred craft for display of spiritual pride, religious beliefs and display of customs. Example artworks include the Bamana n'tomo mask. Other statues were created for people such as hunters and farmers so others could leave offerings after long farming seasons or group hunts. The stylistic variations in Bambara art are extreme sculptures, masks and headdresses display either stylized or realistic features, and either weathered or encrusted patinas. Until quite recently, the function of Bambara pieces was shrouded in mystery, but in the last twenty years field studies have revealed that certain types of figures and headdresses were associated with a number of the societies that structure Bambara life. During the 1970s a group of approximately twenty figures, masks and TjiWara headdresses belonging to the so-called 'Segou style' were identified. The style is distinct and recognizable by its typical flat faces, arrow-shaped noses, all-over body triangular scarifications and, on the figures, splayed hands.

Masks

There are three major and one minor type of Bambara mask. The first type, used by the N'tomo society, has a typical comb-like structure above the face, is worn during dances and may be covered with cowrie shells. The second type of mask, associated with the Komo society, has a spherical head with two antelope horns on the top and an enlarged, flattened mouth. They are used during dances, but some have a thick encrusted patina acquired during other ceremonies in which libations are poured over them.

The third type has connections with the Nama society and is carved in the form of an articulated bird's head, while the fourth, minor type, represents a stylized animal head and is used by the Kore society. Other Bambara masks are known to exist, but unlike those described above, they cannot be linked to specific societies or ceremonies. Bambara carvers have established a reputation for the zoomorphic headdresses worn by Tji-Wara society members]. Although they are all different, they all display a highly abstract body, often incorporating a zig-zag motif, which represents the sun's course from east to west, and a head with two large horns. Bambara members of the Tji-Wara society wear the headdress while dancing in their fields at sowing time, hoping to increase the crop yield.

Statuettes

Bambara statuettes are primarily used during the annual ceremonies of the Guan society. During these ceremonies, a group of up to seven figures, measuring from 80 to 130 cm in height, are removed from their sanctuaries by the elder members of the society. The sculptures are washed, re-oiled and sacrifices are offered to them at their shrines. These figures - some of which date from between the 14th and 16th centuries - usually display a typical crested coiffure, often adorned with a talisman.

Two of these figures were ascribed great significance: a seated or standing maternity figure called Guandousou - known in the West as 'Bambara Queen' - and a male figure called Guantigui, who usually appears holding a knife. The two figures were surrounded by Guannyeni attendant figures standing or seated in various positions, holding a vessel, or a musical instrument, or their breasts. During the 1970s, numerous fakes from Bamako which were based on these sculptures entered the market. They were produced in Bamako.

Other Bambara figures, called Dyonyeni, are thought to be associated with either the southern Dyo society or the Kwore society. These female or hermaphrodite figures usually appear with geometric features such as large conical breasts and measure between 40 and 85 cm in height. The blacksmith members of the Dyo society used them during dances to celebrate the end of their initiation ceremonies. They were handled, held by dancers and placed in the middle of the ceremonial circle.

Among the corpus of Bambara figures, Boh sculptures are perhaps the best known. These statues represent a highly stylized animal or human figure, and are made of wood which is repeatedly covered in thick layers of earth impregnated with sacrificial materials such as millet, chicken or goat blood, kola nuts and alcoholic drinks. They were employed by the Kono and the Komo societies and served as receptacles for spiritual forces, and could in turn be used for apotropaic purposes.

Each special creative trait a person obtained was seen as a different way to please higher spirits.

Dogon

Dogon art is primarily sculpture. Dogon art revolves around religious values, ideals, and freedoms (Laude, 19). Dogon sculptures are not made to be seen publicly, and are commonly hidden from the public eye within the houses of families, sanctuaries, or kept with the Hogon (Laude, 20). The importance of secrecy is due to the symbolic meaning behind the pieces and the process by which they are made.

Themes found throughout Dogon sculpture consist of figures with raised arms, superimposed bearded figures, horsemen, stools with caryatids, women with children, figures covering their faces, women grinding pearl millet, women bearing vessels on their heads, donkeys bearing cups, musicians, dogs, quadruped-shaped troughs or benches, figures bending from the waist, mirror-images, aproned figures, and standing figures (Laude, 46-52). Signs of other contacts and origins are evident in Dogon art. The Dogon people were not the first inhabitants of the cliffs of Bandiagara. Influence from Tellem art is evident in Dogon art because of its rectilinear designs (Laude, 24).

Dogon art is extremely versatile, although common stylistic characteristics – such as a tendency towards stylization – are apparent on the statues. Their art deals with the myths whose complex ensemble regulates the life of the individual. The sculptures are preserved in innumerable sites of worship, personal or family altars, altars for rain, altars to protect hunters, in market. As a general characterization of Dogon statues, one could say that they render the human body in a simplified way, reducing it to its essentials. Some are extremely elongated with emphasis on geometric forms. The subjective impression is one of immobility with a mysterious sense of a solemn gravity and serene majesty, although conveying at the same time a latent movement. Dogon sculpture recreates the hermaphroditic silhouettes of the Tellem, featuring raised arms and a thick patina made of blood and millet beer. The four Nommo couples, the mythical ancestors born of the god Amma, ornament stools, pillars or men's meeting houses, door locks, and granary doors. The primordial couple is represented sitting on a stool, the base of which depicts the earth while the upper surface represents the sky; the two are interconnected by the Nommo. The seated female figures, their hands on their abdomen, are linked to the fertility cult, incarnating the first ancestor who died in childbirth, and are the object of offerings of food and sacrifices by women who are expecting a child. Kneeling statues of protective spirits are placed at the head of the dead to absorb their spiritual strength and to be their intermediaries with the world of the dead, into which they accompany the deceased before once again being placed on the shrines of the ancestors. Horsemen are remainders of the fact that, according to myth, the horse was the first animal present on earth. The Dogon style has evolved into a kind of cubism: ovoid head, squared shoulders, tapered extremities, pointed breasts, forearms, and thighs on a parallel plane, hairdos stylized by three or four incised lines. Dogon sculptures serve as a physical medium in initiations and as an explanation of the world. They serve to transmit an understanding to the initiated, who will decipher the statue according to the level of their knowledge. Carved animal figures, such as dogs and ostriches, are placed on village foundation altars to commemorate sacrificed animals, while granary doors, stools and house posts are also adorned with figures and symbols.

There are nearly eighty styles of masks, but their basic characteristic is great boldness in the use of geometric shapes, independent of the various animals they are supposed to represent. The structure of a large number of masks is based on the interplay of vertical and horizontal lines and shapes. Another large group has triangular, conic shapes. All masks have large geometric eyes and stylized features. The masks are often polychrome, but on many the color is lost; after the ceremonies they were left on the ground and quickly deteriorated because of termites and other conditions. The Dogon continue an ancient masquerading tradition, which commemorates the origin of death. According to their myths, death came into the world as a result of primeval man's transgressions against the divine order. Dama memorial ceremonies are held to accompany the dead into the ancestral realm and restore order to the universe. The performance of masqueraders – sometimes as many as 400 – at these ceremonies is considered absolutely necessary. In the case of the dama, the timing, types of masks involved, and other ritual elements are often specific to one or two villages and may not resemble those seen in locations only several miles distant. The masks also appear during baga-bundo rites performed by small numbers of masqueraders before the burial of a male Dogon. Dogon masks evoke the form of animals associated with their mythology, yet their significance is only understood by the highest ranking cult members whose role is to explain the meaning of each mask to a captivated audience.

Kenya

Kenyan art has changed much in the post colonial years. Painters emerged in the 1950s after training in Makerere University College; they include such artists as Elimo Njau Elizabeth Karuga. The 1970s saw the self-taught African painters mostly inspired by the demand for original African paintings. These include the Ancient Soi, Macua Ngethe, and Moses Gichuiri. Kenyatta Universityalso produced artists but more so taught in western art styles of painting. Among these include John Dianga and Moses Gichuiri. Others include the late Dr. Sylvester Maina, Stephen Mayienga and others. The '80s was the produced many contemporary artists. From Teachers Training colleges came Stephen Mbatia, Rix Butama, Shake Makelele, and Meube to name but a few. From the University of Nairobi School of Fine Art and Design came the following artists: Bulinya Martins and Sarah Shiundu. The two by virtue of having learned many basic techniques in design are highly innovative both in style, use of color and execution. Unlike most contemporary Kenyan artist they paint using oils, acrylics and watercolors and/or combination. Pure abstract art is rare in Kenya. Most artists paint semi-abstract with distorted human figures. The initial paintings by Bulinya Martins were a combination of cubism and original African abstractions. The late Mainga's abstractions were 2D and highly embellished on leather. As for material, the use of Acrylics and oil is more frequent than watercolors. Oil paint is by far the preferred medium today and it lasts much longer. The art items in Kenya include sisal baskets, elephant hair bracelets, Maasai bead jewelry, musical instruments, silver and gold jewelry, soapstone sculptures, wooden carvings, tribal masks, Maasai figurines, paintings, prints and sculptures. These art items are available in the arts and craft markets and shops throughout the main tourist centers of Kenya.

Cloth in Kenya also represents interesting art, with batik cloth, kangas (women's wraparound skirts) with patterns and even Kenyan proverbs printed on them and kikois (type of sarong for men) that come in many different colours and textiles. Kenya offers African jewelry containing cowry shells, and soapstone carvings from Western Kenya, carved by the Gusii and Abagusii ethnic groups in Kisii stone.

Gabon

The Fang people make masks and basketry, carvings, and sculptures. Fang art is characterized by organized clarity and distinct lines and shapes. Bieri, boxes to hold the remains of ancestors, are carved with protective figures. Masks are worn in ceremonies and for hunting. The faces are painted white with black features. Myene art centers around Myene rituals for death. Female ancestors are represented by white painted masks worn by the male relatives. The Bekota use brass and copper to cover their carvings. They use baskets to hold ancestral remains. Tourism is rare in Gabon, and unlike in other African countries, art is not spurred on by commerce.

Botswana

In the northern part of Botswana, women in the villages of Etsha and Gumare are noted for their skill at crafting baskets from Mokola Palmand local dyes. The baskets are generally woven into three types: large, lidded baskets used for storage large, open baskets for carrying objects on the head or for winnowing threshed grain, and smaller plates for winnowing pounded grain. The artistry of these baskets is being steadily enhanced through color use and improved designs as they are increasingly produced for commercial use.

The oldest evidence ancient paintings from both Botswana and South Africa. Depictions of hunting, both animal and human figures were made by the San people dating before civilization over 20,000 years old within the Kalahari desert.

Burkina Faso

Burkina Faso is a small, landlocked country north of Ghana and south of Mali and Niger. Economically, it is one of the four or five poorest countries in the world. Culturally, it is extremely rich. In part this is because so few people from Burkina have become Muslim or Christian. Many of the ancient artistic traditions for which Africa is so well known have been preserved in Burkina Faso because so many people continue to honour the ancestral spirits, and the spirits of nature. In great part they honour the spirits through the use of masks and carved figures. Many of the countries to the north of Burkina Faso had become predominantly Muslim, while many of the countries to the south of Burkina Faso are heavily Christian. In contrast many of the people of Burkina Faso continue to offer prayers and sacrifices to the spirits of nature and to the spirits of their ancestors. The result is that they continue to use the sorts of art that we see in museums in Europe and America.

One of the principal obstacles to understanding the art of Burkina Faso, including that of the Bwa, has been a confusion between the styles of the Bwa, "gurunsi", and Mossi, and a confusion of the Bwa people with their neighbours to the west the Bobo people. this confusion was the result of the use by French colonial officers of Jula interpreters at the turn of the century. these interpreters considered the two peoples to be the same and so referred to the Bobo as "Bobo-Fing" and to the Bwa as "Bobo-Oule." In fact these two peoples are not related at all. Their languages are quite different, their social systems are quite different, and certainly their art is quite different. In terms of artistic styles the confusion stems from the fact that the Bwa, "gurunsi'" and Mossi make masks that are covered with red white and black geometric graphic patterns. This is simply the style of the Voltaic or Gur peoples, and also includes the Dogon and other peoples who speak Voltaic languages.

Ivory Coast

The Baoulé, the Senoufo and the Dan peoples are skilled at carving wood and each culture produces wooden masks in wide variety. The Ivorian people use masks to represent animals in caricature to depict deities, or to represent the souls of the departed.

As the masks are held to be of great spiritual power, it is considered a taboo for anyone other than specially trained persons or chosen ones to wear or possess certain masks. These ceremonial masks are each thought to have a soul, or life force, and wearing these masks is thought to transform the wearer into the entity the mask represents. Ivory Coast also has modern painters and illustrators. Gilbert G. Groud criticizes the ancient beliefs in black magic, as held with the spiritual masks mentioned above, in his illustrated book *Magie Noire*.

Tanzania

Tinga Tinga art has roots in decorating hut walls in central and south Tanzania. It was first in 1968 when Edward Said Tingatinga started to paint on wooden sheets with enamel colours when Tinga Tinga art became known. The art of the Makonde must be subdivided into different areas. The Makonde are known as master carvers throughout East Africa, and their statuary that can be found being sold in tourist markets and in museums alike. They traditionally carve household objects, figures and masks. Since the 1950s years the socalled Modern Makonde Art has been developed. An essential step was the turning to abstract figures, mostly spirits (Shetani) that play a special role. Makonde are also part of the important contemporary artists of Africa today. An outstanding position is taken by George Lilanga.

Egypt

Persisting for 3,000 years and thirty dynasties, the "official" art of Ancient Egypt was centred on the state religion of the time. The art ranged from stone carvings of both massive statues and small statuettes, to wall art that depicted both history and mythology. In 2600 BCthe maturity of Egyptian carving reached a peak it did not reach again for another 1,500 years during the reign of Rameses II.

A lot of the art possesses a certain stiffness, with figures poised upright and rigid in a most regal fashion. Bodily proportions also appear to be mathematically derived, giving rise to a sense of fantastic perfection in the figures depicted. This most likely was used to reinforce the godliness of the ruling caste.

TRADITIONAL AFRICAN RELIGION

The traditional beliefs and practices of African people include various traditional religions. Generally, these traditions are oral rather than scriptural, include belief in a supreme creator, belief in spirits, veneration of ancestors, use of magic, and traditional medicine. The role of humanity is generally seen as one of harmonizing nature with the supernatural.

While adherence to traditional religion in Africa is hard to estimate, due to syncretism withChristianity, Islam, and Judaism, practitioners are estimated to number over 100 million, or at least 10 percent of the population of the continent. African diasporic religions are also practiced in the diaspora in the Americas, such as Candomble, Santeria, and Vodou.

Terminology

African traditional religions and *Indigenous African religions* are both common terms used to discuss the subject of indigenous faiths found within Africa. Each term is debated among scholars. Some challenge the word "traditional" and prefer "indigenous" since traditional can also include traditional African Islam and Christianity, and are established traditions in African societies. Some, such as Mbiti, contend that while using the singular "religion" a plural understanding is needed. Some suggest that these thousands of "religions" are only differing expressions of the same basic "religion." However, many suggest this is problematic as there is no "genetic" relationship between these plural beliefs to create ideological homology, and the observed similarities can subjectively also be found outside of Africa.

Statistics

Practitioners of traditional religions in Sub-Saharan Africa are distributed among 43 countries, and were estimated to number over 100 million, although the largest religions in Africa are Christianityand Islam.

Ceremonies

West and Central African religious practices generally manifest themselves in communal ceremonies and/or divinatory rites in which members of the community, overcome by *force* (or *ashe,nyama,* etc.), are excited to the point of going into meditative trance in response to rhythmic or mantric drumming and/or singing. One religious ceremony practiced in Gabon and Cameroon is theOkuyi, practiced by several Bantu ethnic groups. In this state, depending upon the types of drumming or instrumental rhythms played by respected musicians (each of which is unique to a given deity or ancestor), participants embody a deity or ancestor, energy and/or state of mind by performing distinct ritual movements or dances which further enhance their elevated consciousness, or, in Eastern terms, excite thekundalini to a specific level of awareness and/or circulate chi in a specific way within the body. When this trance-like state is witnessed and understood, practitioners are privy to a way of contemplating the pure or symbolic embodiment of a particular mindset or frame of reference. This builds skills at separating the feelings elicited by this mindset from their situational manifestations in daily life. Such separation and subsequent contemplation of the nature and sources of pure energy or feelings serves to help participants manage and accept them when they arise in mundane contexts. This facilitates better control and transformation of these energies into positive, culturally appropriate behavior, thought, and speech. Further, this practice can also give rise to those in these trances uttering words which, when interpreted by a culturally educated initiate or diviner, can provide insight into appropriate directions which the community (or individual) might take in accomplishing its goal.

Spirits

Followers of traditional African religions pray to various spirits as well as to their ancestors. These secondary spirits serve as intermediaries between humans and the primary God. Most African societies believe in a single Supreme Creator God (Chukwu, Nyame, Olodumare,Ngai, Roog, etc.). Some recognize a dual God and Goddess such as Mawu-Lisa.

Practices and rituals

There are more similarities than differences in all traditional African religions. Often, the supreme God is worshiped through consultation or communion with lesser deities and ancestral spirits. The deities and spirits are honored through libation, sacrifice (of animals, vegetables, cooked food, flowers, semi-precious stones, precious metals, etc.). The will of God is sought by the believer also through consultation of oracular deities, or divination. In many traditional African religions, there is a belief in a cyclical nature of reality. The living stand between their ancestors and the unborn. Traditional African religions embrace natural phenomena – ebb and tide, waxing and waning moon, rain and drought – and the rhythmic pattern of agriculture. According to Gottlieb and Mbiti:

The environment and nature are infused in every aspect of traditional African religions and culture. This is largely because cosmology and beliefs are intricately intertwined with the natural phenomena and environment. All aspects of weather, thunder, lightning, rain, day, moon, sun, stars, and so on may become amenable to control through the cosmology of African people. Natural phenomena are responsible for providing people with their daily needs.

For example, in the Serer religion, one of the most sacred stars in the cosmos is called Yoonir the (Star of Sirius). With a long farming tradition, the Serer high priests and priestesses (Saltigue) deliver yearly sermons at the Xoy Ceremony (divination ceremony) in Fatickbefore Yoonir's phase in order to predict winter months and enable farmers to start planting.

Divination

Since Africa is a large continent with many ethnic groups and cultures, there is not one single technique of casting divination. The practice of casting may be done with small objects, such as bones, cowrie shells, stones, strips of leather, or flat pieces of wood. Some castings are done using sacred divination plates made of wood or performed on the ground (often within a circle). They are classified in two ways:

- Casting marked bones, flat pieces of wood, nuts, shells, or leather strips and numerically counting up how they fall – either according to their markings or whether they do or do not touch one another – with mathematically based readings delivered as memorized results based on the chosen criteria.

- Casting a special set of symbolic bones or an array of selected symbolic articles, e.g., a bird's wing bone to symbolize travel, a round stone to symbolize a pregnant womb, and a bird's foot to symbolize feeling.

In traditional African societies, many people seek out diviners on a regular basis. There are generally no prohibitions against the practice. Those who divine for a living are also sought for their wisdom as counselors in life and for their knowledge of herbal medicine.

Duality of person and divinities

Most traditional African religions have a dualistic concept of the person. In the Igbo language, for instance, a person is said to be composed of a body and a soul. The Yoruba language includes a tripartite concept: in addition to body and soul, there is said to exist a spirit or an *ori*, an independent entity which mediates or otherwise interacts between the body and the soul. Some traditional religious systems have a similar duality, with a specific "devil-like" figure (e.g., Ekwensu), who is believed to be the opposite of God.

Virtue and vice

Virtue in traditional African religion is often connected with carrying out obligations of the communal aspect of life. Examples include social behaviors such as the respect for parents and elders, raising children appropriately, providing hospitality, and being honest, trustworthy, and courageous.

In some traditional African religions, morality is associated with obedience or disobedience to God regarding the way a person or a community lives. For the Kikuyu, according to their primary supreme creator, Mbiti, acting through the lesser deities, is believed to speak to and be capable of guiding the virtuous person as one's conscience. In traditional African religions, such as the Azande religion, a person is said to have a good or bad conscience, depending on whether he does the bidding of God or malevolent spirits. In many cases, Africans who have converted to other religions have still kept up their traditional customs and practices, combining them in a syncretic way.

Sacred places

Some sacred or holy locations for traditional religions include Nri-Igbo, the Point of Sangomar, Ile-Ife, Oyo, Dahomey, Benin City, Ouidah,Nsukka, Kanem-Bornu, Igbo-Ukwu among others.

Mythology

Many traditional African religions have elaborate stories that explain how the world was created, how humans were created, how culture and civilization came about, or what happens when a person dies (e.g., Kalunga Line). Other mythologies are meant to explain or enforce social conventions on issues relating to age, gender, class, or religious rituals. Myths are popular methods of education; they communicate religious knowledge and morality while amusing or frightening those who hear or read them.

RELIGION IN AFRICA

Religion in Africa is multifaceted and has been a major influence on art, culture and philosophy. Today, the continent's various populations and individuals are mostly adherents of Christianity, Islam, and to a lesser extent Traditional African religion. In Christian or Islamic communities, religious beliefs are also sometimes characterized with syncretism with the beliefs and practices of traditional religions.

African Traditional Religion

Africa encompasses a wide variety of traditional beliefs. Although religious customs are sometimes shared by many local societies, they are usually unique to specific populations or geographic regions. According to Dr J Omosade Awolalu, The "traditional" in this context means indigenous, that which is foundational, handed down from generation to generation, meant as to be upheld and practised today and forevermore. A heritage from the past, yet not treated as a thing of the past but that which connects the past with the present and the present with eternity.

Often spoken of in the terms of a singularity, deliberate; yet conscious of the fact that Africa is a large continent with multitudes of nations who have complexed cultures, innumerable languages and myriads of dialects. The essence of this school of thought is based mainly on oral transmission; that which is written in people's hearts, minds, oral history, customs, temples and religious functions. It has no founders or leaders like Gautama the Buddha, Christos, Ashoka, or Muhammed. It has no missionaries or the intent to propagate or to proselytise. Some of the African traditional religions are those of the Yoruba, Serer and Igbopeoples. Also among the Ashanti, the Fon/Ewe of Benin, Ghana and Nigeria.

Abrahamic religions

The majority of Africans are adherents of Christianity or Islam. African people often combine the practice of their traditional belief with the practice of Abrahamic religions. Abrahamic religions are widespread throughout Africa. They have both spread and replaced indigenous African religions, but are often adapted to African cultural contexts and belief systems. The World Book Encyclopedia has estimated that in 2002 Christians formed 40% of the continent's population, with Muslims forming 45%. It was also estimated in 2002 that Christians form 45% of Africa's population, with Muslims forming 40.6%.

Bahá'í Faith

The Bahá'í Faith in Africa has a diverse history. It is the 3rd most widespread organized Abrahamic religion in Africa after Islam and Christianity after its wide-scale growth in the 1950s and extend in the 1960s. TheAssociation of Religion Data Archives (relying on World Christian Encyclopedia) lists many large and smaller populations in Africa with Kenya, the Democratic Republic of the Congo, South Africa and Zambia among the top ten numerical populations of Bahá'ís in the world in 2005 (each with over 200,000 adherents), andMauritius in terms of percentage of the national population.

All three individual heads of the religion, Bahá'u'lláh, 'Abdu'l-Bahá, and Shoghi Effendi, were in Africa at various times. More recently the roughly 2000 Bahá'ís of Egypt have been embroiled in the Egyptian identification card controversy from 2006 through 2009. Since then there have been homes burned down and families driven out of towns. On the other hand, Sub-Saharan Bahá'ís were able to mobilize for nine regional conferences called for by the Universal House of Justice 20 October 2008 to celebrate recent achievements in grassroots community-building and to plan their next steps in organizing in their home areas.

Christianity

Christianity is now one of the two most widely practiced religions in Africa and is the largest religion in Sub-Saharan Africa. Most adherents outside Egypt, Ethiopia and Eritrea are Roman Catholic or Protestant. Several syncretistic and messianic sects have formed throughout much of the continent, including the Nazareth Baptist Church in South Africa and the Aladura churches in Nigeria.There is also fairly widespread populations of Seventh-day Adventists and Jehovah's Witnesses. The oldest Christian denominations in Africa are the Coptic church in Egypt and the Ethiopian Orthodox Tewahedo Church and theEritrean Orthodox Tewahedo Church, all Oriental Orthodox, which rose to prominence in the fourth century AD after King Ezana the Great made Ethiopia one of the first Christian nations.

In the first few centuries of Christianity, Africa produced many figures who had a major influence outside the continent, including St Augustine of Hippo, St Maurice, Origen, Tertullian, and three Roman Catholic popes (Victor I, Miltiades and Gelasius I), as well as the Biblical characters Simon of Cyrene and the Ethiopian eunuch baptised by Philip the Evangelist. Christianity existed in Ethiopia before the rule of King Ezana the Great of the Kingdom of Axum, but the religion took a strong foothold when it was declared a state religion in 330 AD, becoming one of the first Christian nations. The earliest and best known reference to the introduction of Christianity to Africa is mentioned in the Christian Bible's Acts of the Apostles, and pertains to the evangelist Phillip's conversion of an Ethiopian traveler in the 1st century AD. Although the Bible refers to them as Ethiopians, scholars have argued that Ethiopia was a common term encompassing the area South-Southeast of Egypt.

Other traditions have the convert as a Jew who was a steward in the Queen's court. All accounts do agree on the fact that the traveler was a member of the royal court who successfully succeeded in converting the Queen, which in turn caused a church to be built. Tyrannius Rufinus, a noted church historian, also recorded a personal account as do other church historians such as Socrates and Sozemius. Some experts predict the shift of Christianity's centre from the European industrialized nations to Africa and Asia in modern times. Yale University historian Lamin Sanneh stated, that "African Christianity was not just an exotic, curious phenomenon in an obscure part of the world, but that African Christianity might be the shape of things to come." The statistics from the World Christian Encyclopedia (David Barrett) illustrate the emerging trend of dramatic Christian growth on the continent and supposes, that in 2025 there will be 633 million Christians in Africa.

Islam

According to the World Book Encyclopedia, Islam is the largest religion in Africa, with 47% of the population being Muslim, accounting for 1/4 of the world's Muslim population. The faith's historic roots on the continent stem from the time of the Prophet Muhammad, whose early disciples migrated to Abyssinia (hijira) in fear of persecution from the pagan Arabs.

The spread of Islam in North Africa came with theexpansion of Arab empire under Caliph Umar, through the Sinai Peninsula. Spread of Islam in West Africa was through Islamic traders and sailors.

Islam is the dominant religion in North Africa and the Horn of Africa. It has also become the predominant religion on the Swahili Coast as well as the West African seaboard and parts of the interior. There have been several Muslim empires in Western Africa which exerted considerable influence, notably the Mali Empire, which flourished for several centuries and theSonghai Empire, under the leadership of Mansa Musa, Sonni Ali and Askia Mohammed.

The vast majority of Muslims in Africa are Sunni, belonging to either Maliki or Shafi schools of jurisprudence. However, Hanafi school of jurisprudence is also represented, mainly in Egypt. There are also sizeable minorities of Shias, Ahmadis and Sufis.

Judaism

Adherents of Judaism can be found scattered in a number of countries across Africa; including the Beta Israel of Ethiopia, the Abayudayaof Uganda, the House of Israel in Ghana, the Igbo Jews of Nigeria and the Lemba of Southern Africa.

Hinduism

Hinduism has existed in Africa mainly since the late 19th century. It is the largest religion in Mauritius, and several other countries have Hindu temples. Hinduism is said to be the fastest growing religion in Ghana.

Buddhism and Chinese religions

Buddhism is a tiny religion in Africa with around 250,000 practicing adherents, and up to nearly 400,000 if combined with Taoism and Chinese Folk Religion as a common traditional religion of mostly new Chinese migrants (significant minority in Mauritius, Réunion, and South Africa). About half of African Buddhists are now living in South Africa, while Mauritius has the highest Buddhist percentage in the continent, between 1.5% to 2% of the total population.

Other religions

Other faiths are practiced in Africa, including Zoroastrianism and Rastafarianism among others.

Irreligion /Agnosticism/Atheism

A Gallup poll shows that the irreligious comprise 20% in South Africa, 16% in Botswana, 13% in Mozambique, 13% in Togo, 12% in Libya and Côte d'Ivoire, 10% in Ethiopia and Angola, 9% in Sudan, Zimbabwe and Algeria, 8% in Namibia and 7% in Madagascar.

Syncretism

Syncretism is the combining of different (often contradictory) beliefs, often while melding practices of various schools of thought. In the commonwealth of Africa syncretism with indigenous beliefs is practiced throughout the region. It is believed by some to explain religious tolerance between different groups. Kwesi Yankah and John Mbiti argue that many African peoples today have a 'mixed' religious heritage to try to reconcile traditional religions with Abrahamic faiths. Jesse Mugambi claims that the Christianity taught to Africans by missionaries had a fear of syncretism, which was carried on by current African Christian leadership in an attempt to keep Christianity "pure." Syncretism in Africa is said by others to be overstated, and due to a misunderstanding of the abilities of local populations to form their own orthodoxies and also confusion over what is culture and what is religion. Others state that the term syncretism is a vague one, since it can be applied to refer to substitution or modification of the central elements of Christianity or Islam with beliefs or practices from somewhere else. The consequences under this definition, according to missiologist Keith Ferdinando, are a fatal compromise of the religion's integrity. However, communities in Africa (e.g. Afro-Asiatic) have many common practices which are also found in Abrahamic faiths, and thus these traditions do not fall under the category of some definitions of syncretism.

CLOTHING IN AFRICA

African clothing is the traditional clothing, often vibrantly coloured, worn by the people of Africa. In some instances these traditional garments have been replaced by western clothing introduced by European colonialists.

In Northeastern Africa, particularly in Egypt, styles of traditional dress have been influenced by Middle Eastern culture, this can be exemplified by the simply embroidered jelabiya which are similarly worn in the Gulf states. The Northwest Africans are less influenced by foreign elements and have remained more in antiquity. The djellaba (worn in Northwest Africa) shares similar properties with the grand boubou, the dashiki, and the Senegalese kaftan. In Nigeria, women wear headbands In Sahelian Africa, the dashiki, Senegalese kaftan, and the grand boubou are worn more prominently, though not exclusively (thebògòlanfini, for instance, is worn in Mali). The dashiki is highly stylized and is rendered with an ornate V-shaped collar. In contrast the grand boubou is simpler, even more so than the djellaba, though the color designs reach impressive proportions, especially among the Tuareg, who are known for their beautifully dyed indigo robes.

In East Africa, the kanzu is the traditional dress worn by Swahili speaking men. Women wear the kanga and the gomesi.

In Southern Africa distinctive shirts are worn, like the long dresses they wear. For instance, South Africa is known for the Madiba shirt, whereas, Zimbabwe is known for the safari shirt.

In the Horn of Africa, the attire varies by country. In Ethiopia, men wear the Ethiopian suit and women wear the habesha kemis. In Somalia, men wear the khameez with a small cap called a koofiyad.

AFRICAN POPULAR MUSIC

African popular music, like African traditional music, is vast and varied. Most contemporary genres of African popular music build on cross-pollination with western popular music. Many genres of popular music like blues, jazz, salsa, zouk, and rumba derive to varying degrees on musical traditions from Africa, taken to the Americas by African slaves. These rhythms and sounds have subsequently been adapted by newer genres like rock, and rhythm and blues. Likewise, African popular music has adopted elements, particularly the musical instruments and recording studio techniques of western music.

Afropop

Afropop (also spelled Afro-Pop or Afro Pop) is a term sometimes used to refer to contemporary African pop music. The term does not refer to a specific style or sound, but is used as a general term for African popular music.

Afro-Cuban comes home

Cuban music has been popular in sub-Saharan Africa since the mid twentieth century. It was Cuban music that more than any other, that provided the initial template for Afropop. To the Africans, clave-based Cuban popular music sounded both familiar and exotic. *The Encyclopedia of Africa v. 1.* states:

"Beginning in the 1940s, Afro-Cuban [son] groups such as Septeto Habanero and Trio Matamoros gained widespread popularity in the Congo region as a result of airplay over Radio Congo Belge, a powerful radio station based in Léopoldville (now Kinshasa DRC). A proliferation of music clubs, recording studios, and concert appearances of Cuban bands in Léopoldville spurred on the Cuban music trend during the late 1940s and 1950s."

Congolese bands started doing Cuban covers and singing the lyrics phonetically. Soon, they were creating their own original Cuban-like compositions, with French lyrics. The Congolese called this new music *rumba*, although it was really based on the son. The Africans adapted guajeos to electric guitars, and gave them their own regional flavor. The guitar-based music gradually spread out from the Congo, increasingly taking on local sensibilities. This process eventually resulted in the establishment of several different distinct regional genres, such as soukous.

Cuban popular music played a major role in the development of many contemporary genres of African popular music. John Storm Roberts states: "It was the Cuban connection, but increasingly also New York salsa, that provided the major and enduring influences—the ones that went deeper than earlier imitation or passing fashion. The Cuban connection began very early and was to last at least twenty years, being gradually absorbed and re-Africanized." The re-working of Afro-Cuban rhythmic patterns by Africans brings the rhythms full circle.

The re-working of the harmonic patterns reveals a striking difference in perception. The I IV V IV harmonic progression, so common in Cuban music, is heard in pop music all across the African continent, thanks to the influence of Cuban music. Those chords move in accordance with the basic tenets of Western music theory. However, as Gerhard Kubik points out, performers of African popular music do not necessarily perceive these progressions in the same way: "The harmonic cycle of C-F-G-F [I-IV-V-IV] prominent in Congo/Zaire popular music simply cannot be defined as a progression from tonic to subdominant to dominant and back to subdominant (on which it ends) because in the performer's appreciation they are of equal status, and not in any hierarchical order as in Western music."

The largest wave of Cuban-based music to hit Africa was in the form of salsa. In 1974 the Fania All Stars performed in Zaire (known today as the Democratic Republic of the Congo), Africa, at the 80,000-seat Stadu du Hai in Kinshasa. This was captured on film and released as*Live In Africa* (*Salsa Madness* in the UK). The Zairean appearance occurred at a music festival held in conjunction with the Muhammad Ali/George Foreman heavyweight title fight. Local genres were already well established by this time. Even so, salsa caught on in many African countries, especially in the Senegambia and Mali. Cuban music had been the favorite of Senegal's nightspot in the 1950s to 1960s. The Senegalese band Orchestra Baobab plays in a basic salsa style with congas and timbales, but with the addition of Wolof and Mandinka instruments and lyrics.

According to Lise Waxer: "African salsa points not so much to a return of salsa to African soil (Steward 1999: 157) but to a complex process of cultural appropriation between two regions of the so-called Third World." Since the mid-1990s African artists have also been very active through the super-group Africando, where African and New York musicians mix with leading African singers such as Bambino Diabate, Ricardo Lemvo, Ismael Lo and Salif Keita. It is still common today for an African artist to record a salsa tune, and add their own particular regional touch to it.

Modern Afrobeats

From early in the 21st century, a new type of sound, originating in West Africa, has become increasingly prominent in African popular music. This sound was initially referred to simply as 'Naija music' after the common slang term for Nigeria but has become known as Afrobeats. This name echo's Afrobeat, the 1970s fusion of jazz and traditional Ghanaian and Nigerian music which is an important influence, but Afrobeats is a largely different style combining influences from Congolese rumba, hip hop and dancehall. Early hits included "African Queen" by2face Idibia (2004) and "No One Like You" by P-Square (2007).

More recently the Azonto style of dance from Ghana has become closely associated with Afrobeats and more up-tempo songs have become popular. More recent hits include

"Bumper2Bumper" by Wande Coal (2008), "Oleku" by Ice Prince (2010) and "Kukere" by Iyanya (2011).

Since 2012, Afrobeats have gained mainstream recognition outside of Africa, especially within the UK. UK hits have included "Oliver Twist" by D'banj which reached 9 in the UK singles charts in 2012, and "Million Pound Girl (Badder Than Bad)" by the British artist Fuse ODG which reached 5 in the UK singles charts in 2014. Afrobeats nightclubs are now primary features of UK's nightlife with clubs opening in most major cities.

MUSIC OF AFRICA

Given the vastness of the continent, the traditional music of Africa is historically ancient, rich, and diverse, with the different regions andnations of Africa having distinct musical traditions.

Traditional music in much of the continent is passed down orally (or aurally) and is not written. In Sub-Saharan African music traditions, it also frequently relies heavily on percussion instruments of every variety, including xylophones, drums, and tone-producing instruments such as the mbira or "thumb piano."

The music and dance of the African diaspora, formed to varying degrees on African musical traditions, include American music and many Caribbean genres, such as Soca, Calypso and Zouk. Latin American music genres such as the Bachata, Danzón, Samba,Rumba, Salsa, Tango, Cumbia, Bomba del Chota, Mambo, Merengue, Reggae, Compas, Milonga, Son, Guaracha, Punta, Cha-Cha-Cha,Plena, Conga, and other clave (rhythm)-based genres, were also founded on the music of enslaved Africans, and have in turn influenced African popular music.

Music by regions

North Africa and the Horn of Africa

North Africa *(red region on map below)* is the seat of ancient Egypt and Carthage, civilizations with strong ties to the ancient Near East and which influenced the ancient Greek and Roman cultures. Eventually, Egypt fell under Persian rule followed by Greek and Roman rule, while Carthage was later ruled by Romans and Vandals. North Africa was later conquered by the Arabs, who established the region as the Maghreb of the Arab world.

Like the musical genres of the Nile Valley and the Horn of Africa *(sky-blue and dark green region on map),* its music has close ties with Middle Eastern music and utilizes similar melodic modes (maqamat). North African music has a considerable range, from the music of ancient Egypt to the Berber and the Tuareg music of the desert nomads. The region's art music has for centuries followed the outline of Arabic and Andalusian classical music: its popular contemporary genres include the Algerian Raï.

With these may be grouped the music of Sudan and of the Horn of Africa, including the music of Eritrea, Ethiopia, Djibouti and Somalia. Somali music is typically pentatonic, using five pitches peroctave in contrast to a heptatonic (seven note) scale such as the major scale. The music of the Ethiopian highlands uses a fundamental modal system called *qenet,* of which there are four main modes: *tezeta, bati, ambassel,* and*anchihoy*. Three additional modes are variations on the above: tezeta minor, bati major, and bati minor. Some songs take the name of their qenet, such as tizita, a song of reminiscence.

West, Central, Southeast and South Africa

The ethnomusicological pioneer Arthur Morris Jones (1889–1980) observed that the shared rhythmic principles of Sub-Saharan African music traditions constitute *one main system*. Similarly, master drummer and scholar C. K. Ladzekpo affirms the "profound homogeneity" of sub-Saharan African rhythmic principles.

African traditional music is frequently functional in nature. Performances may be long and often involve the participation of the audience. There are, for example, little different kinds of work songs, songs accompanying childbirth, marriage, hunting and political activities, music to ward off evil spirits and to pay respects to good spirits, the dead and the ancestors. None of this is performed outside its intended social context and much of it is associated with a particular dance. Some of it, performed by professional musicians, is sacral music or ceremonial and courtly music performed at royal courts.

Musicologically, Sub-Saharan Africa may be divided into four regions:

- The eastern region *(light green regions on map)* includes the music of Uganda, Kenya, Rwanda,Burundi, Tanzania, Malawi, Mozambique and Zimbabwe as well as the islands of Madagascar, the Seychelles, Mauritius and Comor. Many of these have been influenced by Arabic music and also by the music of India, Indonesia and Polynesia, though the region's indigenous musical traditions are primarily in the mainstream of the sub-Saharan Niger–Congo-speaking peoples.
- The southern region *(brown region on map)* includes the music of South Africa, Lesotho, Swaziland, Botswana, Namibia and Angola.
- The central region *(dark blue region on map)* includes the music of Chad, the Central African Republic, the Democratic Republic of the Congo and Zambia, including Pygmy music.
- West African music *(yellow region on map)* includes the music of Senegal and the Gambia, of Guinea and Guinea-Bissau, Sierra Leoneand Liberia, of the inland plains of Mali, Niger and Burkina Faso, the coastal nations of Cote d'Ivoire, Ghana, Togo, Benin, Nigeria, Cameroon, Gabon and the Republic of the Congo as well as islands such as Sao Tome and Principe.

Southern, Central and West Africa are similarly in the broad Sub-Saharan musical tradition, but draw their ancillary influences primarily from Western Europe and North America.

Musical instruments

Besides vocalisation, which uses various techniques such as complex hard melisma and yodel, a wide array of musical instruments are used. African musical instruments include a wide range of drums, slit gongs, rattles and double bells, different types of harps, and harp-like instruments such as the Kora as well as fiddles, many kinds of xylophone and lamellophone such as the mbira, and different types of wind instrument like flutes and trumpets. Additionally, string instruments are also used, with the lute-like oud serving as musical accompaniment in some areas.

Drums used in African traditional music include talking drums, bougarabou and djembe in West Africa, water drums in Central and West Africa, and the different types of ngoma drums (or engoma) in Central and Southern Africa. Other percussion instruments include many rattles and shakers, such as the kosika (kashaka), rain stick, bells and wood sticks. Also, Africa has lots of other types of drums, and lots of flutes, and lots of stringed and wind instruments.

The playing of polyrhythms is one of the most universal characteristics of Sub-Sarahan music, in contrast to polyphony in Western music. Several uniquely designed instruments have evolved there over time to facilitate the playing of simultaneous contrasting rhythms. The mbira, kalimba, Kora and dousn'gouni are examples of these instruments which organize notes not in the usual single linear order from bass to treble, but in two separated rank arrays which allows additional ease in playing cross rhythms. The continuing influence of this principle can be seen in the gravikora and gravikordmodern examples.

Relationship to language

Many languages spoken in Africa are tonal languages, leading to a close connection between music and language in some local cultures. These particular communities use vocal sounds and movements with their music as well. In singing, the tonal pattern or the text puts some constraints on the melodic patterns. On the other hand, in instrumental music a native speaker of a language can often perceive a text or texts in the music. This effect also forms the basis of drum languages (talking drums).

Influences on African music

Historically, several factors have influenced the tribal music of Africa. The music has been influenced by language, the environment, a variety of cultures, politics, and population movement, all of which are intermingled. Each African tribe evolved in a different area of the continent, which means that they ate different foods, faced different weather conditions, and came in contact with different tribes than other societies did. Each tribe moved at different rates and to different places than others, and thus each was influenced by different people and circumstances. Furthermore, each society did not necessarily operate under the same government, which also significantly influenced their music styles.

Influence on North American music

Although African American music is widely known and loved, and much popular North American music emerged from it, White American music also has strong African roots. The musical traditions of the Irish and Scottish settlers merged with African African musical elements to become old-time and bluegrass, among other genres.

African music has been a major factor in the shaping of what we know today as Dixieland, the blues and jazz. These styles have all borrowed from African rhythms and sounds, brought over the Atlantic ocean by slaves. African music in Sub-Saharan Africa is mostly upbeat polyrhythmic and joyful, whereas the blues should be viewed as an aesthetic development resulting from the conditions of slavery in the new world.

On his album *Graceland,* the American folk musician Paul Simon employs African bands, rhythms and melodies as a musical backdrop for his own lyrics; especially Ladysmith Black Mambazo. In the early 1970s, Remi Kabaka, an Afro-rock avant-garde drummer, laid the initial drum patterns that created the Afro-rock sounds in bands such as Ginger Baker's Airforce, The Rolling Stones, and Steve Winwood's Traffic. He continued to work with Winwood, Paul McCartney, and Mick Jaggerthroughout the decade.

Certain Sub-Saharan African musical traditions also had a significant influence on such well-known works as Disney's *The Lion King* and *The Lion King II: Simba's Pride,* which blend traditional tribal music with modern culture. Songs such as "Circle of Life" and "He Lives in You" combine of Zuluand English lyrics, as well as traditional African styles of music with more modern western styles. Additionally, the Disney classic incorporates numerous words from the Bantu Swahili language. The phrase *hakuna matata,* for example, is an actual Swahili phrase that does in fact mean "no worries". Characters such as Simba, Kovu, and Zira are also Swahili words, meaning "lion", "scar", and "hate", respectively.

Popular music

African popular music, like African traditional music, is vast and varied. Most contemporary genres of African popular music build on cross-pollination with western popular music, Many genres of popular music, including blues, jazz and rumba, derive to varying degrees from musical traditions from Africa, taken to the Americas by enslaved Africans. These rhythms and sounds have subsequently been adapted by newer genres like rock and rhythm and blues. Similarly, African popular music has adopted elements, particularly the musical instruments and recording studio techniques of western music.

One of the most important 20th century singers of South African popular music was Miriam Makeba, who played a key-role, in the 60s, in drawing global audience's attention to African music and its meaning.

The Afro-Euro hybrid style, the Cuban son, has had an influence on certain popular music in Africa. Some of the first guitar bands on the continent played covers of Cuban songs. The early guitar-based bands from the Congo called their music *rumba* (although it was son rather than rumba-based). The Congolese style eventually evolved into what became known as soukous.

LANGUAGES OF AFRICA

There are 1,250 to 2,100 and by some counts over 3,000 languages spoken natively in Africa, in several major language families:

- Afroasiatic is spread throughout the Middle East, North Africa, the Horn of Africa, and parts of the Sahel
- Nilo-Saharan is centered on Sudan and Chad (disputed validity)
- Niger–Congo (Bantu and non-Bantu) covers West, Central, Southeast and Southern Africa
- Khoe is concentrated in the deserts of Namibia and Botswana

- Austronesian is spoken in Madagascar.
- Indo-European is spoken on the southern tip of the continent.

There are several other small families and language isolates, as well as obscure languages that have yet to be classified. In addition, Africa has a wide variety ofsign languages, many of which are language isolates.

About a hundred of the languages of Africa are widely used for inter-ethnic communication. Arabic, Somali, Berber, Amharic, Oromo, Swahili, Hausa, Igbo, Fulani and Yoruba are spoken by tens of millions of people. If clusters of up to a hundred similar languages are counted together, twelve are spoken by 75 percent, and fifteen by 85 percent, of Africans as a first or additional language.

The high linguistic diversity of many African countries (Nigeria alone has over 500 languages, one of the greatest concentrations of linguistic diversity in the world) has made language policy a vital issue in the post-colonial era. In recent years, African countries have become increasingly aware of the value of their linguistic inheritance. Language policies being developed nowadays are mostly aimed atmultilingualism. For example, all African languages are considered official languages of the African Union (AU). 2006 was declared by the African Union as the "Year of African Languages". However, although many mid-sized languages are used on the radio, in newspapers, and in primary-school education, and some of the larger ones are considered national languages, only a few are official at the national level.

Language groups

Most languages spoken in Africa belong to one of three large language families: Afroasiatic, Nilo-Saharan, and Niger–Congo. Another hundred belong to small families such as Ubangian (sometimes grouped within Niger-Congo) and the various families called Khoisan, or the Indo-European and Austronesian language families which originated outside Africa; the presence of the latter two dates to 2,600 and 1,500 years ago, respectively. In addition, the languages of Africa languages include several unclassified languages and sign languages.

Afroasiatic languages

Afroasiatic languages are spoken throughout North Africa, the Horn of Africa, the Middle East, and parts of the Sahel. There are approximately 375 Afroasiatic languages spoken by over 350 million people. The main subfamilies of Afroasiatic are the Berber languages, Semitic languages, Chadic languages and the Cushitic languages. The Afroasiatic Urheimat is uncertain. However, its most extensive sub-branch, the Semitic languages (including Arabic, Amharic and Hebrew among others), seems to have developed in the Arabian peninsula. The Semitic languages are the only branch of the Afroasiatic family of languages that is spoken outside of Africa.

Some of the most widely spoken Afroasiatic languages include Arabic (a Semitic language, and a recent arrival from West Asia), Somali (Cushitic), Berber (Berber), Hausa (Chadic), Amharic (Semitic), and Oromo (Cushitic). Of the world's surviving language families, Afroasiatic has the longest written history, as both the Akkadian language of Mesopotamia and Ancient Egyptian are members.

Nilo-Saharan languages

Nilo-Saharan is a controversial grouping uniting over a hundred extremely diverse languages from southern Egypt to northern Tanzania and into Nigeria and DR Congo, with the Songhay languages along the middle reaches of the Niger River as a geographic outlier. Genetic linkage between these languages has not been conclusively demonstrated, and among linguists, support for the proposal is sparse. The languages share some unusual morphology, but if they are related, most of the branches must have undergone major restructuring since diverging from their common ancestor. The inclusion of the Songhay languages is questionable, and doubts have been raised over the Koman, Gumuz, and Kadu branches.

Some of the better known Nilo-Saharan languages are Kanuri, Fur, Songhay, Nubian, and the widespread Nilotic family, which includesLuo, Dinka, and Maasai. The Nilo-Saharan languages are tonal.

Niger–Congo languages

The Niger–Congo language family is the largest group of Africa (and probably of the world) in terms of the number of languages. One of its salient features is an elaborate noun class system with grammatical concord. The vast majority of languages of this family are tonal such as Yoruba and Igbo, Ashanti, and Ewe language. A major branch of Niger–Congo languages is the Bantu family, which covers a greater geographic area than the rest of the family put together.

The Niger–Kordofanian language family, joining Niger–Congo with the Kordofanian languages of south-central Sudan, was proposed in 1950s by Joseph Greenberg. Today, linguists often use "Niger–Congo" to refer to this entire family, including Kordofanian as a subfamily. One reason for this is that it is not clear whether Kordofanian was the first branch to diverge from rest of Niger–Congo. Mande has been claimed to be equally or more divergent. Niger–Congo is generally accepted by linguists, though a few question the inclusion of Mande and Dogon, and there is no conclusive evidence for the inclusion of Ubangian.

Other language families

Austronesian

Several languages spoken in Africa belong to language families concentrated or originating outside of the African continent: for example, Malagasy, the language of Madagascar, is an Austronesian language.

Indo-European

Afrikaans is Indo-European, as are the lexifiers of most African creoles. Afrikaans is the only Indo-European language known to have developed in Africa, thus it is an African language. Afrikaans is spoken throughout Southern Africa. Most Afrikaans speakers live in South Africa, in Namibia it is the lingua franca and in Botswana and Zimbabwe it is a minority language of roughly several ten thousand people. Over the entire world 15 to 20 million people are estimated to speak Afrikaans.

Since the colonial era, Indo-European languages such as Afrikaans, English, French, Italian, Portuguese and Spanish have held official status in many countries, and are widely spoken, generally as lingua francas. German was once used in Germany's colonies there from the late 1800s until World War I, when Britain and France took over and revoked German's official status. Despite this, German is still spoken in Namibia, mostly among the white population. Although it lost its official status in the '90s, it has been redesignated as a national language. Indian languages such as Gujarati are spoken by South Asian expatriates exclusively. In earlier historical times, other Indo-European languages could be found in various parts of the continent, such as Old Persianand Greek in Egypt, Latin and Vandalic in North Africa, and Modern Persian in the Horn of Africa.

Small families

The three small Khoisan families of southern Africa have not been shown to be closely related to any other major language family. In addition, there are various other families which have not been demonstrated to belong to one of these families.

- Mande, some 70 languages, including the major languages of Mali and Guinea. These are generally thought to be divergent Niger–Congo, but debate persists.
- Ubangian, some 70 languages, including the languages of the Central African Republic. May also be Niger–Congo.
- Khoe, about 10 languages, the primary family of Khoisan languages of Namibia and Botswana
- Sandawe, an isolate of Tanzania, possibly related to Khoe
- Kx'a, a language of Southern Africa
- Tuu, or Taa-Ui, two surviving languages
- Hadza, an isolate of Tanzania
- Bangi-me, a likely isolate of Mali
- Jalaa, a likely isolate of Nigeria
- Laal, a possible isolate of Chad

Khoisan is a term of convenience covering some 30 languages spoken by around 300,000–400,000 people. There are five Khoisan families which have not been shown to be related to each other: Khoe, Tuu, and Kx'a (these are found mainly in Namibia and Botswana), as well asSandawe and Hadza of Tanzania, which are language isolates. A striking feature of Khoisan languages, and the reason they are often counted together, is their use of click consonants. Some neighboring Bantu languages (notably Xhosa and Zulu) have clicks as well, but these were adopted from Khoisan languages. The Khoisan languages are also tonal.

Creole languages

Due partly to its multilingualism and its colonial past, a substantial proportion of the world's creole languages are to be found in Africa. Some are based on Indo-European languages (e.g. Krio from English in Sierra Leone and the very similar Pidgin in Nigeria and parts ofCameroon, Cape Verdean Creole in Cape Verde and Guinea-Bissau Creole in Guinea-Bissau and Senegal both from Portuguese,Seychellois Creole from French in the Seychelles, or Mauritian Creole in Mauritius); some are based on Arabic (e.g., Juba Arabic in the southern Sudan, or Nubi in parts of Uganda and Kenya); some are based on local languages (e.g., Sango, the main language of the Central African Republic); while in Cameroon a creole based on French, English and local African languages known as Camfranglais has started to become popular.

Unclassified languages

A fair number of unclassified languages are reported in Africa. Many remain unclassified simply for lack of data; among the better-investigated ones that continue to resist easy classification are:

- possibly Afroasiatic: Ongota, Gomba
- possibly Nilo-Saharan: Shabo
- possibly Niger–Congo: Jalaa, Mbre, Bayot
- possibly Khoe: Kwadi
- unknown: Laal, Mpre

Of these, Jalaa is perhaps the most likely to be an isolate.

Less-well investigated languages include Irimba, Luo, Mawa, Rer Bare (possibly Bantu), Bete (evidently Jukunoid), Bung (unclear), Kujarge(evidently Chadic), Lufu (Jukunoid), Meroitic (possibly Afroasiatic), Oropom (possibly spurious), and Weyto (evidently Cushitic). Several of these are extinct, and adequate comparative data is thus unlikely to be forthcoming. Hombert & Philippson (2009) list a number of African languages that have been classified as language isolates at one point or another. Many of these are simply unclassified, but Hombert & Philippson believe Africa has about twenty language families, including isolates. Beside the possibilities listed above, there are:

- Aasax or Aramanik (Tanzania) (South Cushitic? contains non-Cushitic lexicon)
- Imeraguen (Mauritania) - Hassaniyya Arabic restructured on an Azêr (Soninke) base
- Kara (Fer?) (Central African Republic)
- Oblo (Cameroon) (Adamawa? Extinct?)

Roger Blench notes a couple additional possibilities:

- Defaka (Nigeria)
- Dompo (Ghana)

Sign languages

Many African countries have national sign languages, such as Algerian Sign Language, Tunisian Sign Language, Ethiopian Sign Language, while other sign languages are restricted to small areas or single villages, such as Adamorobe Sign Language in Ghana. Tanzania has seven, one for each of its schools for the Deaf, all of which are discouraged. Not much is known, since little has been published on these languages.

Language in Africa

Throughout the long multilingual history of the African continent, African languages have been subject to phenomena like language contact, language expansion, language shift, and language death. A case in point is the Bantu expansion, in which Bantu-speaking peoples expanded over most of Sub-Equatorial Africa, displacing Khoi-San speaking peoples from much of Southeast Africa and Southern Africaand other peoples from Central Africa. Another example is the Arab expansion in the 7th century, which led to the extension of Arabic from its homeland in Asia, into much of North Africa and the Horn of Africa.

Trade languages are another age-old phenomenon in the African linguistic landscape. Cultural and linguistic innovations spread along trade routes and languages of peoples dominant in trade developed into languages of wider communication (lingua franca). Of particular importance in this respect are Berber (North and West Africa), Jula (western West Africa), Fulfulde (West Africa), Hausa (West Africa),Lingala (Congo), Swahili (Southeast Africa), Somali (Horn of Africa) and Arabic (North Africa and Horn of Africa). After gaining independence, many African countries, in the search for national unity, selected one language, generally the former colonial language, to be used in government and education. However, in recent years, African countries have become increasingly supportive of maintaining linguistic diversity. Language policies that are being developed nowadays are mostly aimed at multilingualism.

Used Languages

Besides the former colonial languages of English, French, Portuguese and Spanish, the following languages are used at the national level in Africa:

Afroasiatic

- Arabic in Comoros, Chad, Djibouti, Egypt, Eritrea, Mauritania, Somalia, Sudan, Tunisia, Algeria, Libya and Morocco
- Berber in Morocco and Algeria
- Amharic in Ethiopia
- Somali in Somalia
- Tigrinya in Eritrea

Austronesian

- Malagasy in Madagascar

Indo-European

- Afrikaans

Niger-Congo

- Chichewa in Malawi

- Comorian in the Comoros
- Kinyarwanda in Rwanda
- Kirundi in Burundi
- Sesotho in Lesotho and South Africa
- Setswana/Tswana in Botswana and South Africa
- Shona, Sindebele in Zimbabwe
- Sepedi in South Africa
- Ndebele in South Africa
- Swahili in Tanzania, Kenya and Uganda
- Swati in Swaziland and South Africa
- Tsonga in South Africa
- Venda in South Africa
- Xhosa in South Africa
- Zulu in South Africa

Creoles

- Sango in the Central African Republic
- Seychellois Creole in the Seychelles

Cross-border languages

The colonial borders established by European powers following the Berlin Conference in 1884-1885 divided a great many ethnic groups and African language speaking communities. In a sense, "cross-border languages" is a misnomer — the speakers did not divide themselves. Nevertheless, it describes the reality of many African languages, which has implications for divergence of language on either side of a border (especially when the official languages are different), standards for writing the language, etc. Some notable cross-border languages include Berber (which stretches across much of North Africa and some parts of West Africa), Somali (stretches across most of the Horn of Africa), Swahili (spoken in the African Great Lakes region) and Fula (in the Sahel and West Africa).

Some prominent Africans such as former Malian president and former Chairman of the African Commission, Alpha Oumar Konaré, have referred to cross-border languages as a factor that can promote African unity.

Language change and planning

Language is not static in Africa any more than on other continents. In addition to the (likely modest) impact of borders, there are also cases of dialect levelling (such as in Igbo and probably many others), koinés (such as N'Ko and possibly Runyakitara), and emergence of new dialects (such as Sheng). In some countries, there are official efforts to develop standardized language versions.

There are also many less widely spoken languages that may be considered endangered languages.

Demographics

Of the 1 billion Africans (in 2009), about 17 percent speak an Arabic dialect . About 10 percent speak Swahili , the lingua franca of Southeast Africa; about 5 percent speak a Berber dialect ; and about 5 percent speak Hausa, which serves as a lingua franca in much of the Sahel. Other important West African languages are Yoruba, Igbo and Fula. Major Horn of Africa languages are Amharic, Oromo and Somali. Important South African languages are Zulu, Xhosa and Afrikaans.

English, French, and Portuguese are important languages in Africa: 130, 115, 30 million Africans speak them as either native or secondary languages. Portuguese has become the national language of Angola. Through (among other factors) sheer demographic weight, Africans are increasingly taking ownership of these three world languages and having an ever greater influence on their development and growth.

Linguistic features

Some linguistic features are particularly common among languages spoken in Africa, whereas others are less common. Such shared traits probably are not due to a common origin of all African languages. Instead, some may be due to language contact (resulting in borrowing) and specific idioms and phrases may be due to a similar cultural background.

Tonal languages are found throughout the world but are especially numerous in Africa. Both the Nilo-Saharan and the Khoi-San phyla are fully tonal. The large majority of the Niger–

Congo languages is also tonal. Tonal languages are also found in the Omotic, Chadic, and South & East Cushitic branches of Afroasiatic. The most common type of tonal system opposes two tone levels, High (H) and Low (L). Contour tones do occur, and can often be analysed as two or more tones in succession on a single syllable. *Tone melodies* play an important role, meaning that it is often possible to state significant generalizations by separating tone sequences ("melodies") from the segments that bear them. Tonal sandhi processes like tone spread, tone shift, and downstep and downdrift are common in African languages.

Syntactic

Widespread syntactical structures include the common use of adjectival verbs and the expression of comparison by means of a verb 'to surpass'. The Niger–Congo languages are famous for having very large numbers of genders (noun classes) which cause agreement in verbs and other words. Case, tense, and other categories may be distinguished only by tone.

Semantic

Quite often, only one term is used for both animal and meat; the word *nama* or *nyama* for animal/meat is particularly widespread in otherwise widely divergent African languages.

INDIGENOUS PEOPLES OF WEST AFRICA

Africa has been late in joining the rest of the world in the indigenous movement. It was the persecuted, oppressed, and sometimes-destroyed nations on the American continent that forced the the so-called modern world to recognize the rights of indigenous peoples. Their efforts compelled the United Nations to launch action to safeguard indigenous peoples' rights in 1982 with the advent of the Working Group on Indigenous Populations.

Some African delegates have participated each year in the working group, which meets every summer in Geneva. But it took 15 years for Africa to draw from the inspiration of other indigenous nations and begin internal work toward implementing a continent-wide network. This is how the Indigenous Peoples of Africa Coordinating Committee (IPACC) was born, in response to the critical need expressed by Africans during the caucuses organized in parallel with the working group. IPACC is the preeminent organization representing indigenous rights on the continent, and has representatives in every region.

West Africa played a major role in the birth of IPACC. Indeed, this area contains very militant peoples who, during the same period, took up arms against Niger, Mali, and Chad so that their identities would be recognized in these young countries born from decolonization in the 1960s. These peoples are the Tuareg (the name given to the southern part of the Amazigh nation, which covers all of northern Africa), the Toubou, the Woodaabè, and the Ogoni of the Niger Delta in Nigeria.

The Tuareg, Woodaabè, and Toubou are nomadic peoples in the Sahelo-Saharan countries (Niger, Mali, Chad, Algeria, Libya, and Mauritania). The balkanization of the African continent resulting from the Berlin Conference in 1885 divided these peoples among several different countries, the leadership of which favored other peoples, generally sedentary farmers, who had a vision closer to colonialism and who continued colonial works. Since decolonization, the suffering of the pastoral nomadic peoples has continued. Indeed, the configurations of these countries do not take their specific political, geographical, and cultural features into account at all. In forming these countries, the nomad component was difficult to control, and the solution was either to ignore them or to persecute them until the end. This is why, since then, each group has been trying to resist this steamroller. They want to continue to exist as completely separate entities within their current countries, as they had done for thousands of years before the colonial phenomenon. The armed fights led by Tuareg and the Toubous in Niger and Mali since the early 1990s ended with negotiations under the aegis of France and countries in the sub-region. These negotiations resulted in peace agreements that provided for the nomads' progressive recognition in government bodies. These agreements are being applied, yet the process is far from what we would consider satisfactory. The problems persist and have even become more complicated. For the moment, the battle continues on the political front to assist the democratic processes in our countries. History will tell us the rest.

The Ogoni people of Nigeria are faced with the same constraints in a country that counts thousands of nations and of peoples, each with its own identity. The Ogoni are a minority, a circumstance complicated even more by the richness of the subsoil of their lands. Their fight is still ongoing in a Nigeria that refuses to recognize the legitimate nature of their aspirations. Opposing them is the machine of the multinationals exploiting the oil in the Niger Delta and a government primarily run by people who are the accomplices of these multinationals in crushing the Ogoni without the world knowing.

Since the birth of the IPACC, our struggles have been better coordinated through sharing our experiences with our brothers and sisters on the continent. Indigenous peoples from South Africa, with the long history of their fight against apartheid, are very helpful to us. Moreover, our permanent secretariat, which received support in its beginnings from the South African San Institute, is located on the Cape of Good Hope. Thanks to the pleas and lobbying that we are conducting through IPACC, the African Commission on Human and Peoples' Rights adopted a charter for indigenous peoples in November 2003. That charter is now in the process of winning approval by the member states of the African Union who have signed the African Charter on Human and Peoples' Rights. The working group set up by the commission for this purpose, of which our experts are members, is crisscrossing the continent. Last February, they passed through Niger, where they met members of the government and civil society, as well as the president of the republic. We are crossing our fingers that this effort will result in improved respect for our rights.

However, this promising picture could become darkened if we are not careful. Indeed, the ambition of the United States of America is to position itself in the Saharan region, our ancestral domain. With the help of the Saharan countries that wish to eliminate us (Niger, Mali, Algeria, Libya and Mauritania), the United States is in the process of setting up a program to militarize our territories, which they say is intended to prevent terrorist threats. The real goal is control of this "empty" space in order to exploit its oil to make up for the loss of Persian Gulf oil, which is becoming increasingly problematic. The pretext invoked—Islamic terrorism—is unknown to us here. Our Sahara is of no interest to anti-American Islamic militants. They prefer their urban centers or the deserts of their own countries, which they defend against occupation. But that seems to make no difference to the United States. We fear that our Sahara may be the next Iraq. Should we let ourselves be brought down without reacting? No!

As for these coveted riches, we would like to share them respectfully with anyone who can exploit them. Why does the United States not approach us directly? Our people are open, but they are also fierce when they are trampled upon. Nobody will be able to take charge of the Sahara without the agreement of the Tuareg, the Toubous, and the Arabic-speaking populations who live there. May the United States hear this call.

4

India-Africa Partnership: Future Directions

The 3rd India-Africa Forum Summit is scheduled to be held in New Delhi from 26th to 29th October 2015, with all 54 heads of African nations having been invited for the Summit. This is the most significant diplomatic outreach by the Government of India underlining the importance of Africa in India's growth trajectory. A closer India-Africa partnership is important for the security and development of both India and Africa. In the coming years, Africa will play an increasing role in shaping global norms and institutions. The India-Africa connectivity, therefore, presents immense opportunities for exploring strategies for mutual cooperation and growth.

To facilitate engagement on the various dimensions of the India-Africa relationship, the Institute for Defence Studies and Analyses (IDSA), in collaboration with Research in Information System for Developing Countries (RIS), Brookings India, and the Confederation of Indian Industry (CII) is hosting a day-long conference on the theme "India-Africa Partnership: Future Directions", on 20th October 2015 to deliberate on the geo-strategic, economic and development aspects of this relationship.

Concept Note

The First India-Africa Forum Summit, held in New Delhi in 2008, marked the beginning of a robust and contemporary partnership. The second Summit, held in Addis Ababa in May

2011, emphasized the renewed focus of India to strengthen and enhance its partnership with countries in the African continent. It brought out two important documents, the Addis Ababa Declaration and the Africa-India Framework for Enhanced Cooperation. Both agreements offer direction to further Indo-African relations in the coming years, and provide a framework for the establishment of a long-term and mutually beneficial partnership encompassing diverse fields. The forthcoming Third India Africa Forum Summit, 26-29 October 2015, at New Delhi, provides an opportune moment to map the future trajectory of this relationship.

The contemporary world order is in a flux. On one hand, multi-polarity has meant more complex relations not only among great powers, but even among developed countries and countries of global south. On the other hand, a multipolar world has also meant that greater engagement is required to manage the international system which is characterised by power diffused among various actors at various levels. In this context, the geo-strategic imperatives and geo strategic interests between India and Africa need to be fully analysed and understood. Their partnership and its potential impact on the world order are issues that need deep deliberation. India Africa relations have hinged on the common struggle against colonialism, apartheid, poverty, disease, illiteracy and hunger. In the contemporary international order, what are the gamut of issues that will define the contours of this partnership?

Greater economic engagement has been crucial to boosting ties between Africa and India. India's trade with Africa amounted to US$71 -billion in 2014-15. The potentialities, scope and complementarities for future economic engagement need to be discussed. Sectorial potentials in energy, pharma, agriculture and mining need to be further explored for a much more dynamic relationship. In the field of energy and mining, the dynamics of engagement need to be versatile enough to take into consideration India's energy security and Africa's economic development. Similarly, agriculture is another area of cooperation where wider implications of climate change on food security of Africa must be taken into consideration.

Against this backdrop, the Institute for Defence Studies and Analyses, the Research and Information System for Developing Countries (RIS), the Confederation Indian Industries (CII), and Brookings India are jointly organizing conference on India-Africa Partnership: Future Directions on 20 October 2015. The objective of this initiative is to build on existing partnerships between African countries and India, and to explore new areas of convergence for mutual engagement.

INDIA-AFRICA: A PARTNERSHIP WITH UNTAPPED POTENTIAL

Africa is drawing a variety of investors in search of natural resources and fast-growing consumer markets. They are eager to benefit from some of the highest economic growth rates in the world – as two-thirds of the countries in the continent will grow at over 5% over the next 5 years – and favourable demographics. Africa's fast-growing, very young and increasingly urban population is currently estimated at 1.2 bn and set to exceed 4 bn by 2100, when around 40% of the global population will be living in Africa, based on projections from the UN. As the EU and China remain Africa's main trade and investment partners and President Obama has given momentum to the US-Africa partnership, India's involvement with Africa has been growing steadily. It is set to intensify further, based on the synergies of needs and interests.

India is in a good position to extend its reach in Africa

While no country can likely replace China's appetite for commodities, India is a large fast-growing economy, expected to grow more rapidly than China over the next years (7.5% vs 6.7% in 2016 according to the latest forecasts from Deutsche Bank). India's commodity hunger is likely to increase in line with the "Make in India" strategy proposed by Prime Minister Narendra Modi. It could partially mitigate slowing demand in China as the country pursues reforms away from investment towards consumption-led growth.

India's growth profile and development needs are similar to those of many African countries which can find parallels with India's development challenges rooted in linguistic, ethnic and religious divisions or colonial heritage. India also shares with 18 African countries a membership of the Commonwealth. With its companies typically inclined towards offering low-cost products and services, India is well-positioned to become an attractive trade partner and investor for Africa.

With trade openness revitalizing historical and cultural links, India-Africa trade has grown steadily in the past years. Bilateral trade amounted to USD 65bn (6% share of Africa's trade with the world) in 2014, up from USD 7 bn (3% share) in 2000. This is still only 40% of Africa's trade with China but now similar to the US. Most of India's trade with Africa takes place below the Sahara. Sub-Saharan Africa's exports to India reached USD 30 bn in 2014 (8% of total exports), overtaking the US (share of 6%). Two-thirds of these exports are oil and gas, 16% gold and other precious stones. India's main trade partners in Africa are Nigeria (USD 17 bn), South Africa (USD 9 bn), Angola (USD 6 bn) and Tanzania (USD 5 bn).

India needs increasingly large amounts of raw materials. It imported USD 195 bn worth of raw materials in 2014 and is particularly dependent on crude oil imports (34% of its total imports), precious metals, other minerals and agricultural products, e.g. cashews and cotton. India's total imports from Africa amounted to USD 33 bn, a small share (6%) of its total imports compared to its main providers China and the GCC (13% each). However, more than a quarter of India's oil and gas imports now come from Africa, particularly Nigeria and Angola, as part of an effort to diversify import origins. Nigeria recently replaced Saudi Arabia as the largest crude supplier to India. Although India has lost out to Chinese oil giants in its search for oil supplies in Africa, Indian oil and gas companies are present on the continent. India is a significant market for a few African countries, including Tanzania, Nigeria, Botswana, Cameroon and Angola. It is now the largest buyer of Nigerian oil. The nature of Africa's exports is likely to change as the continent pursues efforts to process its raw materials and add value to its exports.

In turn, Africa imported USD 32 bn worth from India (5% of total African imports). Africa is a relatively small export market for

India, which exports mostly to the US and the GCC (USD 45 bn to each in 2014), but some African countries import significantly from India, including Tanzania, Mozambique, Kenya and Mauritius. The nature of these imports varies according to the region, with East and Southern Africa receiving mainly refined petroleum products from India, Central Africa pharmaceuticals and North Africa vehicles. Electrical and industrial machinery are other Indian products exported to Africa.

India enjoys a private sector which is rapidly getting global

A number of Indian multinationals already have significant interests and investments in Africa, in diverse sectors including ICT, energy, agribusiness, healthcare and automotives. Indian FDI into Africa exceeded USD 6 bn over the period 2003-2012, ranking fifth behind the US (USD 10 bn), the UAE, France and the UK. However, the figures for Chinese FDI are likely under-estimated – according to calculations from McKinsey. India has approved USD 9 bn of concessional loans to Africa in the past decade and committed a further USD 10 bn over the next five years, according to Indian authorities. India's green-field investments in Africa amounted to USD1.1 bn in 2014 (USD 6 bn from China), according to UNCTAD.

Some Indian conglomerates have been operating for decades in multiple African countries across a wide range of industries such as automobiles, telecommunications and hotels. Indian pharmaceutical companies also operate in Africa, providing generic medicine and vaccines at affordable prices.

Other firms are looking at tapping growing African markets in the consumer goods area. Bollywood is also present in Africa with many Africans, especially in the East and South, very fond of Hindi films.

Like various other countries, India is also looking at Africa as a place to grow food, attracted by massive amounts of cheap land, more abundant water resources and low farming costs while African authorities welcome both the investors and the influx of skilled Indian farmers, working as entrepreneurs and landowners.

There is momentum within India to catch up in Africa

India is looking at boosting political and economic ties with the continent. Since taking office last year, PM Modi has taken a strategic approach to increase India's foreign policy engagement and broaden its trade partners. He has yet to visit mainland Africa. The India-Africa Summit was initiated in 2008 to strengthen bilateral relations and reduce India's reliance on Europe and North America. It took place for the third time at the end of October and New Delhi hosted representatives of most African states including Nigeria's M. Buhari and South Africa's J. Zuma.

There is also a significant Indian diaspora in Africa, estimated in excess of 2 million, that has been living in Africa for generations, especially in southern and eastern Africa (e.g. Kenya, Tanzania, Mauritius and South Africa). Still to be tapped, this diaspora enjoys strong entrepreneurial ties, owning distribution and commodities trading channels, manufacturing facilities and mines. South Africa hosts 1.15 million people of Indian origin who arrived around 1900 to work in plantations. Hosting a large number of Indians, Durban has been named the largest Indian city outside India. (Durban is also the place where Mahatma Gandhi practiced his non-violent struggle against colonial masters during his stay over 1893–1914, before leading the freedom movement in India).

Ties are also strengthening around security and capacity-building

East African coastal states (from Somalia to South Africa, including the islands) are major partners in India's efforts to establish leadership in the Indian Ocean – in combating piracy, securing maritime routes and mitigating disasters. India is also one of the largest contributors to UN-mandated peacekeeping and other operations in Africa, with over 30,000 people involved since 1960.

India has emerged as a major development actor in Africa. Striving to build human capital in fellow developing countries, the country has offered 25,000 scholarships since 2011 for Africans to go and study on Indian campuses. India is also involved in setting up numerous vocational centres across Africa as it has already done in Ethiopia, Burundi and Rwanda. It has committed USD 600 m in grants towards areas such as education, technology and health-care. The world's largest democracy is also increasingly helping African governments on the democratic front, offering training on electronic voting systems, parliamentary procedures, federal governance, and an independent judicial system to strengthen the rule of law.

In a nutshell, India is already involved in Africa and the long-standing presence of Indian business communities on the continent is set to help expand trade and investment between the two countries as deficiencies in transport, logistics and the business environment are worked through. Those African countries with a larger share of private sector in the economy are more likely to attract Indian involvement. PM Modi has promised to make India more competitive in the global economy and Africa may play an important role in that endeavour.

INDIA-AFRICA PARTNERSHIP WILL KEEP CHINA IN CHECK'

In what is being seen as New Delhi's clearly chalked out strategy to reduce the Chinese influence in Africa, Prime Minister Narendra Modi offered everything on the plate — defence and economic cooperation, combating terrorism, clean energy and addressing climate change — when he met the African dignitaries during the four-day India Africa Forum Summit that concluded on Thursday. India's announcement of $10 billion aid to Africa is a demonstration of her willingness to cement ties with the continent, hitherto dependent solely on Beijing to buy its natural resources.

As the economic slowdown in China becomes more apparent by the day, there is apprehension in Africa that the demand for its resources will drop. By hosting 41 heads of state from 54 countries in Africa, PM Modi, hence, sent out a timely message that India is eager to step forward as Africa's natural alternative in that scenario. This move is being hailed by many as a "foreign policy foresight" of the current regime as, in the coming years, India's economy is set to grow further, accelerating the demand for cheap and readily available natural resources.

PM Modi is understood to have also used the opportunity to secure commitment from African leaders to back India's attempt to democratise the United Nations Security Council, signalling to Beijing that New Delhi is not behind it when it comes to assertion of her place as a world power.

Experts believe that although India cannot compete with China in doling out a concessional line of credit, PM Modi is trying to replicate an Aghanistan-like non-militarised partnership with Africa, with focus on capacity building. "I think it is a larger part of the strategy of the Modi government. It is an attempt to increase India's engagement with the African continent and it reflects the robust foreign policy approach of the Modi government," Monika Chansoria, a columnist writing on India's foreign relations, told The Sunday Guardian.

She dismissed cynics who have been sniffing at the India-Africa Forum Summit, the biggest ever assembly of dignitaries in India from abroad since the 1983 Non-Aligned Summit, as a late approach to a continent where China has monopolised the economic and diplomatic zone. "When one talks of foreign policy approaches, be it bilateral or multilateral, I do not think that the attempt should be to see how much of space is left or not. The attempt should be to build a collaborative relationship. And with so many leaders and heads of state visiting India, it is also about India asserting its position as an emerging power to reckon with. Africa is a very important continent where Indian presence and Indian investment shall help in India's assertion as an emerging power."

Despite India's strong political ties with Africa in the first three decades since her independence in 1947, the momentum was gradually lost. Although Indian and African diplomats gathered on two occasions recently, in the New Delhi summit in 2008 and later the Addis Ababa summit in 2011, the erstwhile United Progressive Alliance government led by former Prime Minister Manmohan Singh failed to devote much insight or prepare the blueprint for long-term bilateral relations. In the summit held at the Indira Gandhi National Stadium here, PM Modi, however, indicated without ambiguity that he wanted to re-energise India's bond with the continent. By calling on the heads of states, the PM has signalled that India is going to pay attention to Africa at the appropriate levels and by setting aside a large amount, he has also indicated the country's willingness to partner them in infrastructure projects, human resource development, and institution building, besides the ongoing projects on agriculture, health and education.

Those aware of the nature of Chinese engagement in Africa believe that despite the huge financial grants the latter has received, there has been an element of exploitation. Jayadeva Ranade, a foreign policy commentator, said that although China is way ahead in terms of investment, there are downsides to it. "Almost a million Chinese have settled in Africa. And they have started small businesses in that continent by edging out the local African people. There are questions being raised on the kind of ventures they have got into, and whether their businesses are of any benefit to the people of Africa," Ranade told this newspaper. He added that the slowing down of China's economy may hamper some projects that China had initiated including the "one road, one belt project", and it was a good time for India to build its ties with Africa. "We can impart training in certain kinds of agricultural development, and other areas of capacity building and skill development. Besides that, we have a reservoir of goodwill which we can tap into, and also channel our Diaspora for more engagement with the local. So we have pluses which are not in competition with or are undermined by what the Chinese are doing in Africa," he pointed out.

India's trade with Africa in 2014-2015 stood at nearly $70 billion and Indian companies are estimated to have invested as much as $30-35 billion there over the last 10 years. India's concessional credit, although insignificant compared to that of China, is responsible for 137 projects created in 41 African countries.

However, it will be early to predict that the Indian efforts can fetch a formal nod from the African Union to second New Delhi's aspiration for a permanent membership in the expanded UNSC. "This will be a very important decision on which the African Union will have to come together in a unified manner. But that will be difficult because each country has its own Chinese stake invested in that country, and the Chinese definitely are very adept at playing coercive diplomacy. They will use all the cards in their hand to ensure that they are able to emphasise the Chinese concern," a source in the diplomatic circles told this correspondent.

INDIA-AFRICA PARTNERSHIP – FUTURE DIRECTIONS

In anticipation of the 3rd India-Africa Forum Summit to be held in New Delhi 26-29 October 2015, Brookings India in collaboration with RIS, Institute of Defence Studies and Analysis (IDSA), and Confederation of Indian Industry (CII) jointly hosted a day-long conference to facilitate engagement on various dimensions of the India-Africa relationship. The objective of the conference was to lay the foundation for structured engagement between India and Africa on broad areas of trade and investment, technology, capacity building, infrastructure and geostrategic interests.

The day-long conference started with special remarks by Ambassador Sujata Mehta, Secretary (M&ER), Ministry of External Affairs and keynote address delivered by H.E. Dr. Genet Zewide, Ambassador of Federal Democratic Republic of Ethiopia and Dean of African Diplomatic Corps. The two guests of honour also released three publications – *'India and Africa: Forging a Strategic Partnership'; 'India-Africa Partnership Towards Sustainable Development'; and 'India and Africa: Common Security Challenges for the Next Decade'* - published by Brookings India, RIS and IDSA respectively.

The subsequent three panels revolved around the themes of geo-strategic linkages between India and Africa, trade and investment opportunities, and sectoral perspectives on the Indo-Africa partnership. The valedictory address was delivered by Ambassador Navtej Singh Sarna, Secretary (West), Ministry of External Affairs.

Africa is a continent of paradoxes with 34 of the least developed countries and six of the fastest growing economies in the world, the panel discussed. India is Africa's third largest trading partner with over $70 billion in trade, and over $30 billion in investment. Therefore, trade and investment is a critical dimension of the India-Africa relationship. Until recently, India's trade orientation was focused mostly toward the West: United States and European Union. But with the inevitable Indian economic slowdown in the next few years, India will need to look for consumers with similar patterns of consumption as ours. This is where Africa becomes a desirable market.

The panel discussed how from an African perspective, energy and raw materials were key components which India would be a keen importer of, especially with India's growing needs for energy. Africa has benefitted tremendously from India's Duty Free Tariff Preference for Least Developed Countries (DFTP-LDC) scheme. However, due to lack of logistics and poor infrastructure, many African countries have been unable to take full advantage of its benefits.

Trade and investment opportunities between India and African countries are immense, especially with the changing demographics and growing urban populations. In order to achieve the target of $120 billion in trade and investment by the 2020, there needs to be a simplification of bilateral processes and tax regimes. Institutions such as the African Development Bank can play an increasing role in facilitating the co-operation. Projects such as SITA can support in fostering cooperation between Indian businessmen with African opportunities.

There is also immense potential for India to be a reliable partner in development of sectoral infrastructure within Africa primarily in the energy, sustainable agriculture, health, telecommunications and education sectors. There can be potential for synergy between India and African countries in areas of energy technology, supercritical and advanced coal technologies, nuclear power, micro–grids and smart-grids, and agriculture related energy for lifting water, cold storage etc. India's solar programmes and hydropower, micro-hydel programs could also be very relevant for Africa. Engaging with the Indian model in the long-term could enable Africa to benefit from an open technology platform and foster local innovation. Sustainable agricultural development is also pivotal for Africa as the demand for agricultural produce in expected to go up by a 100% by 2050. The way forward is to ensure that agriculture is science based and technology driven and peasant agriculture transforms to give way to agriculture business.

In terms of higher education, there is ample scope for a mutually beneficial partnership between India and Africa. However, for an effective partnership, the Indian higher education system must first offer incentives for African students in India in the form of a separate accreditation system, create channels to inform African students about Indian universities, offer hands-on experience for African students in Indian companies and take measures to narrow the cultural divide between African and Indian students.

For an effective trade, investment and development partnership, there needs to be enough awareness among Indian investors about the diverse nature of African countries. In order to succeed, Indian companies must understand that each African country is different and has different needs and expectations. India's relationship with Africa is based on a common future with similar demographics and economic opportunities. By overcoming the hurdles faced by both Indian investors in Africa and African investors in India, both India and Africa can strengthen their trade and investment ties.

With increasing economic importance of the African continent, the geo-political linkages between India and Africa are becoming even more imperative. Ensuring peace, security and internal stability are the key to economic investment and growth. In that sense, Africa is no more a continent on the margins of Indian security interests, but very much a focus in its long-term strategic plan. India has had a long engagement with Africa in terms of peacekeeping, dating back to the UN Operation of Congo in 1960. India currently deploys about 4,500 peacekeepers in several African countries like South Sudan and Congo. Indian peacekeeping mainly stems from its support for African initiatives for peace and security. However, India peacekeeping has not always been considered in a positive light by African countries and there is a need to counter this perception. While peacekeeping forms an important aspect of Indian engagement in Africa, there is perhaps a need to reform peacekeeping and move towards peacebuilding.

Meanwhile, Indian bilateral defence cooperation has largely played out in the form of combating piracy off the coast of Somalia in the last few decades. While combating piracy remains an important issue, there is a need to now shift the focus of security cooperation from piracy, which is largely under control, to ensuring security on both the eastern and western coastlines of Africa. To this end, the IBSAMAR exercises conducted by the navies of India, South Africa and Brazil are fast becoming the flagship initiative of the Indian security establishment. Indian military institutions also provide training to officers from countries like Mozambique, Seychelles, South Africa and Tanzania. However, these defence partnerships are largely ad hoc in nature and lack a well-planned strategic outlook. It is a common allegation that India's security aspirations in Africa are largely a reaction to China's increasing influence in the region. Upgradingthe India-Africa partnership to a strategic dialogue level might assuage some of these concerns and ensure long-term cooperation in security and strategic matters. The security establishments of India and Africa also need to establish adequate policy tools to engage with the different security communities in Africa so as to ensure secure maritime systemsand encourage blue powers.

In conclusion, 'chaos, conflict and crises' continue to colour the Indian public's perception of Africa. The message of 'resurgence, renewal, renaissance' of Africa must be more effectively broadcasted to transform this perception. The India Africa Forum Summit will hopefully result in the creation of a commonand integrated intellectual analytical platform where a broad spectrum of issues in the India-Africa relationship can be discussed in a targeted manner.

INDIA-AFRICA: A LIMITED PARTNERSHIP

With the curtains finally drawn on the third India-Africa Forum Summit (IAFS)—one of the biggest and longest diplomatic jamborees ever hosted by India—there is broad consensus that while the summit itself was a resounding success in terms of optics and laid out a clear roadmap for the future of India-Africa relations, the road to forging a closer partnership will be a long, winding and complicated one.

The contours of this complex journey were evident in the Delhi Declaration and the India-Africa Framework for Strategic

Cooperation unveiled at the summit. Moreover, multilateral institutions and organizations, which might otherwise facilitate this partnership, are also likely to contribute to the complexity. While both documents stressed the need for India and African nations to work together to achieve the ambitious Sustainable Development Goals (SDGs) by 2030, there was very little elaboration on how this might work in practice beyond the obvious call that the UN "should function in a transparent, efficient and effective manner". There was no call for closer cooperation to work on SDGs.

In fact, it is the comprehensive reform of the UN system in general and the Security Council in particular that poses the biggest challenge to the partnership. The *Delhi Declaration*, which reaffirms their commitment "to make it (the UN) more regionally representative, democratic, accountable and effective", reflects the divergent views of India and African nations, given that India has chosen to throw in its lot with the G-4 (Brazil, Germany, India and Japan), which is not "regionally representative" of Africa.

Moreover, the summit also did not break, let alone dissolve, the Ezulwini Consensus and Sirte Declaration, which New Delhi considers as one of the primary hurdles to reform of the UNSC. Instead, the Delhi Declaration merely "notes" the common African position on reforms, just as the African nations "note" India's position and aspirations for permanent membership. This is essentially a diplomatic stalemate that will sustain the status quo and be to the advantage of existing Security Council permanent members rather than in the interest of either India or Africa.

Similarly, both documents, particularly the Framework for Strategic Cooperation, are silent on India's contribution to UN peacekeeping in Africa, reflecting another area of divergence. While India considers its peacekeeping role a singular contribution to the continent and the UN, not all African nations have a similar positive outlook. In some instances, alleged sexual and financial misconduct by Indian peacekeepers have marred India's credentials.

Moreover, despite India's flattering self-image of its UN peacekeeping role, New Delhi has not been very successful in converting its peacekeeping efforts into political support, for instance, for reform of the UNSC. For any agreement on this important issue, it is imperative that India and Africa have a sustained dialogue beyond the "gold versus blood" debate between countries that mandate and fund peacekeeping operations (the five permanent UNSC members and large donors, such as Japan and Germany) and the biggest troop contributing countries (such as India, Pakistan and Bangladesh, whose personnel actually carry out the operations in the field) that has stymied UN peacekeeping. However, the summit documents make only a passing reference to how they might support UN peacekeeping reforms.

Finally, while acknowledging common threats to peace and security, ranging from terrorism to piracy and organized crime, the summit documents are singularly conservative in pushing for greater security cooperation on the ground and at sea, primarily on account of New Delhi's shyness in playing the role of an overt security provider. Indeed, India is reported to have turned down requests by African nations to build their maritime capabilities. Similarly, India has not been bold enough to expand IBSAMAR (the joint maritime exercises of India, Brazil and South Africa) to include other littoral African nations.

Clearly, while the IAFS process has laid out a clear path to enhance the India-Africa partnership, the significant difference on one hand and the absence of bold initiative on the other is going to limit the scope of this partnership. That is a missed opportunity.

AFRICA-INDIA - ANALYZING THE CONDITIONS AND STAKES OF A WIN-WIN PARTNERSHIP

India-Africa cooperation that promotes economic and technological exchange and the indigenous transformation of Africa's natural resources could help move the continent up the global value chain.

The Indo-African partnership has been rooted in the spirit of the Afro-Asian conference held at Bandung, Indonesia, in 1955. Cemented by a common stand against colonization and racism, today this partnership is at a turning point motored by the stellar economic growth in the two regions and the growing exchange between them. The goal of shared development through cooperation between the two regions is a perspective that is in line with the reduction of world poverty as enshrined in the Sustainable Development Goals.

Understandably, the third edition of the Africa-India Forum Summit generates a lot of interest. The Summit this year was much larger than in previous years, with participation from 54 African countries.

Participation in the previous two summits, held in 2008 and 2011, was limited to Regional Economic Communities (RECs) in accord with the Banjul Agreement. The 2015 Summit has given greater privilege to bilateral endeavours. That said, the implication of regional actors is an asset of the India-Africa partnership and should continue, in the interest of promoting regional development in Africa. Additionally, regional cooperation provides a platform for opinion building and sharing common positions in international organizations.

Meanwhile, keeping the regional dimension alive, the unprecedented levels of participation in the third Summit is an opportunity to be explored. The scale of this Summit provides an occasion to renew and further accelerate the India-Africa partnership.

This article studies the stakes at play in the 2015 Summit and future perspectives on cooperation between India and Africa. It is based on shared reflections of the two authors hailing from Africa and India.

The African Perspective

Though rich in natural resources, Africa accounts for three percent of total world trade. Hence, enhancing the continent's share in the world economy is a major stake.

In this regard, the Indian experience - with industrialization based on the development of indigenous scientific and technical capital - is worth exploring. Indian technology sells itself as adaptable and affordable. Mangalyan, the Indian mission to Mars, cost $80 million; much less than the $2.5 billion invested in the American mission Curisosity.

The green revolution in the 1960s, and the push for information technology in the 1980s, have been major success stories of India's brush with scientific and technological development. An India-Africa cooperation that promotes economic and technological exchange and the indigenous transformation of Africa's natural resources could be a vector for moving the continent up the global value chain.

The Diamond Institute in Botswana has been one of the flagship projects in this direction. In line with India's initiative "Make in India", a "Make in Africa" project supporting local private sectors and employment generation should be one of the pillars of the growing Africa-India partnership. John Kuffour, the former President of Ghana, underlined that Africa's strategy towards cooperation with India should be based on "marrying African resources with Indian technology".

Countries in Africa should also negotiate better access to the Indian market. An equal partner, Africa's support is crucial to India when it comes to trade negotiations at the World Trade Organization (WTO), climate change talks and the expansion and reform of the Security Council.

India's duty free tariff lines to Africa were revised in August 2014 to further boost trade with African countries. In spite of the revision, which was raised to cover 98 per cent of Indian tariff lines, Africa's exports to India, especially agricultural, remain low.

The reason behind the dismal level of exports could be because products of interest to Africa, such as coffee, tea, vegetables and spices are excluded from the duty free market access scheme. India is either a direct competitor of Africa in the above-mentioned products or is interested in protecting its local producers. A rural and agricultural economy, domestic concerns, and the interests of agricultural producers can have a direct impact on politics and elections in India.

It also has to be noted that most of the products covered under the duty free market access scheme, including cashew nuts and aluminum ore, are in India's interest because the country processes and re-exports them to developed countries. Therefore local processing and further expansion of the duty free scheme are what countries in Africa should push for in their cooperation with India.

When it comes to security and strategic concerns, India should enhance its cooperation with Africa in two domains. India could position itself as the principal 'security provider' in the Indian Ocean region, which we call the strategy of the "Varuna Triangle".

India's readiness to contribute to UN peacekeeping missions in Africa makes it one of the top contributors in this regard, as it provides India with a good knowledge of the African terrain. This experience and willingness can be capitalized and integrated into a security strategy designed at the African Union level, in order to deal with security issues faced by the African continent.

The federal structure of the Indian republic also provides opportunities for decentralized cooperation that countries in Africa could explore. For instance, South Africa and Mozambique were participants in the "Vibrant Gujarat" forum launched by Narendra Modi, the then chief minister of Gujarat and now India's Prime Minister.

The Indian Perspective

When it comes to India's future engagement with Africa, diversification is the word to go by. The Export-Import (EXIM) bank of India is a major actor in India's cooperation with Africa.

Though concessional credit lines by the EXIM bank require that 75 per cent of the goods and services be exported from India, there is an interest for joint ventures with local partners in Africa. In Senegal, for instance, the urban transport project in Dakar was conducted by a joint venture between Tata India and Senbus, a Senegalese company. Similarly, the Senegalese programme of self-sufficiency in the production of rice was supported by the supply of irrigation pump sets by the Indian company Kirloskar, which again was working with a local partner TSE Entreprises.

For more sustainable cooperation, the EXIM bank should continue the promotion of joint ventures in Africa for greater local participation in projects, development of the private sector fabric and for increasing employment opportunities in the country of operation. This has to be reinforced through a diversification of Indian companies involved in the EXIM bank operations in Africa. Recently, an article by P. Vaidyanathan Iyer (Indian Express, October

20, 2015) pointed out that the contracts for most of the EXIM bank projects in Africa have been won by three Indian companies: Angelique International, Lucky Exports and Jaguar Overseas.

This restricted number of Indian companies imposes multiple limitations on cooperation between the two regions. It also points out the low level of exchange and communication between decision-makers and enterprises from Africa and India. A partnership limited to a handful of companies carries the risk of nepotism, and a restricted transfer of technology and know-how.

An increase in the number and type of enterprises is crucial to the renewal of the partnership, and the 2015 Summit should enhance interaction between Indian companies and their African counterparts.

Annual or triennial summits, which only privilege decision-makers and 'big' actors to the neglect of smaller actors, do not engender a bottom-up relationship.

A diversification of actors and resources is integral to sustainable cooperation. Decentralization, greater communication, enhanced engagement of small and medium enterprises, and of federal states with the likes of the previously mentioned "Vibrant Gujarat" forum, are a step forward in strengthening cooperation at the grass-roots level. Trade between India and Africa also needs to look beyond natural resources and raw materials to an emphasis on manufacturing.

Indo-African cooperation is often concentrated in the Anglophone regions of Africa, which house the majority of the Indian diaspora in Africa. Mauritius and South Africa occupy a position of privilege in India's relationship with the African continent. The partnership needs to be extended to other regions in Africa with diverse linguistic profiles, in order to impart a new dynamic to the relationship. The TEAM 9 programme launched in 2004, which includes a diverse set of countries in the West African region, sets an example for a future Indo-African relationship. A holistic engagement with the whole of the African continent is an imperative for an emerging India with global ambitions. Better communication and exchange between the two regions could reduce the risk of isolation and conflicting stands on issues of mutual benefit and shared interests and ideas. In the last round of World Trade Organization (WTO) talks, India stood almost isolated in its stand on domestic food security in spite of a common position on food subsidies with African and G33 countries. This is an instance of diplomatic negligence by the Indian government in mobilizing a shared position and in the chance to build consensus with its African partners on issues of common concern at international organizations.

Though India and its African partners back the stand of differentiated responsibilities, there are incompatibilities in the urgency to respond to climate change issues, especially with certain coastal and the African, Caribbean and Pacific Group of States (ACP). The India-Africa Forum Summit of 2015 would be an occasion for India to revise and formulate a mutually convivial stand on the issue of climate change ahead of the summit in Paris in December 2015.

"Rebranding" Of Africa In New Delhi

In the article titled 'Engaging with an aspirational Africa' published in the Indian daily The Hindu dated 19 October 2015, Sanjay Baru points out that one of the major stakes for the Indo-African relationship is the way Africa is imagined and projected in India. Africa as an equal partner and a 'rising' continent cannot be subject to prejudice of racism and tags of the 'dark continent'. India would have to take a more proactive and clear stand against incidents of racism and physical violence against Africans in India.

These incidents are a blot on the moral standing of the country, which has been pivotal in its relations with Africa. A relationship which claims to build itself on "people to people contact" needs a mutual effort by India and its African partners on raising awareness about the continent in the minds of the Indian public, and in institutions of higher education.

ECONOMIC ANGLE TO INDIA-AFRICA PARTNERSHIP

Laying stress on the importance of Africa-India ties and establishment of Organization of African Unity (OAU), Africa Day was celebrated here last week with emphasis on goals to be achieved in the coming years. Just as in the past, India and Africa have fought against colonialism, they need to establish strong economic ties to emerge victorious in the future. "While celebrating this Africa Day, we should work together to explore new ways of advancing our common objective of establishing a win-win strategic partnership between Africa and India," Dean of African Diplomatic Corps, Carlos Agostinho Do Rosario, who is also envoy of Mozambique, said.

The significance of Africa Day, which falls on May 25, was highlighted at the press conference held at Egyptian embassy (May 23) with several African leaders giving importance to development of Africa-India ties.

Liberation of Africa from colonialism led to OAU taking shape as African Union, in keeping with the "undergoing changes," Rosario said. Tracing Africa-India ties to history, he emphasized: "As together, we were victorious yesterday against colonialism, apartheid and injustice of all sorts, today also nothing will prevent us from being victorious against hunger and poverty. Together we will always succeed."

In this direction, some of the issues that emerging economy of India can contribute in development of Africa, include: – increasing investment in human capital development in Africa; promote technology acquisitions as well as knowledge generation sharing and applications; acceleration of infrastructure development in Africa; enhance economic cooperation, trade and improved market access for African products: and share India's experience on green revolution for boosting agricultural products to combat hunger and disease in Africa, the African leaders said.

The Africa Day was also celebrated with the release of an annual magazine that focused on the new importance given in the recent years to development of Africa-India relations. In the opinion of Egyptian envoy Mohamed Higazy, who was a key speaker at the press conference: "We need to convert framework of cooperation (between Africa and India) into an action plan in all aspects. The action plan will be able to transform the Africa-India partnership into a dynamic, profitable and fruitful endeavor for the benefit of people."

Referring specifically to bilateral Egypt-India economic ties, Higazy said: "The exact figure of Indian investment in Egypt is US $2 billion." Drawing attention to number of projects being submitted by Indian companies in areas such as textiles, petrochemicals, hydrocarbon, steel, plastic, tourism and information technology, he said: "India today is third largest foreign investor in Egypt after United States and Italy. However, by 2010, India shall be number one trading partner of Egypt." The first ever India-Africa summit, held last month (April 8-9), adopted Delhi Declaration and Africa-India Framework for Cooperation resolving to "develop jointly" within a year's time, "a joint plan of action at a continental level and an appropriate follow-up mechanism to implement our Framework for Cooperation."

In response to a question on new emphasis being suddenly given to India-Africa relations, Rosario described it as part of Africa's "Look East, Look India policy." This is linked to India having become a significant player in the global economy. "India's rapid emergence in global economy raises demand for Africa's natural resources, which fortunately are available in the African continent, which need to be industrialized for a better contribution in sustainable development of the continent," Rosario said.

Dismissing speculations of India facing strong competition from China regarding investment in Africa, Rosario said: "We don't see any negative competition. We need both India and China besides the others to convert the continent's natural resources into wealth. We need different partnerships. China, India and Brazil among others, are our partners. The competition brings more benefits."

Earlier, at India-Africa summit, when asked to compare India's approach towards Africa with that of western powers and China, Prime Minister Manmohan Singh replied: "India's renewed focus on Africa has nothing to do with China's growing clout in the continent. We are not in any race or competition with China or any other country. The desire of India and Africa to work together is not new."

Asserting that India-Africa summit has laid foundations, the Indian premier said that it is now time to plan ahead to implement the joint programs of cooperation and to build a meaningful and productive Indo-African partnership.

Emphasis was laid on India and Africa working together with a new momentum at last week's press conference. Quoting the importance given by India's first prime minister, late Jawaharlal Nehru to developing strong ties with Africa, Rosario said: "In his words, 'though separated by the Indian Ocean, Africa is in a sense our next door neighbor."

The African leaders expressed satisfaction with several measures announced by Indian government to strengthen ties with Africa. These include preferential market access to 34 least developed African countries, more than doubling to $5.4 billion the lines of credit over the next five years and increasing the 'Aid to Africa' budget by investing over half a billion dollars in capacity building and human resource development projects. Among other key measures are more scholarships for African students wishing to study in India.

"We are very happy for now. All these decisions will be implemented by the Indian government in this financial year," Rosario said. Expressing optimism on strengthening Africa-India partnership, he said: "I look forward for a bright future of a strong Indo-Africa Partnership in this 21st century and together we will make a difference."

INDIA-AFRICA: A PARTNERSHIP OF PRAGMATISM AND POTENTIAL

The third India-Africa Forum Summit (IAFS) was hosted in New Delhi from 26-29 October. This year's event included representation from 54 African countries, with 41 heads of state or government, and marked the unveiling of Prime Minister Narendra Modi's African foreign policy. The summit was originally scheduled for December 2014but was delayed due to the Ebola outbreak. As a result it had remained ambiguous as to where the African continent fitted within Modi's foreign policy, which aspires to secure India's regional hegemony and project a dominant India on the global stage. Even before the Summit commenced, it became apparent that the BJP government's first IAFS would differ from the two previous summits hosted by the Congress-led government. Past summits extended invitations to 14 least developed countries (LDCs) that were selected by the African Union (AU). However, the October 2015 IAFS opened the invitation to 54 African countries (only Western Sahara was not invited). While past summits highlighted bilateral exchanges, the 2015 summit advocated for the India-Africa partnership to confront global challenges.

Despite a larger guest list and more ambitious agenda, Modi's desired engagements with the African continent follows in the footsteps of his predecessor, Manmohan Singh. The preference for economic diplomacy, or growing the Indian economy through renewed ties with committed global partners, prevails. This invokes a pragmatic and multifaceted foreign policy based on energy needs, security of the Indian Ocean region, Indian comparative advantages in technology and health, and bolstered soft power perceptions. Relations with Africa are premised on India as a nascent global power and a rising Africa that can fulfil India's dire energy needs and serve as a market for Indian products. Furthermore, India's African foreign policy is part of Modi's geopolitical calculations to counter Chinese influence in the Indian Ocean Region.

It is essential to explore what was actually accomplished at the summit. During the inaugural ceremony, Modi outlined the past successes of Indian education opportunities, ICT projects, and affordable pharmaceutical products that have improved African countries' human capital and technological advancements. Additionally, the Prime Minister outlined a vision for the India-Africa partnership (which represents one-third of humanity) to play a vital role in global issues of reducing the global digital divide, respecting the environment, promoting the Doha Development Agenda at the upcoming WTO Nairobi Ministerial, reforming the UN Security Council, and sharing intelligence to combat terrorism. The summit produced the India-Africa Framework for Strategic Cooperation document that commits to reaching Africa's Agenda 2063 and the UN's Sustainable Development Goals.

The soft power of Modi's foreign policy derives from India's offer of concessional lines of credit worth $10 billion over five years and grant assistance of $600 million. The latter will include 50,000 scholarships for Africans to study in India, a proposed expansion of the Pan-Africa E-Network, an India-Africa Development Fund and an India-Africa Health Fund. Since the first IAFS in 2008, India has extended $7.4 billion in concessional credit and $1.2 billion in grants. However, Modi's India is still reluctant to project democratic norms over pragmatic partnerships as demonstrated by the participation in IAFS of President Abdel Fattah el-Sisi, who overthrew a democratically elected government in Egypt, and Sudan's Omar al-Bashir, who is wanted by the International Criminal Court.

The results of the third IAFS illustrate that Africa can fit within Modi's economic diplomacy through bolstering the interactions with the Indian Ocean Region and promoting India's comparative advantages while gaining access to natural resources. The importance of the "blue economy", or the maritime activites, such as trade and security, that link India with other countries bordering the Indian Ocean explains Modi's decision to travel to Seychelles and Mauritius.

When Modi visited Mauritius in March, India offered the country $500 million in concessional lines of credit for infrastructure projects and signed five memoranda of understanding on cooperation and sustainable development of the ocean economy. A recent trip by India's petroleum minister to Nigeria has opened the door to India sharing its knowledge and expertise in refining oil to help modernise Nigeria's domestic oil refining industry. In exchange the India Oil Corporation will gain access to more Nigerian oil blocks, thus resulting in a "win-win scenario" of value-added capabilities for Nigeria and increased access to oil resources for an energy-dependent India. In an effort to expand ties across Africa, India has deepened its relations with Mozambique through ONGC Videsh Ltd investing $24 billion in the African countries' natural gas.

Additionally, the timing of IAFS is perhaps not a coincidence. India is currently overshadowed by China's activities in Africa but Modi is aiming to take advantage of a weaker Chinese economy with a decreased appetite for natural resources and negative African perceptions of a "neo-colonial" China. While India can serve as an alternative to Chinese relations, African responses to continued Chinese engagement must be reassessed after the 6th Forum on China-Africa Cooperation (FOCAC) that will be co-hosted by South Africa in December 2015.

It is unlikely that India can match Chinese engagement in dollars. Chinese bilateral trade with the African continent stood at over $200 billion in 2014.

This figure dwarfs India's trade linkages with Africa valued at $72 billion in 2014. Perhaps more crucial to Modi is continued Indian hegemony in the Indian Ocean Region. The threat of China intruding through its proposed military base in Djibouti sparks a need for India to bolster relations with African countries neighbouring the Indian Ocean. These strengthened ties serve to safeguard India's dominance in this maritime zone.

Finally, it is imperative look at the actors who participated in IAFS –Indian and African politicians, Indian public and private sector businesses, the AU, and African business delegates. Moreover, media coverage was skewed towards analysis in Indian media, while African media engagement (with the notable exceptions of South African think tanks and media outlets, see reports by SAIIA and ISS) was limited to government press releases and brief articles.

Crucially missing from this summit were civil society voices, which will be needed to make this partnership realise its transformative agenda on both local and global platforms.

During the closing ceremony Modi highlighted India and Africa's "solidarity and unity can be a major force in the cause of a more inclusive, fair and democratic global order." However, this "reinvigorated partnership" will be powerful in building a more equal and sustainable global order when Indian and African civil societies participate in shaping the modes of engagement. The agenda laid out by the third IAFS with the inclusion of an active civil society can confront the hubris of myopic "rising" narratives and recognise that India and Africa can learn from one another to overcome shared development challenges stemming from inequality, poverty, young populations and rapid urbanisation.

STRENGTHENING THE ASIA-AFRICA PARTNERSHIP

An event next month is an ideal opportunity to institutionalize a partnership that offers considerable opportunity.

Next month, Indonesia will be hosting the commemoration of the 60th anniversary of the 1955 Asia-Africa Conference. According to Indonesian President Joko Widodo, the commemoration aspires to remind the world that Indonesia played a significant role in the anti-colonial struggle. Amidst complex contemporary global politics, it will be a challenge for Jokowi to convince the world that this Asia-Africa gathering is necessary and relevant. Institutionalizing effective cooperation between the two continents should be a priority.

Ten years ago, Indonesia hosted the Asia-Africa Conference golden jubilee, out of which came the New Asian-African Strategic Partnership (NAASP). At that 2005 summit, Asian and African leaders agreed to revive the 1955 Bandung Spirit, whose one aim was to advance cooperation between the two continents. The NAASP expanded the form of Asia-Africa engagement from merely non-aligned and anti-colonial rhetoric to broader cooperation. Since then, there have been several projects and programs under the NAASP banner, from diplomatic training and technical cooperation to a business forum. Nevertheless, the NAASP receives little in the way of either public attention or political will. Does the NAASP really boost Asia-Africa relations? That is unclear. Certainly, interactions between Asia and Africa are growing, especially on economic matters, but they do not appear to be driven by the NAASP. Asia and Africa currently lack any formal institutional links, despite the long-standing rhetoric of Asia-Africa solidarity. This is in contrast to Asia's relations with other continents, which have been developed in institutions such as the Asia-Europe Meeting (ASEM) and the Forum for East Asia-Latin America Cooperation (FEALAC).

Framework

NAASP did in fact try to institutionalize interregional ties. The 2005 NAASP agreed to hold heads of state/government summits every four years and a foreign ministerial meeting every two years, but neither actually went ahead. There were some meetings under the Asian-African Sub-Regional Organization Conference (AASROC) framework, but the long-term vision of this forum remains unclear.

Leaders in Asia and Africa have ignored the NAASP's commitment to establishing closer contact. Individual Asian powers that see Africa as an enormous economic opportunity, approach African within their own national frameworks. Each Asian country pursues its national interests through bilateral engagement, such as the Forum on China-Africa Cooperation, India-Africa Forum Summit, and Tokyo International Conference on African Development (TICAD). Yet there are few initiatives for African countries to pursue what they might want from cooperation with Asia. On several occasions, South Africa has proposed the inclusion of NAASP into the agenda of the African Union (AU) and the New Partnership for Africa's Development *(NEPAD)*, without success.

If the upcoming Asia-Africa gathering wants to be remembered, it should offer something fresh and substantive. Fail to do so, and the fate of NAASP will follow that of the Non-Aligned Movement (NAM): a lot of rhetoric, but little that is operational or significant. The institutionalization of the NAASP should enable Asian and African officials to meet on a more regular basis. A routine inter-continental meeting could become a venue to exchange views and address global challenges, such as climate change, development and terrorism, areas that are usually outside the scope of the more economically focused bilateral format. This would in turn add to the weight of Asia and Africa, which already account for 75.3 percent of the world's population and 28.5 percent of its GDP, on the global stage.

Institutionalizing the NAASP as a driver of Asia-Africa relations will not be easy, but it is feasible, especially if it is modeled after ASEM and FEALAC, which have a strong tradition of informality. ASEM holds a summit every two years with periodic ministerial meetings on foreign affairs, economic, cultural and other areas. FEALAC, on the other hand, has only biennial foreign ministers' meetings and gatherings of senior official. Neither ASEM nor FEALAC has a structured agenda or any secretariat – FEALAC has a cyber secretariat, but it is more an online database and a source of information on FEALAC activities. Neither ASEM nor FEALAC aspire to become arenas for problem solving. Rather, they are forums for building trust and dialogue, with the potential to open up mutually beneficial opportunities for their members.

Taking ASEM and FEALAC as models, the countries of Asia and Africa could start to seriously explore an informal institutionalization project. Informality will provide flexibility and inclusiveness, enabling all members to contribute. Regular meetings between foreign ministers should be initiated in the upcoming commemoration, with an eventual target of setting up an intergovernmental forum – let's call it "the Asia – Africa Contact (AAC)."

ASEAN and Trade as Drivers

If continent-wide interregional cooperation between Asia and Africa is too complex, then they could begin with ASEAN. The Southeast Asian bloc could have some relevance from the Asian side because it is the only coherent regional community within Asia. ASEAN has the profile to set a "Pan-Asian agenda" for engaging Africa. The 2015 ASEAN Economic Community, which aims to create a Southeast Asian-wide single market and production base, is potentially compatible with Africa's ambition of establishing a trade union comprising three regional organizations: the Common Market for Eastern and Southern Africa (COMESA), the South African Development Community (SADC), and the East African Community (EAC) by 2016. ASEAN, or even broader East Asia, could engage Africa nations through this huge trade union, which covers 27 African countries.

A closer economic engagement between ASEAN with one, if not those three regional entities in Africa will not only help to solidify relations between the continents, it also has the potential to boost trade. Currently, trade volumes between ASEAN and COMESA, for instance, are still just 0.37 percent of ASEAN's total trade with the rest of the world. Given a burgeoning middle class and demographic conditions in both regions, there is a huge potential market, are considerable unexplored economic potential.

A free trade agreement (FTA) between ASEAN and SADC could be one aim. SADC countries offer agricultural products such as fruit, vegetables, meat and livestock. ASEAN's main goods are electrical products, machinery and automobiles, all important imports for SADC. These competitive advantages suggest an ASEAN-SADC FTA could be quite beneficial. For one thing, African consumers would certainly appreciate the removal of the relatively high tariffs SADC and COMESA apply to imports from outside their blocs.

An FTA between Asia and Africa would be challenging to achieve, but in the meantime countries from both continents should aim to improve people-to-people and business-to-business connections, who would be stakeholders in any future FTA. In this sense, the Asia-Africa Business Summit that will be convened on the sidelines of the upcoming commemoration is welcome, and should become routine. This kind of forum can improve trust in the business community.

More The Ceremony

To create a framework that covers wide-ranging engagement between Asia and Africa, Jokowi could take a lesson from Singapore's former Prime Minister Goh Chok Tong, who in the 1990s persistently pursued his vision of establishing ASEM and FEALAC, proactively exchanging ideas with other heads of state and government. And similar effort with Africa will obviously take time, diplomatic energy (and of course money), and will require careful study. But proposing an institutionalization project could certainly provide the bridge the two regions need.

Next month's event should not just be ceremonial. It should have a robust, operational vision. A successful commemoration is one that can reenergize a commitment to creating a platform that eliminates gaps in culture and mindsets. For an Asia-Africa partnership to be relevant, the event next month should chart a course for more tangible, institutionalized cooperation, with economic engagement as the priority.

5

Emerging Global Challenges: The African Perspective

REGIONAL PERSPECTIVES ON CHALLENGES AND OPPORTUNITIES FOR AFRICA

In much of international development literature, Africa's sub-Saharan region represents a prolonged development crisis. Despite the recent remarkable development gains by some sub-Saharan African countries — driven by a combination of factors like increasing democratization and transparency, strengthening and reform of governance institutions, surge in commodity prices, and the adoption and implementation of more effective macro-economic policies, the region still faces daunting sustainable development challenges. With forty-eight countries, a population of over 700 million, and an average per capita income of roughly US$1 a day, sub-Saharan Africa remains, in economic terms, the poorest region in the world.

Put in the context of global development trends, Africa's development hardships are characterised by a stark paradox; whereas extreme poverty levels have declined globally in various regions of the world since 1980, the proportion of people living in abject poverty in Africa has increased. According to economist Dambisa Moyo, in her seminal book Dead Aid: Why Aid is Not Working and How There Is a Better Way for Africa, the number of Africans living in abject poverty nearly doubled in two decades (1991-2002).

Notwithstanding Africa's development crisis, the continent is endowed with abundant renewable and non-renewable natural resources. In the context of sustainability, especially the often complex links between environment and development, how best could Africa's natural resources be harnessed to advance sustainable development of the continent? How can Africa's governance and institutional frameworks and policies be strengthened to respond to the emerging and re-emerging sustainability challenges facing the continent and its people?

Ongoing challenges

While the twenty-first century has witnessed sustained demand for Africa's natural resources — oil, minerals, and other raw materials — the continent continues to lack effective institutional capacity to manage these resources sustainably. Added to the continent's vulnerabilities to climate change, Africa's ongoing sustainable development efforts must, as out of necessity, link the environment (nature), economic growth (wealth) and governance (power) as the essential elements in poverty reduction strategies.

Although the linkages between Africa's socio-economic development and the continent's natural, ecological, and climatic factors have been examined in relevant development literature, this discourse has also identified the need for the continent to develop effective, accountable and transparent governance institutions to manage these complex development-environment-climate linkages.

Economic and investment policies in Africa that recognize and integrate development-environment-climate approaches will likely yield positive development outcomes towards achieving the Millennium Development Goals.

Sustainability science for Africa

Sustainability science is a new academic discipline that "probes interactions between global, social and human systems, the complex mechanisms that lead to degradation of these systems, and concomitant risks to human well-being".

Inter-disciplinary and multi-institutional academic research under the umbrella of sustainability science can be useful for addressing diverse and concurrent research priorities in the African context, including vulnerability in farm incomes, forestry management for climate change, and water supply governance. These priorities have been identified by a University of Nairobi team in the Strategy for Global Environmental Change Research in Africa: Science Plan and Implementation Strategy.

As one example of sub-Saharan Africa's unique geographical, ethnic, historical, and political features, Mozambique is a coastal country with a large drainage basin from which to produce hydropower, and a wealth of natural resources. In comparison to Ghana, a top cocoa and gold exporter with similar geographic features, Mozambique has not taken advantage of its resources to develop more sustainably. Researchers Aurélio Bucane and Peter Mulder have found that Mozambique, at the low end of Transparency International's Corruption Index, has a weak institutional infrastructure to the extent that the country's natural resource wealth may, in fact, have a negative impact on the economy.

Sustainability Science journal

While some interesting research has been conducted on sustainability challenges in Africa, the Journal of Sustainability Science has dedicated a special issue — including a message from Wangari Mathaai — that gathers more leading-edge inter-disciplinary research on African regional perspectives.

The first article in this special issue examines climate change impacts and adaptation options in Mozambique using modeling approaches. The UN University World Institute for Development Economics Research (UNU-WIDER) applied economist James Thurlow and co-authors present a modeling framework that investigates the range of impacts on Mozambique's environment and economy by using the wettest and driest climate scenarios, at global and local levels. The first striking result is the contrasting impact depending on whether the extreme scenarios were local or global. The authors predict that the frequency of most severe floods will double or quadruple under the global extreme scenarios, but will remain about the same in the local wet/dry scenarios. Crop yields show both negative and positive impacts under most conditions, but the authors found that hydropower generation and road networks will suffer negative long term impacts from just about all climate change scenarios. The study concludes with transport, agriculture and education adaptation strategies.

This and other articles in this issue, as an overlapping theme, confirm that environmental sustainability must be combined with poverty alleviation for a functioning ecosystem to produce resources and services as a basis for development that improves individual well-being and community resilience. These articles, focusing on selected African regional studies, highlight some of the policy challenges and opportunities for communities — from the local to the national levels — to tackle these interrelated problems sustainably. It is hoped that these studies and others, although limited in scope, offer a microcosm of the larger sustainability challenges facing African societies, and address some of the gaps in sustainable development literature in Africa.

As the African Development Bank observed in its 2007 African Development Report, sound environmental management and effective governance are indispensable policy frameworks to ensure that Africa's natural resource wealth generates rapid development and poverty reduction. In order to be successful, these frameworks must be transparent, accountable, representative, and take into account public participation.

AFRICAN ENGAGEMENT WITH EMERGING GLOBAL POWERS

The BRICS certainly want to engage with Africa yet the consensus is that it is up to the continent to determine how it wants to use its platform to navigate the international system – and many questions remain unanswered. Rebecca Ramsamy, our Young International Professional, reports on discussions at a recent Friedrich-Ebert-Stiftung conference.

African representatives emphasised how they would rather define their own agenda when engaging with the BRICS group. The only way to prevent the "Africa versus superpower" syndrome in summits and negotiations would be to support regional integration, allowing Africa to present a common stance. But what is Africa's stake in the BRICS? How has the relationship between

Africa and BRICS been developing and how do they both engage the international system?

At 'BRICS in Africa: Challenges and Opportunities' a large visual backdrop hung behind panelists, depicting the African continent as a chessboard, with the BRICS and the European Union as chess pieces positioned on the continent.

This image was later analysed amongst the panelists, who agreed it was a misrepresentation of Africa's engagement with the BRICS, and that the image suggested that individual BRICs would dictate their engagement with Africa.

An Agenda-Check on Bottom-Up Development?

A trade union representative from Africa remarked that strategic coherence between the BRICS in trade and development issues is needed, as well as with Africa.

Calls for the BRICS to support participatory social development and ensure fair trade with Africa were abundant, as well as with the BRICs other partners.

European participants noted the dominance of China in African trade, and the broader discussion that ensued suggested that China's engagement in Africa might not have always yielded fairer trade that helps sustainable and long-term development in Africa. China needs to work on providing more equal terms of trade and social development in all African countries, Europeans argued.

Perhaps this is where partnership with Europe shows some advantage? Fairer trade deals and Corporate Social Responsibility (CSR) initiatives for EU companies that operate in African countries represent a qualitative difference absent from BRICS-Africa engagement, as some argued.

From the African perspective, the BRICS formed as a bloc for the Global South in the international system to represent developing countries on an equal platform. Representatives from all sides welcomed the challenge for Europe in engaging with Africa 'beyond aid'. Resonating with the African principle of 'Ubuntu', BRICS may yet host an African civil society platform, supporting a bottom-up form of engagement in Africa.

Banking on the BRICS?

The BRICS Bank, with equal ownership among its founding members, while not solely for Africa, could coordinate projects of the African Development Bank and the Development Bank of South Africa.

The question of conditionalities and responsibility for security loan and bond disbursement has yet to be fully addressed. A real assessment of the BRICS bank can only be made in more detail after its programmes and initiatives have been put into practice.

The possibility of the new BRICS Development bank energising New Partnership for Africa's Development (NEPAD) or other financing instruments was suggested, but it was reasoned by both African and European discussants that more network institutional-building would be needed to facilitate this.

A Foreign Policy Rainbow

Can South Africa adequately represent the diverse opinions of the African continent? Although South Africa would naturally pursue its own foreign policy objectives, an integral part of its foreign policy is to support and promote African continental initiatives and South-South Cooperation. From the African perspective, there are many "gateways" to the continent.

The BRICS certainly want to engage a continent with so much potential economic opportunity. However, it is up to Africa to determine how it wants to engage with the BRICS and use it as a platform to navigate the international system.

Many important questions remain, and this symposium highlighted African agency, integration, the incorporation of civil society and strategic actions by the BRICS as some of the key factors to consider.

THE 'S' IN BRICS: AN AFRICAN PERSPECTIVE

South Africa's foreign policy contends that our national interests are better safeguarded by not just focusing on our own national interests, but broadly on the interests of our region and our continent.

Our country, as a member of the BRICS (Brazil, Russia, India, China and South Africa) bloc, is playing an important role towards the shifting and distribution of power internationally. This shift is expected to give rise to a multi-polar world order.

Our interaction with fellow BRICS states is premised on three levels of engagement: firstly, national, where we advance our national interests; secondly, regional, where we promote regional integration and interaction with specific emphasis on the African Union mandate given to President Jacob Zuma to promote infrastructure development across the continent; and, thirdly, on a global level, where we advocate for a more inclusive global governance system.

The BRICS bloc represents 43% of the world's population, approximately one-fifth of global gross domestic product (GDP), estimated at US$13.7-trillion, as well as combined foreign reserves estimated at $4.4-trillion.

Last year, 2012, the BRICS countries accounted for approximately 11% of global annual foreign direct investment (FDI) flows ($465-billion) and 17% of world trade.

Promoting the African agenda

South Africa's membership of BRICS contributes to further leveraging economic opportunities for our own development agenda as well as that of the continent.

We want to ensure that our membership of BRICS also benefits the entire continent. The Fifth BRICS Summit scheduled for 26-27 March 2013 in Durban will constitute another high-level opportunity to further support key priority areas of the African agenda.

Asset Management Global chairman, Mr Jim O'Neill, published an article entitled "South Africa's BRICS Score: Not All Doom and Gloom". O'Neil argued objectively that South Africa could more than justify its presence in BRICS if it helped Africa to fulfill its remarkable potential by exploring cross-border expansion in trade and infrastructure, as well as improvements in domestic productivity. Africa is emerging as one of the fastest growing markets with the potential of future growth due to the demographic basis underpinning this growth and the new consumer market that is emerging.

BRICS-Africa trade set to treble

The BRICS countries now constitute the largest trading partners of Africa and the largest new (not total) investors.

The BRICS investment portfolio in Africa is very encouraging and promising. Over the past decade, we have seen a seismic acceleration of commercial and strategic engagements between the BRICS and Africa.

BRICS has nourished Africa's economic emergence and elevated the continent's contemporary global relevance. The recession and recovery period has enhanced this shift. In 2010, Standard Bank economists predicted that BRICS-Africa trade will "see an additional increase in the velocity of BRIC-Africa engagements, with trade and investment spearheading the commercial charge".

According to Standard Bank, BRICS-Africa trade will increase threefold, from $150-billion in 2010 to $530-billion in 2015.

The exponential growth potential of BRICS over the years to come will impact considerably on the future of emerging markets and developing economies - especially in the case of Africa.

Tackling SA's, Africa's challenges

South Africa's membership of this emerging markets bloc must be understood within the context of what we wish to achieve against the current challenges we face as a country and a continent.

As part of the developing world, South Africa faces the challenges of poverty, unemployment and inequality. BRICS Leaders engage in peer learning and share best practices and development models.

The Indian Prime Minister, Manmohan Singh, outlined 10 specific priority areas at the New Delhi Summit last year. These included job creation; skills upgrading; energy, food and water security; sustainable growth through expanded trade opportunities; clean energy; income inequality; urbanisation; and the impact of the external geo-political environment. Due to the complex nature of our challenges, the South African government has singled out infrastructure development as a key vehicle for improving the quality of life of the people. Infrastructure development is also expected to boost our competitiveness and create jobs.

Supporting Africa's industrialisation

Our BRICS partners view South Africa as a springboard into the African continent and a partner for economic development opportunities.

At the New Delhi Summit, President Zuma met with captains of industry from fellow BRICS member states and invited them to join hands with South African companies in the development of Africa, pointing out that in the infrastructure sector alone, $480-billion in investments will be required over the next 10 years.

BRICS leaders already expressed support in the Sanya Declaration for infrastructure development in Africa. They are committed to the continent's industrialisation within the framework of the New Partnership for Africa's Development (Nepad).

In the Delhi Declaration, the leaders expressed further support for Africa's industrialisation, saying they "attach the highest importance to economic growth that supports development and stability in Africa, as many of these countries have not yet realised their full economic potential".

The BRICS economies, which already constitute between 20 and 25 percent of global GDP, will link a large part of Africa with the fastest growing economies in the world.

SECURITY THREATS IN AFRICA: A CRITICAL PERSPECTIVE

The events of 9/11 brought increased engagement with the African continent. Yet, while Africa's significance to U.S. foreign policy has shifted since the Cold War—particularly with the formation of the U.S. Africa Command (AFRICOM) in 2007—security doctrine remains rooted in political realist thought. The "state," for example, has kept its place of importance in security narratives through government-to-government interactions and consultations as well as weapons sales and training. Likewise, responses to poverty and under-development have become militarized, demonstrated by increasing numbers of U.S. civil affairs operations concurrent with shrinking Congressional allocations for traditional foreign assistance. In challenging the assumptions that are primary in traditional U.S. security approaches in Africa, a critical framework provides a context-specific and realistic view of security threats. The result is more effective security policy.

Western Dalliances

U.S. engagement with Africa has been selective. During the Cold War, Africa was one of several battlegrounds for the containment of the communist influence; the United States and other Western allies used various African leaders to limit Soviet power by supporting authoritarian regimes such as Zaire's Mobutu and Liberia's Samuel Doe, as well as resourcing insurgent groups that fought leftist governments such as Jonas Savimbi's National Union for the Total Independence of Angola (UNITA). The United States also provided emergency assistance in the face of famines and other humanitarian emergencies.

The end of the Cold War saw a significant decline in U.S. assistance to Africa. This new era of retreat was in part due to the failure of the U.S.-led and UN-authorized Unified Task Force (UNITAF) in Somalia (1992-1993). During this period, intermittent attention was drawn to Africa by continued conflict in Somalia and the U.S. Embassy bombings in Kenya and Tanzania. Still, at the end of the 20th century, for all intents and purposes Africa remained geopolitically insignificant.

While security challenges have shifted since the Cold War, the way in which threats in Africa are framed remains entrenched in traditional or mainstream security thinking. Using such an approach, the West understands itself as living in a world threatened by hostile opponents, leading to security policy that requires urgent and radical defense measures. Furthermore, in a traditional framework, the state is the entity that must be secured; little attention is paid to what is *inside* the state. A critical approach reveals the underlying social, political, and historical structures that must be taken into account to successfully assess what is and what is not a true security threat. What follows is a discussion of two oft-identified "threats" in Africa framed in mainstream security approaches. These are then problematized using a critical approach.

Failed States and Ungoverned Spaces

The threat posed by states that do not control areas within their borders is a central security issue, and addressing them has become a basic strategic and moral imperative. Narratives on threats originating from Africa are riddled with phrases of "ungoverned spaces" and "failed states." U.S. State Department officials and defense analysts write about Africa's "anarchic zones" giving rise to "dangerous chaos," while threat briefings claim that the "vast stretches of ungoverned areas"—lawless zones, veritable "no man's lands"—demand constant levels of scrutiny.

As one analyst claimed, Africa, with its "war-ravaged areas and vast swathes of ungoverned territory," offers ideal conditions for extremists looking for a foothold. According to U.S. Army General Martin Dempsey, some of the most significant future security challenges will emanate from ungoverned spaces. Such narratives paint an alarming picture of Africa, full of desolate areas where young men ride in "technicals," waving and shooting AK-47s.

The mainstream security rationale for addressing such spaces and states is that the chaotic conditions of these areas are the primary locations for operations by groups that Western powers designate as foreign terrorist organizations. Such areas are inextricably linked to terrorism, terrorist "safe havens," and other emerging security threats because such locales are used for planning, organizing, training, and preparing operations against the West. In the traditional view of security, territories that states do not control are geopolitical vacuums that illegal actors occupy. The governments in which these spaces are found are considered threats because they fail in their Westphalian responsibility to stop non-state actors from using their territory and populations to prepare and stage attacks against Western interests. A critical approach does not ask what is *not* in these spaces and states, (a formal, Western-looking government) but what *is* there and why the West cannot work with it. Mainstream approaches to security analysis mask our ability to see that what often appears to be the breakdown of political and social order can hide the emergence of informal order.

There is no such thing as a failed state; whole areas do not fail and spaces do not become ungoverned; order exists in these areas, yet it is neither the kind of order the West recognizes, nor the institutions with which the West normally works. Furthermore, groups that are unfavorable to U.S. interests often govern these spaces. Such forms of order may look like the *Nande* traders in the Democratic Republic of the Congo who have developed self-sustaining, successful, transnational economic enterprises in the absence of a strong central government and in the presence of several violent armed groups. The*Nande,* who have built commercial enterprises and trust networks, challenge the assumption that a failed state signals a failed society. This community demonstrates how self-governing entities and property rights systems can coexist and reinforce one another—an idea that is inconceivable in a mainstream security perspective, which assumes that governmental institutions and state sovereignty are necessary.

Using a critical lens, the term "ungoverned space" is geographically subtle, referring to both a physical area and an absence of effective state sovereignty and control. The specification of a "space" rather than a whole area acknowledges the improbability of an entire territory failing uniformly and in geographically similar terrain. In some areas, *formal* institutions are ineffective, or the government in the capital has little to no legitimacy. Yet, these areas will possess informal institutions. For example, local chiefs may have more legitimacy among people in some rural areas than do government-appointed officials. Painting an oversimplified picture of regions and states that host terrorist organizations and operations as "failed" or "ungoverned" decontextualizes such developments, treating them as discrete phenomena divorced from political, social, and historical lineages.

Furthermore, generalizations about such spaces and states do not reflect the logistical necessities and strategies of violent actors. Attempting to organize rebellions from peripheral areas is ineffective if the organization aims to gather supporters in advance and engage with enemy forces. "In chaos, not even terrorists are safe or, more to the point, in order to be safe to train, and plan, terrorists would have to divert their already limited resources to provide their own security or pay protection money to others."

Operating in a "failed state" involves terrorists in local politics, which distracts them from their grander objectives. Furthermore, the infrastructure and logistical problems in such areas are disincentives for actors seeking a reliable base of operations. There has also been a trend toward assuming that all violence occurring in Africa (and elsewhere) is the work of terrorist groups. Branding all groups "terrorist" in nature is a tactic of national and foreign governments to attract attention of foreign policymakers and additional foreign resources.

Groups operating in isolated areas are more likely to be insurgents dedicated to the overthrow of the state, or militias organized by local elites. The considerable attention paid to the Sahel, for example, seems generated by the presence of Al Qaeda in the Islamic Maghreb (AQIM), an organization that does not act beyond the Sahel and is more like an insurgency than a global threat. Furthermore, violent actors that *do* engage with international forces do not require vast ungoverned spaces to do so. The argument that ungoverned territory is necessary for violent actors implies that when an organization focuses on Western interests it automatically becomes a terrorist group whose development is blamed on a lack of state control when, in reality, the group employs a strategy that takes advantage of its own institutional environments.

The Obsession with "Stability"

The danger posed by instability in Africa is another commonly identified threat in the post-9/11 narrative. Instability can range from the extremely violent—terrorist attacks, civil war, ethnic cleansing, massacres, coups, and revolutions—to lesser forms of instability such as protests, strikes, riots, and declarations of emergencies. The traditional security framework is preoccupied with external threats. Security involves the engagement of radical threat and consequently the adoption of equally radical measures.

The idea that localized violence in Africa threatens the stability of the international community is based on the assumption that politically unstable environments breed terrorists.

Furthermore, the political realism of mainstream security narratives focuses on maintaining the status quo: change is dangerous and stability is safe. Reinforcing stability in Africa has led to an increasing Western military presence largely for the training of local forces and the reinforcement of democratic institutions in post-conflict settings. Hence, what has developed is a narrative focused on bolstering African military capabilities and establishing democratic institutions. When viewed critically, however, increased Western military presence on the African continent can be seen to have negative effects on stability because it can create more, not less, radicals.

Furthermore, working with Western governments can make Africans targets of retaliatory violence. For example, the 2013 attack on the Westgate Mall in Nairobi was a response to Kenya's military presence in Somalia battling al-Shabaab along with other U.S. allies. The mainstream focus on stability plays out in international peace building efforts as well. These efforts result in pressure on post-conflict states to adopt democratic institutions. Such a perspective identifies and prioritizes elections, for example, but does not consider that elections are often a veneer that authoritarian regimes adopt to hide weak government institutions and deep-seated corruption. The focus on formal institutions underrates the impact of the informal realm, a bias that may be appropriate for established democracies where the rule of law is more apt to guide actors and where the ethic of constitutionalism reinforces a written constitution. Such conditions often do not exist in emerging democracies where the boundaries of state power have not yet been tested.

Under such conditions, formal institutions fail when political actors ally themselves along lines of personal relations and informal institutions. A critical approach reveals that elections are merely one part of the stabilization process. It also problematizes elections, demonstrating that they can have negative consequences if they are not timed correctly or not designed to fit local conditions.

Elections can mobilize rival factions, encourage the airing of grievances, and provide incentives for political abuse. Instability is more likely to occur when elections are used as a mode of conflict management. According to Salehyan, nearly all conflicts in Africa since 1990 were affiliated with elections. A result of the realist-influenced view that the status quo equates to safety is that many instances of instability are lumped into the broad category of "crisis." The general labels assigned to violence in Africa obscure the variation in violent acts that occur across states and demonstrate the casualness with which Africa is treated as "in crisis." Riots in one community or protests in a capital city are not the same as large-scale conflict. Yet the differences between such events and the characteristics that distinguish them from one another are unacknowledged or misunderstood. Policymakers and analysts often focus on areas with a history of instability as indicative of future violence and subsequent threats to security. Yet, the notion that conflict in the past equates to conflict in the future is a double-edged sword from a threat analysis standpoint. Conflict can be a precursor to future instability, though focusing on such states runs the risk of missing conflicts-in-the-making in "stable" countries.

Such was the case in Mali. A 2010 security brief published by the National Defense University-based Africa Centre for Strategic Studies, described Mali as a stable country with "great credibility in dealing with ... competing interests" from civil society, including Islamist ones. Two years later, members of the U.S.-trained Malian military overthrew the regime, leading to a weak interim government and an Islamist insurgency in the north. Given that the U.S. military had been working with Malian forces for several years prior to the coup as part of the U.S.-initiated Trans-Saharan Counterterrorism Initiative (TSCTI), the lack of awareness of local political, historical, and social issues is surprising. As one observer remarked, "How was it possible for the Special Forces and their Pentagon bosses and the CIA to have had such a total lack of understanding of the Malian officers they'd trained and the country they'd been operating in for over five years?" A critical framework disaggregates political violence and makes room for analysis that uncovers the politics behind it, revealing the underlying causes, which leads to understanding and more effective security policy.

Such an assessment reveals, for example, that instability in the Sahel was not an effect of terrorist influences from groups such as AQIM. Instead, instability in the Sahel was a result of underlying tensions that scholars had been writing about for years. The crisis in Mali was a conflagration of government corruption, continued armed rebellion in the north by the Tuaregs, and the illicit trafficking of arms, drugs, and other resources. A critical approach would have necessitated an examination of the layers of politics, history, and culture that led to the larger crisis, and could have informed more careful U.S. interaction with the Malian military.

Conclusion

The mainstream view of security depoliticizes Africans, characterizing them either as passive victims of underdevelopment, internal wars, and hunger, or in a negative light by their opposition as insurgents and terrorists. In part this reflects the continent's enormous social, historical, political, and cultural complexities. As the dominant narrative, a traditional approach to security proliferates a lack of understanding of Africa on the part of United States and other Western security officials. The traditional security framework, like any system that dominates primary (elite) narratives, defines what is reality and what is not. Given that the narrow confines of a mainstream security approach offer little to see other than the effect of insecurity, analysis that informs decision-makers does not portray fully the security challenges.

While the mainstream approach to security continues to dominate the West and the United States in particular, it is not the narrative that comes from Africans and the African continent. Though many African elites appeal to this perspective, whether to curry favour and resources from Western governments, or because they truly believe in its reality, the larger African population is witness to the enormous complexities that are compounded into insecurity. In many ways, African citizens (like much of the developing world) are the architects of the critical perspective if only because they live it.

This article makes no claim that terrorists do *not* use Africa to recruit, train and plan for their operations. They do. Yet locales where these processes occur and the issues that lead to them are grossly misunderstood and over-simplified. Understandably, in the military and policy world, the need to make swift decisions does not lend itself to lengthy, in-depth research. Still, this results in analysis that is at a minimum off the mark, and at the most dangerously incorrect. The problem is, "We don't know what we don't know." Such ignorance can be detrimental to sound defense policy. In fact it takes a broadminded approach to a complex situation to produce the kind of understanding that leads to effective policy decisions. Characterizing non-Western institutions as having a lack of governance and generalizing about political violence can lead to grave errors in assessing the threat environment.

Actual indicators of insecurity remain unknown and decontextualized if sources of information are limited only to encounters with fellow elites while ignoring institutions (formal and informal) outside government hallways. Knowledge acquired outside the context of high level officials, from the local, practical realities of daily life, along with an understanding of the social, political, and historical environments, will serve analysts and policymakers well when identifying threats in Africa.

COMPETING FOR AFRICAN MARKETS: STRATEGIES TO WIN NEW BUSINESS NOW

The future for Africa has never looked brighter. Over the next several decades, sub-Saharan Africa will continue to attract the highest rates of foreign direct investment (FDI) inflows per capita of any developing region. Business case studies on the continent suggest that risk-adjusted returns for new investors on the continent have never been higher.

Perhaps counter-intuitively—since most US and EU companies still think of Africa as only a natural-resource commodity play—growing consumer demand, including at the retail level, is becoming the main catalyst for this investment bonanza. By 2030, countries in Africa with large populations—such as Ethiopia, Nigeria, and South Africa—could spend as much as $2.2 trillion on consumer goods, about 3 percent of worldwide consumption. Trade with Africa has been steadily on the rise: Between 2000 and

2010, trade between African countries and the rest of the world increased by 200 percent.

Today, there's real muscle behind the "trade, not aid" refrain. In 2011 alone, trade exceeded aid by $7 billion. Social venture funds, which used to be seen as pioneering in Africa, have increasingly become routine, combining the best elements of aid and trade to invest in health, sanitation, energy, housing, and agriculture in Kenya, Tanzania, Uganda, Rwanda, and Ghana.

As Ann MacDougall, Chief Operating Officer of the Acumen Fund—one of the more innovative social venture funds—recently noted, "We invest in sustainable, scalable businesses that illustrate both financial and social impact." She explains, "We use the term 'patient capital' to describe our long-term objective. Entrepreneurs have up to 10 years to achieve financial sustainability—and, hopefully, lasting social impact."

Even Bob Geldof, who founded Band Aid and Live Aid in the mid-1980s to raise money for Africa, now heads a private equity fund looking to invest $450 million in African agribusiness, financial services, and telecommunications. In fact, access to high-growth economies with large populations, rising affluence, and the potential for innovation makes a presence in African markets essential for many companies. This is especially true for the consumer goods, telecommunications, and financial services sectors—industries that many multinationals don't typically associate with Africa.

The shifting global business landscape

Despite the data, not everyone has jumped on the Africa bandwagon. Surprisingly, among many of the most sophisticated international businesses and investors—even some of the keenest of the geopolitical Africa-watchers—there is scant recognition of its growth.

However, as American and European companies look for new global growth opportunities, they are beginning to reverse long-held views about Africa. In fact, 74 percent of respondents to PwC's *16th Annual Global CEO Survey* said they expect to expand their operations in Africa going forward.

A growing number of African countries are distinguishing themselves from other emerging markets with newfound resilience to global economic shocks. They are also standouts as major targets of MNCs from other emerging markets, for example, Chinese and Indian businesses that invest in Africa. This trend reflects the explosion of so-called "south-south" commerce, a term used to describe trade and investment between emerging economies, in contrast to the traditional "north-south" pattern of commerce, that is, multinationals from the advanced countries (for example, the US and EU) investing in emerging markets.

Although many African countries have made greater strides in economic, social, and political reforms over the past two decades than most investors realize, they continue to be dominated by nascent institutions, weak governance structures, poor infrastructure, and underdeveloped health care and educational systems.

Which means doing business successfully in Africa will involve innovative approaches to identify rapidly emergent—but not yet fully apparent—new market opportunities. Those include competing with non-traditional MNCs, leveraging national-level and regional markets to find economies of scale, and nurturing local talent.

Africa's resilience

The steady evolution of Africa's political reform progress is among the primary reasons behind Africa's economic resilience. Over the past 20 years, the number of democracies in sub-Saharan Africa has increased almost eight-fold.

In Ghana, for example, the transition of power from the recently deceased president occurred without incident. A stable democracy, Ghana has held peaceful elections for more than a decade. But Ghana is not alone. With several decades of multi-party democracy under its belt, Botswana has made huge progress in fighting corruption. And recent tax reform in Rwanda has decreased tax preparation time with a lower total tax rate and fewer total payments.

As depicted by the World Bank's Doing Business Index (DBI), 36 of 48 economies in sub-Saharan Africa have enhanced their business environments over the past year. And since 2005, the average DBI throughout the region has more than doubled. Part and parcel of these changes is greater economic diversification; for example, resource-rich countries like Gabon, Nigeria, and Angola have begun significant growth in their technology, services, and manufacturing sectors to reduce their dependence on commodity prices.

Benefits of south-south commerce

While companies from the US and Europe have a decades-long tradition of investing in Africa—90 percent of the existing stock of FDI accumulated in Africa originates from companies based in the "north"—Chinese and Indian multinationals and other businesses from the "south" now dominate the rates of new flows of FDI into Africa.

Africa's south-south trade flows are also growing rapidly. India's two-way trade target with Africa is $90 billion for 2015, up from $3 billion a decade ago. China, meanwhile, is now Africa's largest trading partner, having surpassed the US in 2009. Bilateral trade between China and Africa tallied $160 billion in 2011, up from $10.6 billion 10 years ago.

Technology has played a role in this new wave of "south-south" commerce. Up-to-the-minute tracking of raw materials and finished products allows companies to import raw materials from one destination, process them in another, and then ship them to a third. Ghana and Kenya already have a reputation for apparel manufacturing while Tanzania specializes in food processing, and South Africa is well known for manufacturing automobiles.

As noted by Hussein Hachem, CEO, Middle East and Africa, for shipping and logistics company Aramex, "In the next three to four years, we will have active operations in at least 20 African countries. Many multinationals are talking about coming to Africa, but not many are moving into Africa. I think that will change. Because of the economic situation in Europe and in the US and because of China as a major trade partner with Africa, people will invest more in Africa so they can capitalize on that trade route."

Of course, "northern" companies with an established presence in Africa are also beginning to reap rewards. General Electric (GE), which had a sales office in South Africa more than 100 years ago, began actual operations on the continent about a decade ago. It is now in 22 countries and expects to grow approximately 15 percent a year in Africa over the next few years, given the continent's infrastructure needs. The World Bank estimates that sub-Saharan Africa needs to spend $93 billion a year on infrastructure over the next decade.

New market, new business model

The complexity of Africa often requires turning conventional thinking on its head, as illustrated by South Africa-based Shoprite, the largest food retailer on the continent. Shoprite has expanded from eight supermarkets in Capetown in 1979 to 1,500 stores in 16 African countries today, thanks in large part to an automated supply chain that leverages centralized procurement—resulting in reduced costs and improved service levels.

Gerhard Fritz, Divisional Manager for the Shoprite Group of companies, says, "What works in other parts of the world may not work in Africa. People in Africa have a proud heritage; they don't take kindly to others coming in and telling them what to do. Our perspective is to think of every business as local. For example, Shoprite in Nigeria is a Nigerian business. We run and compete as a Nigerian business; we follow the local culture in every part of the company."

Sometimes, that requires significantly innovating traditional business models, according to Neil Brimacombe, executive director at consumer packaged goods company Tiger Brands. A keynote speaker at PwC's 14th Annual Africa Tax and Business Symposium in Nairobi, Kenya, Brimacombe said African consumers, despite their income levels, "still have aspirations to buy and enjoy certain brands. The consumer class is expected to top 300 million by 2025. So making those brands affordable to them in everyday, on-the-go options is compelling."

Indeed, despite high food and fuel prices, consumers in Africa continue to spend; the growing middle class has boosted consumption, residential construction, and private investment.

Brimacombe notes the importance of understanding local participation, saying it's "part and parcel of working with subdistributors and sub-subdistributors." Sometimes, the route to market is a 150-pound man hefting a 100-pound bag of rice on his shoulders; other times, a makeshift delivery cart consists of a bicycle balancing buckets of chocolate paste that Tiger produces in Cameroon as a spread for bread.

Understanding on-the-ground sensibilities allowed SABMiller to compete more effectively on price terms with locally made products. While the South African brewer competes with global brands in many parts of the rest of the world, in Africa, the biggest source of competition is inexpensive home brews. So SABMiller makes competitively priced beers from locally sourced cassava (a local root) in Mozambique and sorghum in Uganda.

The role of regional economic communities

One potentially effective path to navigating some of the challenges and complexities of Africa (especially the small size of most of the national markets on the continent and the fact that many African countries are landlocked) is via regional economic communities (RECs). Many of these have established free trade areas—where tariffs on internal trade among members are at, or close to, zero—and some have even established customs unions, where all members of a free trade area also put in place uniform tariffs on imports coming from outside a REC.

Three of these RECs—the Common Market for Eastern and Southern Africa (COMESA), Eastern African Community (EAC), and Southern African Development Community (SADC)—have begun to take their cooperation a step further: They have established the Tripartite Free Trade Area agreement spanning 26 African countries from Cape Town to Cairo, although the initiative is still in the implementation process.

In West Africa, the Economic Community of West African States (ECOWAS) has helped secure much-needed infrastructure and telecommunications as well as diplomatic progress, brokering peace in many of the region's unstable economies. In Ghana, the Tema Free Zone has attracted more than 200 companies, including Nestlé and L'Oréal.

One of the most effective trading blocs, the EAC has formally established a common market, which has reduced barriers to investment and increased regional trade 50 percent by guaranteeing free movement of labor, capital, goods, and services among its member countries of Burundi, Kenya, Rwanda, Tanzania, and Uganda.

Many companies investing in Africa traditionally have set up hubs in larger markets, like Nigeria and South Africa, and manage regional operations from there. From these hub markets, they can leverage shared services and better source local talent. However, companies coming to Africa are now increasingly also being well served by engaging with RECs to build scale among otherwise smaller markets. They are also building relationships with the RECs' constituent individual governments to gain support and secure incentives for meaningful policies such as job creation, tax reform, and education.

Nurturing skilled talent

Talent shortages represent another reality in Africa: A third of the CEOs in PwC's 15th Annual Global CEO Survey said a shortage of talent curbed innovation or stifled a market opportunity. And almost half said talent costs climbed higher than expected. Recruitment and retention of skilled middle managers was particularly challenging for 67 percent of CEOs.

In response, some companies actively train the next generation's workforce. In Kenya, mobile telecommunications provider Safaricom partners with Strathmore University to teach consumer insight and project viability. Safaricom also offers secondments to university lecturers in this two-way partnership of knowledge and skills.

Meanwhile, Tullow Oil, a UK-based energy company, received 2,818 applicants to a call for interested students in Uganda to pursue industry-related graduate degrees at UK and French universities; 20 made the final cut. As part of the Tullow Group Scholarship Scheme, the company offers up to 110 fully paid scholarships in Ghana, Uganda, Kenya, Ethiopia, Gabon, Mauritania, and Côte d'Ivoire.

"We proactively engage and build relationships with local people in countries in which we operate," said Rosalind Kainyah, Tullow's Vice President of External Affairs and Corporate Social

Responsibility. In Ghana, for example, Tullow listed on the domestic stock exchange to ensure that local financial institutions and residents can participate in the company's success. Tullow's success has been impressive: The company has opened three new oil basins in five years in sub-Saharan Africa after rigorous analysis of local seismic activity.

After 25 years in Africa, Tullow has proven that it does not expect immediate success. The optimal approach, said Kainyah, is to "take a long-term perspective and don't expect overnight wins." She added, "African markets are no different from any other developing markets and carry with them huge opportunities for investment. Every country in Africa is different—each with its own government, infrastructure, politics, markets, and opportunities. As with investment anywhere else, it is important to do the research to find what matches your business the best."

Not without risk

As with all emerging markets—and even some advanced countries, as the current global financial crisis demonstrated—doing business in Africa is not without risk. Cautionary tales abound of companies stymied on the continent by myriad regulations, corrupt behavior, unilateral changes in tax policies, new cross-border restrictions, high transportation costs, power grid outages, and poor distribution channels.

To this end, Chris Okeke, CEO of Nigerian Starch Mills Ltd., notes: "Money is a problem, seeds are a problem, infrastructure is a problem, input and output markets don't exist and where they do, they're primordial." Okeke advocates patience along with "chipping away slowly" at the challenges.

In fact, more than half the CEOs in Africa surveyed by PwC said they wish they had more time to spend managing risk. A joint report by the World Economic Forum, the World Bank, and the African Development Bank lists the top three challenges in sub-Saharan Africa as access to financing, corruption, and inadequate infrastructure.

The Export-Import Bank, the US Trade and Development Agency, and the Overseas Private Investment Corporation are among the various US governmental agencies that can help companies secure financing. The Export-Import Bank has already provided a record $1.5 billion for exports to sub- Saharan Africa in the first three quarters of 2012, exceeding the total $1.4 billion provided in 2011. Demand for machinery, vehicles, parts, commodities, and aircraft fueled this growth; Nigeria and South Africa were the top markets.

More efficient government goes a long way toward eliminating—or at least reducing—corruption. Bitange Ndemo, Permanent Secretary in Kenya's Ministry of Information and Communications, agrees, saying internal efficiencies in government reduce costs, creating a more productive environment for labor, thus reducing corruption. So does holding those responsible accountable for their actions. As democracy continues to spread across the continent and with it, the various mechanisms of governance, corruption is likely to abate.

As in other geographies, risk is a routine part of the business environment in Africa. As Jay Ireland, President and CEO of GE Africa, remarks, "Be it violence, political turmoil, or economic instability, there is always some risk somewhere and you just have to deal with it." GE uses a "flag-planting" approach to Africa. Says Ireland, "Flag planting is a process that we've done historically," referring to gradually establishing a local presence in a particular region over the long term. "What we do is go in with a few people, scout out what's there, and eventually you put in an investment and more people, resources, facilities, and really become part of the local infrastructure."

Balancing opportunities and risk

Ireland and other CEOs agree that properly managed, the risks of doing business in Africa are worth the rewards. They advocate striking the right balance between risk and reward. Shane Govender, Group Executive, Head of Tax, at mobile telephone services provider Vodacom, agrees.

Says Govender, "How do we repatriate our profits? How do we deal with exchange control issues? And withholding taxes?" Headquartered in South Africa, Vodacom serves more than 45 million customers in South Africa, Lesotho, Mozambique, Tanzania, and the Democratic Republic of Congo. Govender adds, "The IMF has said that seven of the 10 fastest-growing economies in the next five years will be in Africa—so the rewards are great."

Indeed, mobile phone penetration is exploding in Africa, from 2 percent of the population in 2000 to 28 percent in 2009 to a projected 70 percent in 2013. And M-Pesa, Vodacom's widely used mobile money platform—invented in Kenya—allows users to deposit, withdraw, and transfer money with a mobile device. M-Pesa continues to gain ground not only in Africa but also in the rest of the world: In a remarkable example of reverse innovation, it is now penetrating the US and EU markets.

Despite the tremendous opportunities, Govender offers a cautionary note. He says, "There are also challenges. The regulations we face are massive. Realistically, we have to balance the reward with the risk."

Companies cannot do business in Africa without taking into account the risks of inadequate infrastructure—and their attendant costs. In many parts of the continent, for example, where the power grid is unreliable, companies generate their own electricity to keep their plants running.

"We have expensive systems infrastructure that needs to keep running and that needs to be protected from power fluctuations," says Nasim Devji, Group CEO of the Diamond Trust Banks in East Africa. "It is costly to have backup generators and backup servers but for us the costs of planning for this are low compared to the severe impact that system downtime would have on our business and customers. Therefore, we accept energy costs as a reality of doing business in our markets and build backup capability to ensure business continuity."

The time is today

Much of the world has been slow to recognize the substantial economic progress in Africa. However, a significant number of African countries began focusing on economic fundamentals two decades ago. Their policymakers implemented more sustainable fiscal policies, controlled inflation, and managed their debt.

Some went further: They divested from private-sector activity, opened up historically public-dominated sectors like telecommunications, and reduced public-sector borrowing from banks, which was crowding out private investment.

Granted, as with most emerging markets, reform is needed across the continent—in many cases, the implementation of very significant reforms is urgent.

Today, Africa is a complex and diverse continent requiring deep layers of insight. Its potential is unmistakable: a decade of sustained growth with several more to come. In the years ahead, agribusiness, financial services, consumer goods, infrastructure, and telecommunications will continue to power growth and employment.

New products and services will require new ways of configuration to suit the distinctive needs of a young, increasingly more urban population—a population that aspires to consume more sophisticated products and services.

Companies must be prepared to invest time, resources, and talent in a rigorous, consistent approach in order to succeed. However, the rewards can be significant. Opportunities abound for first-mover advantage.

6

India–Africa Forum Summit

The India–Africa Forum Summit (IAFS) is the official platform for the African-Indian relations. IAFS will be held once in every three years. It was first held from April 4 to April 8, 2008 in New Delhi, India. It was the first such meeting between the heads of state and government of India and 14 countries of Africa chosen by the African Union. Libya and Egypt's heads of state did not attend.

Agenda

Rising oil and food prices were the top concerns for the African and Indian leaders during the summit.

Topics

- agricultural sector
- trade
- industry and investment
- peace and security
- promotion of good governance and civil society
- information and communication technology

African representation

- Chairperson of the African Union (AU)
- Chairperson of the AU Commission
- Chairpersons of the eight recognised Regional Economic Communities (REC's)

- Chairpersons of the New Partnership for Africa's Development (NEPAD)
- Heads of State and Government Implementation Committee (HSIGC)
- the five African NEPAD initiating countries

2008 First India–Africa Forum Summit - New Delhi, India

The first such summit was held from April 4 to April 8, 2008 in New Delhi, India. It was the first such meeting between the heads of state and government of India and 14 countries of Africa chosen by the African Union. Libya and Egypt's heads of state did not attend.

2011 Second India–Africa Forum Summit - Addis Ababa, Ethiopia

The second summit was held at the Ethiopian capital Addis Ababa, with India and 15 African Countries participating. The leaders discussed significant aspects of the India-Africa partnership with the objective of enhancing and widening its ambit for mutual benefit.

2015 Third India–Africa Forum Summit - New Delhi

The third summit in a rotation basis is held in New Delhi, India from 26-30 October 2015. The 5 day summit started with consultations on official level followed by the Head of States/ governments level summit on 29 October 2015 with scheduled bilateral meetings on 30 October 2015. This was Modi government's biggest diplomatic outreach involving delegates from a large number of African nations.

Earlier the summit in a rotation basis was scheduled to be held in New Delhi, India in December 2014. But lately Syed Akbaruddin, the official spokesperson of Indian Foreign Ministry told the media that the scheduled summit postponed to 2015 and will include more no. of African leaders unlike previous two occasion where the event was restricted to only 10-15 African countries. In the largest-ever turnout of African leaders in India, at least 41 leaders-including South African president Jacob Zuma, Egyptian president

Abdel Fattah el-Sisi, Zimbabwe president Robert Mugabe and Nigerian President Muhammadu Buhari-have confirmed their presence in New Delhi for the India-Africa forum summit on October 29-30.

THIRD INDIA AFRICA FORUM SUMMIT

The Third India-Africa Forum Summit (IAFS-III) is held in New Delhi, India from 26–30 October 2015. The five-day summit started with consultations on official level followed by the head of states/governments level summit on 29 October 2015 with scheduled bilateral meetings on 30 October 2015. This is going to be India's biggest diplomatic outreach involving delegates from a large number of African nations.

Background

The summit was earlier scheduled to be held in December 2014, with a three-year gap after the 2011 Adis Ababa summit. But Syed Akbaruddin, the official spokesperson of Indian Foreign Ministry, told the media that the scheduled summit was postponed to 2015 and would include a higher number of African leaders unlike the previous two summits where the event was restricted to only 10–15 African countries. Although media reports claimed that Ebola outbreak in Western African nations played key role behind the postponement of the summit.

Invitations were sent out to all 54 African nations through the respective Indian missions but it was not delivered only in Libya, as there is no government functioning at the time, and the Indian embassy also had to move to Tunisia. India's Foreign Minister Sushma Swaraj herself handed over the invitation to South African President Jacob Zuma during her visit to the African country in May 2015.

Logo

The logo depicts a Lion with one half of an African lion and another half of an Indian lion. The official website mentioned about the logo: "Proud, Courageous, Bold and on the Prowl, ready to take on the future and seize every opportunity". In the background African map overlapping merges with Indian map in a reference to ancient Gondwanaland when Indian subcontinent used to be part of today's Africa's continental landmass millions of years ago. The India Gate, one of the iconic land mark of Delhi, the host city will be illuminated with 3D laser projection showing India-Africa shared heritage and India's contribution in African peace and prosperity, through out the summit week.

Participants

The host country, India, had sent invitations to all 54 African head of state/government and trying to ensure maximum participation at the highest level. As of September 2015, the following dignitaries were expected to attend the summit in Delhi, India.

Dignitaries

Country	Title	Leader
Algeria	Prime Minister	Abdelmalek Sellal
Angola	Vice President	Manuel Vicente
Benin	President	Yayi Boni
Botswana	Foreign Minister	Phandu Skelemani
Burkina Faso	President	Blaise Compaoré
Burundi	President	Pierre Nkurunziza
Cape Verde	President	Jorge Carlos Fonseca
Chad	President	Idriss Déby
Cameroon	President	Paul Biya
Comoros	President	Ikililou Dhoinine
Cote d'Ivoire	Prime Minister	Daniel Kablan Duncan
Congo–Brazaville	President	Denis Sassou Nguesso
Djibouti	President	Ismaïl Omar Guelleh
DR Congo	President	Joseph Kabila
Egypt	Prime Minister	Sherif Ismail
Equatorial Guinea	President	Teodoro Obiang Nguema Mbasogo
Ethiopia	Prime Minister	Hailemariam Desalegn
Gabon	President	Ali Bongo Ondimba

Gambia	President	Yahya Jammeh
Ghana	President	John Dramani Mahama
Guinea	President	Alpha Condé
Guinea-Bissau	President	José Mário Vaz
Kenya	President	Uhuru Kenyatta
Lesotho	Prime Minister	Tom Thabane
Liberia	Vice President	Joseph Boakai
Libya	Prime Minister	Abdullah al-Thani
Madagascar	President	Hery Rajaonarimampianina
Malawi	President	Peter Mutharika
Mali	President	Ibrahim Boubacar Keïta
Mauritania	President	Mohamed Ould Abdel Aziz
Mauritius	Prime Minister	Navin Ramgoolam
Morocco	Prime Minister	Abdelilah Benkirane
Mozambique	President	Armando Guebuza
Namibia	President	Hifikepunye Pohamba
Niger	President	Mahamadou Issoufou
Nigeria	President	Muhammadu Buhari
Rwanda	President	Paul Kagame
São Tomé and Príncipe	Prime Minister	Gabriel Costa
Senegal	President	Macky Sall
Seychelles	President	James Michel
Sierra Leone	Foreign Minister	Samura Kamara
Somalia	President	Hassan Sheikh Mohamud
South Africa	President	Jacob Zuma
South Sudan	President	Salva Kiir Mayardit
Sudan	President	Omar Hassan Ahamed Albashir
Swaziland	King	Mswati III
Tanzania	President	Jakaya Kikwete
Togo	President	Faure Gnassingbe
Tunisia	President	Beji Caid Essebsi
Uganda	President	Yoweri Museveni
Zambia	Acting President	Guy Scott

WELCOME TO THE INDIA-AFRICA FORUM SUMMIT 2015

The India-Africa Forum Summit (IAFS) is a celebration of the close partnership between Africa and India. It is an acknowledgement of our shared history as well as our future prospects. From our struggle against colonialism and apartheid, we have emerged to jointly accept the challenges of a globalizing world. Even as we combat with common threats - the threat from international terrorism; the scourge of poverty, disease, illiteracy and hunger; the challenge of climate change - and collectively promote the socio-economic advancement of all our people, we believe that India and Africa traverse the same path, share the same values and cherish the same dreams.

A vibrant India and a resurgent Africa have a vision of a close partnership. A partnership that is anchored in the principles of equality, mutual respect and mutual benefit.This vision takes us beyond our strong bilateral relationships, our close ties with regional economic communities and aims to develop a new paradigm of cooperation which takes into account Africa's own aspirations for pan-African institutions and development programmes.

The third edition of the four day IAFS summit which will take place during 26th-29th October 2015 enables consultations at the highest political level between the heads of government of 54 nations across Africa and the Indian government to give a new thrust to our age-old partnership. It provides an opportunity to not only reflect on the past, but to define the road ahead in tune with the times we live in.

PHILOSOPHY OF THE FORUM SUMMIT

India and Africa have a historic relationship and this has grown into a sustainable partnership. From our struggle against colonialism and apartheid, we have emerged to jointly accept the challenges of a globalising world. Whether we have to deal with threats to international peace and security, the threat from international terrorism or the scourge of poverty, we believe that

India and Africa traverse the same path, share the same values and cherish the same dreams.

We have a vision for a partnership with Africa for the 21st century. This vision will take us beyond our strong bilateral relationships, our close ties with regional economic communities and develop a new paradigm of cooperation which will take into account Africa's own aspirations for pan-African institutions and development programmes.

Given our wide ranging cooperation and developing partnerships ranging from human resource development, health, capacity building, ICT utilisation all of which are perhaps symbolised in the Pan-African e-Network Project. We hope to take this experience to a new level.

India will host the India-Africa Forum Summit in New Delhi. This will be held between 4 & 9 April, 2008 with the Senior Officials Meeting on 4th April, the Foreign Ministers' Meeting on 7th April and the Summit on 8th April.

The participation and the format of the Summit have been decided in consultation with the African Union Commission and the permanent representatives of the member states. This is the beginning of a process. How we take this forward will depend on the outcome of the Summit.

Thus we have invited the Chairs of the regional economic communities and their Secretaries General and the founding members of the NEPAD initiative besides the current and preceding Chairs of the African Union. We believe that this representative group which would have appropriate regional balance will provide the impetus for a fulsome discussion on how India could enhance its engagement with Africa in the future keeping in view Indian capacities and African aspirations.

It is also agreed that the formal outcome documents of the Summit would be a Declaration and an Action Plan. The draft Action Plan is under preparation and a draft has been circulated by the AU Commission to the member states. We await the response of the member states. The second document which will be a Declaration will address broader areas of cooperation and our common views on regional and international issues including the fight against terrorism, climate change and WTO negotiations. After the Annual Summit meeting of the African Union, the officials on both sides will meet for further discussions on the draft Declaration and the draft Plan of Action. The areas on which we have agreed to focus in the Action Plan will include human resources and institutional capacity building and education, science & technology, agricultural productivity and food security, industrial growth including small & medium enterprises and minerals, development in the health sector, development of infrastructure, ICT and establishment of judicial system with police and defence establishments under civilian control, etc.

INDIA AFRICA FORUM SUMMIT 2015

The recently-concluded India Africa Forum Summit involved perhaps the largest participation of African countries on one platform. It has been estimated that almost 1000 delegates represented 54 countries that presently call themselves the members of the African Union.

Normally, such events would have their usual diplomatic importance, but if Sushma Swaraj is to be believed then the summit has also provided a golden opportunity to improve the trade and investment scenario. The Union External Affairs Minister even termed this gathering as a family reunion. She further stated that it is important to collaborate with other countries in order to be able to develop in the long run, citing an African proverb in order to substantiate her statement.

Bettering relationship with Africa

One of the major aims behind this event was to improve the relations between India and Africa. As a part of the stated aim, India and the members of the African Union will look to partake in more trade and investments. At present, China is the greatest bilateral trade partner of India with the estimated worth of trade between the countries being more than 200 billion dollars. While speaking to the media on the event, Narendra Modi has expressed hope that the present summit will take relations between both the countries to new heights.

The Humanitarian Context

Together India and the 54 African countries that participated in the recently-concluded summit comprise one-third of the global population. So, in that context it can be called one of the most important global meets of recent times, considering the fact that they represent the aspirations of so many people. This is also something that Narendra Modi has alluded to in his recent speech. The Indian Prime Minister has described the bond between India and Africa as being an emotional one, something that is beyond the normal strategic relationships that define these events. This is also supposed to be the largest gathering of African countries outside their own continent, thus giving India an excellent opportunity to reach out to these countries and establish their importance in the region.

Modi's Speech

In his speech, the Indian Prime Minister has professed commitment on behalf of India to play an important role in the development of African countries and in helping them counter the different challenges that are impeding their growth. He also spoke in great detail about the bonds that the two regions share in terms of civilization and history, bringing up how both have fought against ills such as colonialism, hunger, and poverty, and for values such as dignity and liberty.

The Demographic Advantage

Both India and Africa have a major advantage in the sense that majority of the population in these areas is under the 35 year limit. This is something that Narendra Modi referred to in his speech as well. He has said that this is a capital to be invested in keeping their future in mind. He has gone so far as to say that the coming century could very well be theirs if youth was the watchword for development. He has pointed out Africa has taken massive leaps in various social and economic areas. Over the years Africa has faced many problems such as terrorism, but continued to attain a greater rate of development nonetheless. In his speech, the Prime Minister of India has further asked the African countries to come together and combat terrorism and ensure greater security from the maritime perspective. He has also asked the United Nations Security Council (UNSC) to be reformed so that India and African countries can get the representation that they deserve.

How can India help?

In his speech the Indian Prime Minister has made clear the pathways in which India will be able to play a role in Africa's growth. He has stated that India can help bring down the digital gap in Africa and also cooperate with them from an economic viewpoint. Both India and Africa will also collaborate at the upcoming environmental summit in Paris. There they can ask the developed countries to take heed of the greater measures for adoption and mitigation that need to be taken so that the developing countries get the technology and finance needed to implement them properly.

INDIA-AFRICA FORUM SUMMIT: CHINA IS AHEAD, BUT AFRICA'S NEEDS AND INDIA'S EXPERIENCE ARE A GOOD FIT

The India-Africa Forum Summit, one of New Delhi's most ambitious diplomatic outreach events in over two decades, is underway in the capital though the gathering of heads of states is slated for the 29-30 October.

This is not the first meeting of the India-Africa Forum. The UPA began it at a modest scale with the unassuming Manmohan Singh hosting some African leaders in 2008. This was followed by another forum summit in Addis Ababa in Ethiopia in 2011, on an even smaller scale. But the third India-Africa summit, will be an extravaganza in keeping with Prime Minister Narendra Modi's personal preference for mega shows. Much is being made of the fact that leaders of all 54 African countries have been invited and that the majority of them have agreed to attend. Indian officials say it will be the largest gathering of African leaders outside the continent A former foreign secretary sees it as an indication of the faith that African leaders have in Modi.

The outcome of the summit will be judged by converting the promises that are likely to be made on both sides into action in a continent where China's footprint is all over. China has been wooing Africa for the last 15 years or so. It has been pouring billions of dollars into ports, rail tracks, football stadiums, highways, dams and other major infrastructure projects.

China is Africa's largest trading partner doing an annual trade of roughly $200 billion, though the figures keep changing according to price of commodities. Much of the trade is related to getting Africa's oil and minerals shipped to mainland China to fuel its insatiable hunger. With the slowing down of the Chinese economy there is anxiety among some in Africa.

India is also wooing mineral-rich Africa for the same reasons as China. As India's economy takes off again, the need for natural resources will steadily mount. Already India is buying oil from Nigeria Algeria, Mozambique and Angola, ONGC Videsh is now looking to invest in West Africa. India realises it cannot compete with China's cheque book diplomacy. Nor is it trying to do so.

Instead India has been concentrating on institution building, on education, telemedicine and skill development projects. None of this is spectacular, but touches the lives of ordinary Africans.

Agriculture is the next big thing New Delhi is looking at in Africa. This will probably come up for discussions at the summit. Senior officials meet on Monday was devoted to working out a development charter for what India and Africa can do together. This will be finalised and made public at the end of the summit.

Africa's needs and India's experience are a perfect fit

One important lesson India has learnt with its experience in Afghanistan is not to dictate what it wants to do. The focus now is on asking Africa what it wants of India. Considering that India and many countries in Africa face similar challenges, both can learn from each other. India is looking at Africa's successful experiment with mobile banking and hoping to adopt some of this to conditions in certain states here.

India's pharma products, the generic drugs which have been opposed by big multinational drug companies, have saved millions of lives in Africa. The copy-cat drugs made by Indian pharmaceutical companies have brought down the prices of drugs, and brought down the cost of treating Aids to affordable levels. All this has been noted in Africa. Today Indian pharmaceutical products provide 80 percent of medicines in poorer African nations.

New Delhi has extended concessional credit to various countries in Africa to the tune of $7.4 billion, most of which stands approved and at least half of that already disbursed. This concessional credit is responsible for the creation of about 137 projects in 41 countries today. The Pan-African e-Network, the brainchild of former president APJ Abdul Kalam is working well for Africa. This connects universities and hospitals in 48 African nations to counter parts in Indian cities for professional advice and training. A fibre optic network built provides satellite connectivity to the centres. Capacity building has been one of India's strongest planks of cooperation. New Delhi has awarded 25,000 scholarships for students across Africa.

A resurgent continent is now taking charge of its own affairs and has worked out a blueprint for development for the year 2063. India has smartly studied the agenda document and hopes to align African priorities with India's activities. India is not interested in flooding Africa with cheap goods as China has done. Its key is human resource development, helping to replicate successful Indian experiences in Africa and taking what suits India.

UN Reforms

India is hoping to get the support of as many African countries as possible for its bid for permanent membership in an expanded UN Security Council. The African Union (AU) has not yet worked out its strategy as nations are all wrestling to get in. India believes that India and Africa are not at odds on UN membership and can work together. But unless AU finalises its stand it is hard to predict what can happen.

INDIA'S INTERESTS AT THE AFRICA FORUM SUMMIT: FROM DEALS TO DELIVERY?

The third India-Africa Forum Summit gets underway in New Delhi today. It is the most ambitious to date. All 54 African countries were invited and at least 40 will participate at the level of president, vice president, prime minister or king. For the first two summits, only 15 countries were invited and were chosen by the African Union based on the Banjul formula; 14 countries participated in 2008 and 11 in 2011. But this time some 2,000 delegates are expected at the refurbished Indira Gandhi Indoor Stadium. Why New Delhi's upgrade now?

Summits with Africa have increasingly become international beauty contests, with hopeful international partners lining up to parade their partnership offers and trade deals, in the hope of winning the big prizes – access to Africa's resources and markets. The US, Turkey and the EU held Africa summits last year, China will hold its sixth Forum on China-Africa Cooperation in Johannesburg this December and Japan and South Korea have their Africa summits planned for 2016. Indian policy makers have been pushed to compete by their business and military leaders, keen to capitalize on a slowing Chinese economy and the desire of African states to diversify their international partnerships. The result has been a broadening of the invitation list, and a more relaxed approach to human rights concerns than Brussels or Washington – allowing invitations to be extended to controversial figures such as Sudanese President Omar al-Bashir.

There has been some momentum built already. Over the last decade trade between India and Africa has expanded by 14 times to more than $70 billion. India has also given concessional credit to the tune of $7.4 billion, of which $3.5 billion has been disbursed. These credit lines have helped create 137 projects in 41 countries. An Indian-managed Pan-African e-Network for education and health is functional in 48 countries. Since 2008, India has extended 40,000 scholarships, and there are some 22,000 African students in India. Medical tourism from Africa has also become big business.

India has an urgent need to diversify energy supplies. It imported $125 billion worth of crude oil and products in FY15, and has oil investments in Mozambique, Sudan, South Sudan, Egypt and Libya. India has become the prime importer of crude oil from Nigeria and the second-largest from Angola. Low oil prices could open up new opportunities for India, including for private investors.

India's ocean

Prime Minister Narendra Modi's only Africa visits during his premiership have been to the Seychelles and Mauritius in March as part of a focus on the Indian Ocean. The 'blue economy' remains a key theme of the forthcoming summit, aimed at building links with African states on the ocean's littoral. Indian anti-piracy efforts, naval visits and defence partnerships, commerce, fisheries, offshore oil and gas, and hydrographical science all fit into this. Countries like Mozambique are now the centre of multi-faceted Indian engagement — investment, trade, military training and development aid. President Filipe Nyusi of Mozambique conducted a state visit to India in August.

There are also bigger geo-political dynamics at play. During his Seychelles visit, Modi signed agreements aimed at expanding India's surveillance capacity, strengthening its footprint on Assumption Island, which it leases from the Seychelles. A similar surveillance agreement was signed with Mauritius for Agalega Island and was already in place with Madagascar. The goals are to enhance maritime security and to monitor expanding Chinese naval activity in the region " India fears a 'string of pearls' of Chinese-supported security placements across the Indian Ocean, and has followed-up agreements with sales of naval technology, including a 1,200 tonne vessel for the Mauritian coast guard.

India's long-term international ambitions will also need African support – fulfilling hopes to become a permanent member of the UN Security Council will mean engaging with all 54 African countries. New Delhi also wants a stronger partnership with Africa on climate change ahead of the COP21 in Paris.

India's pitch

So the summit will be on an impressive scale. The challenge for India will be to follow it with measurable progress in investment and partnerships, while at the same time advocating effectively for India's private sector. Indian companies, such as IOC and ONGC Videsh, have not been particularly successful in Africa to date " research by Chatham House has shown that China's response has been better coordinated. India failed to win key oil concessions in Nigeria and Angola. ONGC Videsh, Oil India and Bharat PetroResources are facing delays on the issue of exploration and production concession contracts for the giant Rovuma Area 1 off-shore gas field in Mozambique. Indian coal investments have also run into problems. The Indian government will need to support its companies better, including through its 48 embassies in Africa.

African states are very much the judges in the investment beauty contest, not the contestants, and the onus will be on India to up its offer. Prime Minister Modi has promised that this summit will 'set substantially higher targets for our development partnership'. In an era when African leaders are being courted by all of the world's big economies, and get promised much at such summits, delivery is key. India needs to prove that this summit is not just about international rivalries, particularly with China, or a vehicle for hectoring African governments on expediting individual deals. Otherwise the next summit will not attract such African attention; those who deliver on their promises may see their African partnerships deepen further.

INDIA-AFRICA SUMMIT: WILL IT GIVE A NEW THRUST TO AGE-OLD TIES?

New Delhi is in the midst of intensive diplomatic activity in preparation for the Third India Africa Forum Summit (IAFS) that will take place October 26-29.

It was under the aegis of the Congress-led UPA government that the first and second IAFS were held in 2008 and 2011. Arriving slightly late on the scene after Japan, the EU, and China had already held numerous African summits, India's the first and second IAFS were rather modest affairs, with limited outreach. They were held adopting the so-callled Banjul Formula recommended by the African Union, according to which only 14-15 African states' representatives were invited.

Yet, the IAFS signalled a radical transformation of India-Africa relations by elevating them to summit level and by establishing an institutional platform for engagement and cooperation at bilateral, regional and continental level.

Nevertheless, there have been concerns in the past few years that Africa has slipped quietly off the Indian radar. Last year, the Third IAFS was postponed to an unspecified date in 2015 due to the Ebola crisis. Equally the 11th edition of the CII India-Africa Conclave was also postponed. This is significant since it is there that deals worth of millions are signed between Indian government and businesses and their African counterparts. To The Economist this was a clumsy decision on the part of New Delhi for, whilst in this period, India-Africa bilateral trade did not grow as predicted, China-Africa bilateral trade soared to US $210bn making China Africa's largest trading partner.

Narendra Modi's packed foreign travelling agenda seemed to confirm these concerns. Since becoming Prime Minister in 2014, Modi has travelled extensively, but beside his Indian Ocean-nation visits (Mauritius and Seychelles) in the spring of this year, he has yet to visit an African country. In fact, Modi has been more preoccupied with engaging with the world's powerful nations than with other fellow-developing countries.

It is in this context, therefore, that this Third IAFS holds much promise.

Some view this larger India-Africa summit just as a showpiece of diplomatic activity. In line with Modi's penchant for the spectacular, this is going to be remembered as the largest diplomatic gathering in India since the Non-Alignment Summit in 1983. Diplomatic spectacles aside, it will be wrong to dismiss it as another example of Modi's modus operandum. There's ground to believe that the Third IAFS may be the occasion to chart a new road for India-Africa relations.

Not only this is the first India-Africa summit to be held under Modi, but this is also the most important public occasion in which India's Prime Minister will engage with a large number Southern countries. Even though we cannot talk yet of a Modi doctrine, Narendra Modi has certainly brought a number of changes to India's foreign policy. His extensive trips abroad have signalled a dynamism and willingness to assume world leadership - something that has been welcomed by those who complained about India's lack of direction in its foreign engagements.

There is also a perceptible shift in the ways in which India's economic agenda is being pursued through foreign engagements with the promotion of the 'Make in India' campaign. In it is in this light that this much-awaited Third IAFS has the potential to reinvigorate the relations between Africa and the subcontinent. Indeed, many observers and officials have lamented of the lack of direction and co-ordination in India-Africa engagements. This lack of foresight has damaged some Indian interests in the African continent. Modi's proactive foreign policy and his self-projection as a decisive leader promises to deliver in these regards.

Second, by extending invitations to all African leaders rather than revert to the Banjul Formula signals a recognition of Africa's diversity and Delhi's desire to strengthen relations with all African countries individually as well as with the continent and its various regional institutions. Wanting to engage with all African countries also indicates that India has finally realised that it has a lot of catching up to do and it is willing to throw itself into the fray with more determination.

Lastly, this much larger and spectacular IAFS is a not-so-subtle message to China, whose FOCAC (Forum on China-Africa Cooperation) will take place in South Africa in December. By holding the IAFS just three weeks ahead of the China-Africa summit, New Delhi is hoping to out-smart and out-do China. FOCAC has been recently upgraded to a summit.

But there is another reason why the Third IAFS is expected to transform India-Africa relations. The ideological and strategic drivers at the heart of New Delhi's relationship with the African continent have very much been couched in a Nehruvian discourse of southern solidarity for the creation of a more equitable and just world. Whilst this rhetoric has often been seen largely as a mask to conceal India's real economic and strategic intentions in Africa, commitments to Third Worldism and alternative ideas of sovereignty and economic development are still relevant in India's engagements with the developing world, more than realist accounts would want us to believe. Yet, this may be bound to change.

That Modi is not a Nehru fan is no secret. Since being elected, Modi has ostensibly tried to distance himself from anything

Nehruvian. As the historian Sunil Khilnani suggests, if the arrival of Modi has brought with it a rewriting of the history of India, Nehru will not be a leading chapter any more. Indeed, Modi has refrained from using terms dear to Nehruvism in describing India's relations with the South. Whilst abroad, he has instead often talked of Vasudhaiva Kutumbakam (a old Sanskrit saying that means that the world is one family) - a concept that many other Indian leaders had used before him - and, in describing India-Africa linkages, so far Modi has preferred to highlight Gandhi's role in cementing India-Africa relations rather than revert back to the Nehruvian discourse of Southern solidarity.

It is possible that Modi's calculated neglect of South-South rhetoric (so prominent in previous official India-Africa declarations) is nothing more that a simple distaste for the Nehruvian. However these rhetorical changes may be more substantial, indicating the diminishing importance of the developing world to India's economic and strategic future. Yet, Africa is a key source of energy and natural resources for India. It is also an important strategic and trading partner that can play a decisive role in Modi's development goals, his 'Make in India' campaign, not to speak of New Delhi's ambitions to reform global governance institutions.

New Delhi can ill afford to neglect Africa. Modi has the political capital to undertake bold foreign policy initiatives. The upcoming IAFS may be the occasion for Modi to reveal his vision for India-Africa relations and to give new thrust to this age-old partnership.

INDIA-AFRICA FORUM SUMMIT: AFRICA INVITES INDIA TO DO BUSINESS

PM Narendra Modi on Thursday described India and Africa as bright spots of hope and economic opportunity and offered technology and credit to match rival China at a summit with more than 40 African leaders.

From seeking help in fighting terror group Al Shabab to inviting India to do business in diamonds, African leaders discussed a wide range of issues with Prime Minister Narendra Modi on the sidelines of the third India-Africa Forum Summit.

Mali President Ibrahim Boubacar Keita on Thursday invited Modi to visit his country and told him that he will personally take him to Timbuktu, which he said was a heritage site that faced the threat of being destroyed by extremist groups. Stating that his country was badly affected by terrorism, he sought India's cooperation in counter-terrorism.

Somalian President Hassan Sheikh Mohamoud, who did his Masters' in Education from Bhopal, told Modi that he was the "shining example" of a beneficiary of education cooperation. He went back to Somalia and set up an educational institute, which has now become an university with 5,000 students.

While praising Indian Navy's role in curbing piracy, he said terror outfit Al Shabab was "in retreat" and sought India's cooperation in counter-terrorist activities. Modi told him that India can send counter-terrorism experts if Somalia needs them.

Angola's Vice-President Manuel Domingos Vicente said India should do business with his country, which is rich in diamonds. To this, Modi said it will be a "win-win partnership".

In a gesture of goodwill, Egyptian President Abdel Fattah el-Sisi decided to release two Indians languishing in Egyptian jails for 16 and 22 years, respectively, under the transfer of sentenced persons agreement between the two countries.

India had requested Egypt in December 2014 to release the two Indians as per provisions of the sentenced persons pact.

"Sisi, in a goodwill gesture, agreed to the release of two long-term Indian prisoners in Egypt who had been in jail for 16 and 22 years. They will be extradited to India under the transfer of sentenced persons agreement," the Ministry of External Affairs spokesperson Vikas Swarup said.

He said there were certain charges against the two Indians due to which they served long prison terms and added that New Delhi had never questioned the judicial process.

During the talks, Modi also thanked Sisi for attending the Summit and asserted that without Egypt, the Summit would have been "incomplete". The two leaders agreed to take bilateral ties to a "much higher and broader level".

Referring to Indian investments, the Egyptian President invited more joint ventures in his country. "He referred to the new Suez canal as a complete corridor of integrated development and said that numerous industrial zones in Egypt would be very attractive to Indian businesses," said Swarup.

India-Africa Summit: Special Envoys to Invite Heads of Government

With just four months left, preparations are in top gear for one of India's most ambitious diplomatic engagement to date - the Third India-Africa Forum Summit (IAFS) here in October that is likely to see the heads of all the 54 countries of the African Union attending with their entourages.

In early July, a dozen "special envoys" will take off for Africa to extend an invite to each of the 54 African heads of state or government for the October 26-30 event, with the actual summit being held on October 29.

Each of the special envoys, who will not be bureaucrats, would be charged with inviting a few countries. While 42 of the African countries have their missions in Delhi, India has missions in 28 countries with many of the Indian ambassadors also appointed concurrent envoy of a neighbouring country as well.

The Third IAFS is set to be the largest gathering of foreign leaders in India since the Non Aligned Summit in New Delhi in 1983 and the Commonwealth Summit the same year.

The logo for the event, as shown to African diplomats during a briefing earlier this month, would be the face of a lion, with one half an Indian lion and the other half an African lion. The lion face is an attempt to focus on the commonalities of India and the African countries.

With 54 African Union leaders, plus the AU commissioner Nkosazana Dlamini Zuma, and their entourages, as well as the Indian side, and business delegations and media - all together would see more than 1,000 people at one spot for the event.

The Indira Gandhi Indoor Stadium, located close to the Delhi Secretariat, will be the venue for the summit. The centrally air-conditioned stadium, built in 1982 to host indoor sports events of the 1982 Asian Games, has a central floor area of 4,500 sq m which would be able to host around 1,000 people comfortably at any time.

Vigyan Bhavan, the convention centre, was shot down as it has a stage that can hold only around 20 delegates at one time The two major hotels of Taj Palace and Ashoka, which have capacious halls, were also rejected as the floor area of around 1,500 sq m would be insufficient, an African diplomat who attended the briefing told IANS.

A large stage would be erected inside the Indira Gandhi Indoor Stadium, on which all the African leaders plus Prime Minister Narendra Modi, the host, would be able to comfortably stand together in semi circle formation for the photo op.

Below the stage, separate desks for each African head would be set up in a semi circle formation. Behind each dignitary would be an additional desk to seat two senior officials, including ministers, of each country. Behind that another desk would be set up to seat three more officials. The ministry of external affairs is making arrangements at the stadium to accommodate around five to seven delegates from each country.

Besides the seating, which would be in semi-circle formation with all dignitaries in a single row, the stadium area has enough space for setting up lounges, in the form of prefabricated tents, for the leaders to relax and chat, separate desks for each country, cubicles for their staff, lounges for business meets and bilateral leaders' meetings, and also a large media lounge.

The stadium complex with an area of around 100 acres, has enough space for car parking too. The complex, which hosts table tennis, badminton and wrestling events, has several entry and exit points, which would be utilised to keep the entry gates of dignitaries separate from that of the other delegates.

The stadium is being given an urgent facelift and renovmation, including doing up the toilets, to cater to the diplomatic extravaganza.

Suites and rooms in 10 top hotels in Delhi have been booked and the routes from each hotel to the stadium venue have been chalked out. The movement of cars of so many dignitaries along the streets would see Delhi Police blocking the roads for some hours during the summit.

Colourful panels with information about each country, plus large lion logos of the event would be strung up around the hall to block the view to the fixtures of the indoor stadium.

On October 26, senior officials of the 54 African nations would meet, followed by a meeting of the foreign ministers the next day. On October 28, the heads of the African states would arrive and meet with President Pranab Mukherjee, who will also host them for an official banquet on the final day. The summit would be held on October 29 and the following day would be reserved for bilateral interactions.

The summit, earlier scheduled to be held in December last year, had to be postponed in view of the Ebola epidemic in western Africa.

The first India-Africa Forum Summit was held in April 2008 in New Delhi, with 14 countries attending it. The second summit was held at Addis Ababa, Ethiopia, with 15 African countries and India participating. But the Modi government decided to invite all 54 African heads of government, instead of a representative number of countries chosen by the African Union as was the norm, to give the message that Africa matters.

India-Africa bilateral trade is $70 billion, while India has extended soft loans of about $7 billion to the African countries where incomes are rising and the continent is increasingly been seen as stable and prosperous. India has investments worth over $32 billion in Foreign Direct Investment in Africa. There are more than three million people of Indian origin in Africa today, with South Africa being home to the largest population of people of Indian descent in the continent, at 1.3 million.

INDIA-AFRICA SUMMIT: 12 AFRICAN LEADERS TALK TERROR, DEFENCE WITH PM NARENDRA MODI

The Prime Minister met President John Dramani Mahama of Ghana during which both sides reviewed the "warm" bilateral ties.

In twelve of nineteen bilateral conversations Prime Minister Narendra Modi had Wednesday, leaders of African countries focused on counter-terrorism, defence cooperation and anti-piracy operations, South Block officials said.

This is being seen as a significant shift in the bilateral conversation with African leaders who would otherwise focus on concessional lines of credit, agriculture, education and increased investments in infrastructure.

"This is a major change which we observed on the first day of bilateral meetings with the African leaders who are battling the rising spectre of terrorism and piracy in their backyard. They want to increase the capability of their defence forces and have a robust intelligence-sharing mechanism," a top South Block official told The Indian Express.

The African continent has been witness to the rise of the Boko Haram and Al Shabab terrorist groups which have been carrying out terror attacks.

Recalling the Westgate mall attack in Nairobi, Kenyan President Uhuru Kenyatta said "both countries, India and Kenya, are victims of terrorism" and New Delhi and Nairobi should "widen" anti-terrorism and security cooperation. "He asked for Indian help in capacity building and better information exchange between governments," Tanmaya Lal, Joint Secretary (East and South Africa) in the Ministry of External Affairs, said, alluding to scope for "intelligence-sharing".

Nigerian President Muhammadu Buhari, who went to the Defence Services Staff College in Wellington as a young army officer, called for increased training of military officers. Officials said that this is what Buhari feels is needed to fight the dreaded Boko Haram.

Boko Haram, which means 'western education is forbidden', has ravaged large parts of north-east Nigeria and carried its violence into Cameroon, Chad and Niger. Early this year, Boko Haram declared its allegiance to the Islamic State.

While Cameroon Tuesday asked for help, Niger President Issoufou Mahamadou too raised the subject of security and counter-terrorism. He explained the difficulty in the neighbourhood. "This was a clear reference to the menace of Boko Haram and they asked for assistance," an official said.

Lesotho Prime Minister Bethuel Pakalitha Mosisili also discussed defence cooperation, and praised the Indian armed forces who have been training officers from Lesotho. "He asked for more slots to train their officers," the official said.

Zimbabwe President Robert Mugabe, who holds the African Union's Presidency, also discussed closer cooperation in the fight against terror.

Ghana's President John Dramani Mahama raised the issues of maritime security and cyber security. According to the official, the Gulf of Guinea is emerging as a hub of piracy, and is a "concern".

Djibouti President Ismail Omar Guelleh also talked of assistance in anti-piracy operations, and recalled Indian ships visiting his country's ports. He also called for cooperation in maritime security, cyber security and defence cooperation.

Chad President Idriss Deby Itno too raised the issue of security and counter-terrorism cooperation, while South African President Jacob Zuma said they need to take more concrete steps to fight terrorism.

Mozambique Prim Minister Carlos Agostinho do Rosario, who once served as ambassador to India, sought greater defence and security cooperation with India.

Gabon President Ali Bongo Ondimba not only raised the issues of terrorism but also transnational crimes and the need for cooperation to take on the menace. Ghana President Yoweri Kaguta Museveni too pushed for greater cooperation between the defence forces of the two countries.

INDO-AFRICA SUMMIT: PM NARENDRA MODI HOLDS BILATERAL TALKS WITH AFRICAN LEADERS

Prime Minister Narendra Modi on Wednesday held bilateral talks with heads of several African nations during which UN reforms, combating challenge of terrorism and boosting trade and investment, particularly in oil and gas sector, figured prominently. The African leaders appreciated India's development projects in the continent and sought deepening of ties in diverse sectors including health care, education and capacity building.

In his meeting, South African President Jacob Zuma strongly called for reform of global governance system and said the UN structure which was set up after the second world war cannot remain relevant in 21st century. He said it was important that all like minded countries come together to ensure reform of the UN, particularly the UN Security Council, observing that many conflicts in the world including the Syrian crisis could not be resolved because of veto powers of the UNSC member countries, sources in the Ministry of External Affairs said.

The heads of state and government of African countries are here to participate in the India Africa Forum Summit on Thursday. There was a detailed discussion between Zuma and Modi on ways to tackle threat of terrorism, with both stressing that there was a need for concrete strategy to fight the menace in a united way.

The South African leader said coming together of African countries with India showed to the world that they no longer are dependent on former colonial powers.

The Prime Minister also met Robert Mugabe, President of Zimbabwe, and Chairman of African Union. Both the leaders discussed issues of common interest, including UN reforms and the threat of terrorism. Mugabe is the co-chair for the India Africa Forum Summit, and the two leaders reviewed the preparations for the Summit.

The Prime Minister also met President John Dramani Mahama of Ghana during which both sides reviewed the "warm" bilateral ties. Growing bilateral trade came up for discussion and both leaders stressed on the need to step up engagement in sectors like agriculture, IT, skill development, cyber security and maritime security.

The Prime Minister met King of Swaziland Mswati III. The King spoke of his vision for his country's development, including areas such as infrastructure, renewable energy and skill development and sought India's assistance. The Prime Minister complimented the Swaziland King on his leadership and vision, and offered assistance in the country's development.

Modi also met Boni Yayi, President of Beni and both the leaders deliberated on growing economic relationship between the two countries, particularly in areas of agricultural, power generation, water supply and transportation.

In the meeting between Modi and President of Nigeria Muhammadu Buhari, issues relating to India's oil exploration projects in that country were discussed besides cooperation in defence cooperation. The issue of UN reforms also figured.

During the meeting between Uhuru Kenyatta, President of Kenya, and the Prime Minister, areas of cooperation including healthcare, infrastructure and mutual trade and economic relations came up for discussion. The historical ties between the two countries and the large Indian diaspora in Kenya were mentioned. Terrorism and UN reform also came up for discussion. The Prime Minister also met the President of Uganda, Yoheri Museveni, and the two leaders discussed ways to enhance prosperity and mutual understanding between the two countries.

African leaders unveil wish list of projects they want India to help in

African leaders on Wednesday unveiled a wishlist of projects that they wanted Indian assistance with, including the setting up of a science and technology park, an industrial park, the continued availability of Indian generic drugs at affordable prices, more soft loans on concessional terms, more scholarships for African students and infrastructure development. India, on its part, sought deeper collaboration from Africa in the energy sector—oil, natural gas as well as uranium—and appealed for African support on issues such as UN Security Council reforms and terrorism. The two sides also discussed the prospects of setting up a fertilizer unit in Ghana even as countries like Chad and Equatorial Guinea expressed desire to open diplomatic missions here.

The airing of expectations of both sides came during the bilateral meetings Prime Minister Narendra Modi had with visiting heads of state and government of African nations who are in New Delhi to participate in the third India-Africa Summit on Thursday.

The summit has been billed as the biggest gathering of foreign dignitaries in New Delhi since the 1983 Non-Aligned Summit.

Previous India-Africa summits—the first in New Delhi in 2008 and the second in Addis Ababa in 2011—were smaller events, with India and representatives of select African countries participating. The forum is aimed at deepening bonds between India and Africa against the backdrop of growing influence of countries like China,

Foreign minister Sushma Swaraj, who addressed an India-Africa Business Forum in New Delhi on Wednesday, called on Indian businesses to increase trade with Africa and not "cede" space to "third parties"—a reference to countries like China whose bilateral trade with Africa topped $200 billion in 2014-15, according to various estimates. In contrast, India's combined bilateral trade with African countries was $72 billion.

Those who met Modi on Wednesday included the presidents of Zimbabwe Robert Mugabe, Ghana's John Dramani Mahama, Nigeria's Muhammadu Buhari, Kenya's Uhuru Kenyatta, Uganda's Yoweri Kaguta Museveni, South Africa's Jacob Zuma, Gabon's Ali Bongo Ondimba, vice-president of Botswana Mokgweetsi Eric Keabetswe Masisi and the king of Swaziland Mswati III.

"The broad elements (of the discussions) were how India and Africa can help each other, particularly how Africa can benefit from capacity-building using Indian expertise," Indian foreign ministry spokesman Vikas Swarup said. "PM Modi used an interesting phrase...he said India and Africa are made for each other," Swarup said, referring to the complementarities of the two sides.

Veteran African leader Mugabe, on a visit to India after a gap of almost two decades, sought Indian aid in human resources development and discussed ways to improve trade with India. Bilateral trade currently is about $1 million dollars.

Africa, told reporters. Both sides discussed the feasibility of setting up a fertiliser project. Ghana's Mahama sought India's help in human resource development, information technology and railways, Tanmay Lal, joint secretary-east and south

"The Ghanaian side assured us of the viability of the project and that they had recently discovered two huge reserves of natural gas and as and when they come on stream in a couple of years, gas at a cheaper rate will be made available to that project," Lal said. With Nigeria, India's largest trade partner in Africa, talks centred on how to increase cooperation in the energy sector, Lal said. "During their discussion on cooperation between India and Nigeria in the oil sector, the Nigerian President informed the prime minister that India had become its largest importer of oil, replacing the US," Lal said.

Defence cooperation was a common point of discussion between India and Nigeria as well as Uganda, Lal said. He recalled that Nigerian President Buhari had received military training in India years ago. With Uganda, along with talks on improving Uganda's dairy sector, there were talks on defence cooperation, Lal said.

Swarup clarified that this cooperation was for now in the area of India training African military officers.

The issue of Indian generic drugs being available at affordable prices was discussed with Kenyan President Kenyatta, Lal said. Africa has been a large market for Indian drugs available at a fraction of the price of those manufactured by western pharmaceutical companies.

But with India looking to come up with a new intellectual property rights policy that could see it aligned more with western standards, there are apprehensions that Indian generic drugs will not be as easily available.

With Niger, India discussed sourcing uranium for its nuclear power plants. "There was also a discussion on how to attract Indian investment in the oil sector," Lal said.

Meanwhile, in her address to Indian industry earlier in the day, Swaraj urged Indian companies to invest in Africa, as it offered resources and growth opportunities. "The day you combine your strength with their needs, that would be a win-win for both...their needs would be fulfilled and you would make money," she said at the India-Africa Business Forum.

"Indian investors are aware of the potential of Africa with large land mass, rich natural resources and demand... We hope various countries in Africa will take steps to attract such investments from India, particularly from manufacturing and processing activities," Swaraj said.

INDIA-AFRICA SUMMIT 2015: INDIA SEEKS TO CHALLENGE CHINA'S DOMINANCE THROUGH 'UNPRECEDENTED' CONFERENCE

During an interaction with African journalist on the eve of the third India-Africa Forum Summit in New Delhi, Indian Prime Minister Narendra Modi sought to reaffirm the "strong emotional link" between the Asian nation and Africa. In India, the summit — which kicked off Monday and is witnessing the participation of all 54 African countries — is already being touted as an "unprecedented" event.

"The relations between India and the countries of Africa, these relations and these bonds that we have, are not just political and economic but we also have a very rich cultural tradition," Modi said. "I am convinced that during this summit and following the summit, we are going to have very important decisions which will give both India and Africa a new sense of self confidence, our relations are going to become closer and deeper."

The four-day summit is the biggest gathering of foreign dignitaries in New Delhi since the 1983 Non-Aligned Summit. Two previous India-Africa summits — the first in New Delhi in 2008 and the second in Addis Ababa in 2011 — were smaller events, with only representatives from select African nations participating.

India is Africa's fourth-largest trading partner, after China, the U.S. and the European Union. Over the past decade, the two-way trade between India and Africa has witnessed a massive surge — from $25 billion in 2006 to the current level of over $70 billion. India currently has oil investments in Mozambique, South Sudan, Egypt and Libya, and is also the biggest importer of crude oil from Nigeria.

However, despite the rise, the bilateral trade still lags behind China's trade with Africa, which currently stands at $200 billion.

Like India — which primarily imports crude oil and gas from the region — China's trade with Africa is largely import driven, with the world's second-largest economy taking petroleum mostly from Nigeria, Angola, Equatorial Guinea, Ghana, Cameroon, the Republic of Congo, Gabon, Uganda, South Sudan, and Sudan.

"We can't match the Chinese in terms of resources — but any engagement we do with the Africans at least gives them a choice," C. Raja Mohan, a foreign policy commentator at the Observer Research Foundation in New Delhi, told Reuters. However, in order to challenge China's dominance in the continent, India has sought to distance itself from what it calls an "exploitative" relationship with Africa in favour of one that focuses on "Africa's needs and India's strengths." In addition to economic and trade ties, the Indian government will also seek to focus on engaging all 54 African nations in its ambition to secure a permanent seat in the United Nations Security Council, and in developing a strong partnership on climate change ahead of a crucial conference in Paris later this year. "The discussion [will focus] on several economic, cultural and political issues like green technology, blue economy, space technology, education, skill development, healthcare, food security, connectivity and peace and security," Modi said, in a statement released over the weekend.

INDIA-AFRICA SUMMIT: BEYOND THE EVENT

The India-Africa Forum Summit was, no doubt, a feather in the cap of the government and in particular for the Ministry of External Affairs that pulled out all the stops for it. Like a well-managed wedding, the venue was beautifully arranged, the guests were well taken care of, and dignitaries got a taste of Indian cuisine, culture and hospitality. There were the traditional squabbles within some of the family members of the African Union, and a few sulking relatives, like the Congress party that stayed away from the Prime Ministerial and Presidential banquets, but the events were executed to near-perfection. Yet like all good weddings, it is the success of the marriage, not of the pomp and splendour of the ceremonies, that will eventually count for India-Africa ties, and one must look beyond the optics to judge the summit.

To begin with, much has been made of the fact that a record 41 of the 54 leaders of the African Union (AU) came together in Delhi, compared with the previous participation of just 15 leaders or less in 2008 and 2011. This is misleading, as previously, the India-Africa summit followed what was called the 'Banjul formula', that the AU would be represented by 15 leaders chosen from the five founders of the New Africa Partnership for Africa's Development (NEPAD) – South Africa, Nigeria, Algeria, Egypt and Senegal, eight RECS (or Regional Economic Coordinators), the current and incoming AU Chairperson, and the AU Commission Chair. As a result, there was some consternation when India, under Prime Minister Narendra Modi, now wanted to invite all 54 African Heads of State or Heads of Government, even though this was by far a more democratic format, followed by China and the U.S. Officials from Nigeria and South Africa in particular, two countries which together account for nearly half of the India-Africa trade, wondered if they were being equated with countries which have no relations with India at all. Significantly, after the IAFS this year, African countries have insisted the next conference be held after five years, not three years, a possible fallout.

Territorial dispute

The attendance of all led to an additional problem, as the dispute between the AU and Morocco over the Western Sahara state called SADR (Sahrawi Arab Democratic Republic) erupted. Morocco claims the SADR, while the AU recognises it as a full state, which led Morocco to walk out of the AU in 1984. India recognised the SADR in 1985, but then withdrew recognition in 2000. For the Summit, India said it had invited 'all' African Union countries, although in reality had invited only 53, and then added Morocco. This didn't go down well with several African countries, especially since the King of Morocco chose to arrive first in Delhi with the largest contingent, seen as 'grandstanding'. A full debate erupted at the summit, when Algeria and others tried to insert a clause on 'colonialism' in the draft declaration, clearly aimed at Morocco, but which could also be read as 'anti-Western', which India, given its good relations with the U.S. and Europe, wished to avoid. Eventually, to the credit of senior MEA officials, the situation was smoothed out, but not before significantly delaying the declaration and the subsequent presidential banquet.

The other disappointment was on the language in the IAFS declaration on a Security Council seat, which mirrored the ambiguous language used by countries like China. "Africa takes note of India's position and its aspirations to become a permanent member with full rights in an expanded UN Security Council," it read. Given that both Prime Minister Modi and External Affairs Minister Sushma Swaraj publicly pitched for support to India's case at the summit, this would have been a blow indeed, but one that can be fixed at a more bilateral level.

Focus diverted

On other issues, the declaration has much to commend it. Unfortunately, official comments and headlines sought to portray this as a 'donor conference', more about India's announcements of $10 billion fund, 50,000 scholarships and infrastructure projects than about shared projects. In truth, each of India's Line-of-Credit projects benefit India as much as they do Africa, giving a toehold in a continent where China and the U.S. already have a greater presence. For most countries there, India doesn't represent just a 'white knight' or trading partner; it represents a country with similar problems, tropical climate, and challenges of poverty and disease, but has overcome many of these challenges through low-cost innovations. As a result, India's rural healthcare, water conservation techniques, scientific expertise, educational facilities and programmes for women mean much more than the amount of aid would. In the IAFS declaration, the clauses on cooperation on food security, solar power technology, satellite weather research and the 'blue', or maritime, economy will probably go the longest way on the India-Africa partnership.India and Africa are a country and a whole continent, and can't really be compared as equals. The meeting ground is one of ideas. For years, the common thread was the freedom struggle, with Mahatma Gandhi as a common inspirational link. Going forward, it is still important to unite against new attempts at exploitation, so they are not bullied into adopting unsustainable standards on issues like poverty alleviation or patents for generic drugs that India produces for Africa. It is this futuristic course that draws closer the ties between the African continent and the Indian subcontinent, described once by Nelson Mandela as 'the golden thread woven in the common struggles against injustice and oppression'.

7

Africa-india Framework for Cooperation

The Heads of State and Government and Heads of Delegation of Africa, representing the Continent, the African Union and its Institutions along with the Prime Minister of the Republic of India, recognizing the rich history of Africa-India relationship and noting with satisfaction the existing close, deep and multi-layered relations between the two sides and realizing the need to give a new dimension to this cooperation, have decided to adopt this Framework for Cooperation between Africa and India.

The two parties agree to cooperate in the areas enumerated herein.

ECONOMIC COOPERATION

As a conducive and supportive international economic environment is important for Africa and India in their quest for a mutually beneficial economic development, the two parties hereby recognize the need to foster such environment by reinforcing efforts to promote between them, trade and industry, Foreign Direct Investment (FDI), development of Small and Medium-scale Enterprises (SMEs) and Africa's regional integration. In this regard, the two parties have agreed to cooperate in the following areas:

Agriculture

Africa and India agree that agricultural development is an effective approach to ensure food security, eradicating poverty and improve peoples' livelihood, and agree to strengthen Africa and India cooperation in this sector in order to improve the food security of Africa and to increase its exports to world markets.

They emphasize sustainable development of agricultural and animal resources with effective support for scientific research for conservation of land and environment.

The cooperation will focus on the following areas:

- Capacity building and sharing of experience in policy analysis and planning relating to agriculture sector;
- Cooperation in water resource management and irrigation practices, agro- infrastructure development, transfer of applied agricultural technology and skills transfer;
- Cooperation to combat agro-based diseases;
- Capacity building/ training for increasing the capacity of small land holder African food producers to comply with the required quality and safety standards, including extension activity and agricultural credit policies;
- Sharing experiences and information on appropriate storage and processing technologies and jointly promoting the uptake of African and Indian developed technologies for diversification and value addition in relations to food and agricultural products;
- Sharing of expertise and information between commodity boards of Africa and India with a view to learning from each other's experiences in farm mechanization, post harvest technology, organic farming, policy and regulatory frameworks and setting up of cross border commodity exchange boards;
- Enhancing market opportunities for African value added agricultural products;
- Cooperation in livestock management, breeding technologies, meat processing, dairy industry development, fisheries and aqua-culture, including exchange and transfer of applied technology;
- Establishing linkages between agriculture and industrial

development in order to support and nurture agro-processing industries; and

- Enhancing cooperation between agricultural training centres and relevant research institutes.

Trade, Industry and Investment

Africa and India recognize the need to expand the two-way trade, greater market access and investment facilitation and decide to take the following steps:

- Technical assistance and capacity-building in trade negotiations, dispute settlement and implementation of different agreements under WTO, as well as in enhancing competitiveness in the world economy;
- Strengthening linkages of enterprises on both sides with a view to developing global markets for products and services available on both sides;
- Maximizing the benefits of trade liberalization through improved market access for products of export interest to African countries and India, including striving to provide duty-free and quota-free market access for African products;
- Promoting and facilitating enhanced trade cooperation between the two sides, including through value addition/ processing;
- Organization of business delegations and participation in trade fairs and exhibitions;
- Preparation of a Joint Strategy and Action Plan for mapping of resources and opportunities for entrepreneurship development and facilitation aimed at mutual growth;
- Developing and implementing projects for information dissemination regarding entrepreneurship opportunities on both sides, business-to-business contacts, such as through business conclaves and upgrading of trade facilitation through commercial missions of both sides; and
- Enhancing corporate governance and social responsibility.

Small and Medium-Scale Enterprises (SMEs)

Africa and India recognize that for a sustainable and successful industrial policy, development of micro, small and medium-scale enterprises is necessary as the first step towards industrialization in African countries. With that objective in focus, the following steps will be taken:

- Capacity building through Entrepreneurship Development Programmes;
- Capacity building on policy formulation and institutional framework development for the SMEs;
- Promotion of Joint Ventures between business enterprises of Africa and India;
- Training in Africa and India for upgrading of skills in the areas of conventional and hi-tech training; and
- Promoting the export of SME products, including projects on turnkey basis.

Finance

Recognizing the importance of the financial sector, cooperation in the following areas is decided:

- Sharing of experiences and capacity-building on policy and regulatory frameworks in the financial sector including the microfinance sector;
- Sharing of experiences in mobilization of domestic savings;
- Capacity-building in development of automated trading systems for stock-exchange and development of cross--border stock-exchanges, such as Pan-African Stock exchanges; and
- Mobilization of financial resources to fund the various projects envisaged in the areas of cooperation.

Regional Integration

Recognizing the importance of regional cooperation and economic integration in development endeavours, Africa and India decide as follows:

- Provision of financial support to mutually agreed integration programmes carried out by the African Union

and the RECs, especially those of inter-regional and continental importance;
- Promotion and support for regional and inter-regional projects, including infrastructural development; and
- Provision of technical assistance to support the establishment of the financial institutions of the African Union.

POLITICAL COOPERATION

Bearing in mind that peace, security and development are inseparable as there can be no lasting development without peace and recognizing the need for closer cooperation in the field of governance structures and civil society, India resolves to support Africa in meeting her objectives of sustainable development, prosperity and peace through the following steps:

Peace and Security

- Cross-fertilization of the experiences of the AU and India in peacekeeping and post-conflict reconstruction efforts taking into account the AU's Policy Framework for Post Conflict Reconstruction and Development (PCRD);
- Cooperation in undertaking lessons-learned exercises and sharing of experiences regarding the role of women in peacekeeping operations;
- Cooperation in developing and implementing training of trainers towards enhancing the civilian component of peacekeeping operations;
- Technical assistance and capacity building to tackle the challenge of money laundering and terrorist financing;
- Cooperation in duplication of the Female Formed Police Unit;
- Cooperation in developing and implementing a Training of Trainers Programme towards effective policing and police support as -part of peacekeeping operations;
- Sharing of experiences and information to enhance capacity

to fight international terrorism, including through the African Centre on the Study and Research on Terrorism.

- Cooperation in combating drug trafficking, as well as trafficking in women and children; and
- Technical assistance and capacity building in disaster management and humanitarian intervention.

Civil Society and Good Governance

- Cross-fertilization of ideas on decentralization of governance and building capacity of local governments through administrative reforms and enhancing public participation in local and central government;
- Establishing a platform to initiate, deepen and maintain cooperation in civil establishments and training institutes in Africa and India on various relevant issues;
- Create a joint platform for discussion of global political and economic issues with a view to reinforcing South-South positions that will enable Africa and India to have greater leverage in the international fora;
- Cross-fertilization and sharing of experiences on public service reforms and human rights regimes with a view to strengthening mutual competences in these areas;
- Sharing of experiences on strategies for deepening democratization at the local level, management of ethnic diversity and wealth distribution in a democratic context and the professionalisation of the public services;
- Exchange of expertise and sharing of experiences on the conduct of elections in vast and complex terrains
- Sharing experiences in harnessing resources from Diaspora;
- Helping to strengthen the African Court on Human and Peoples' Rights;
- Interaction of legal experts/lawyers through Bar Associations; and
- Cooperation in legal research methodology and in emerging international legal issues, such as the mechanisms, processes and regulatory frameworks that support outsourcing.

SCIENCE, TECHNOLOGY, RESEARCH AND DEVELOPMENT

Science and Technology

- Developing robust networks among leading institutes for Science and Technology for collaborative research and development;
- Sharing experiences in technology transfer and development of appropriate technology;
- Sharing experiences in capacity building for strengthening the role of science and technology;
- Cooperation in setting quality standards and recognition awards in science, technology and innovation; and
- Cooperation in management of intellectual property, including indigenous knowledge.

Information and Communication Technology (ICT)

Recognizing that Information Technology is emerging as one of the major vehicles of economic growth and has become fundamental part of infrastructure and improvement of myriad sectors of socio-economic activities, Africa and India agree to take the following steps:

- Cooperate closely to ensure quick and effective implementation and roll out of the Pan-African E-Network Project being funded by India. The project will be a major step forward in removing the digital divide, ensure connectivity of all African countries and provide much needed telemedicine and tele-education to the masses of African countries;
- Cooperate in the implementation of the digital solidarity mechanism developed within the framework of NEPAD.
- Cooperation in capacity building in devising model legal and policy frameworks for ICT, such as on e-Commerce, e--Governance, e-Health etc.;
- Cooperation and information sharing among ICT regulatory bodies;

- Development of Information and Communication Technology tools and applications aimed at improving public administration at different levels of government, taxation management, public financing and delivery of public services;
- Promotion of cooperation in the range of non-material knowledge-based human resources such as technology, organization, information, education and skills development;
- Cooperation in setting up Community Information Centers using IT to accelerate socio-economic development, with a view to providing rural connectivity and bridging the digital divides; and

COOPERATION IN SOCIAL DEVELOPMENT AND CAPACITY BUILDING

Education

Africa and India recognize that human resource development is vital to achieve the socio-economic development goals of Africa and universal mass education is a key factor in this endeavor. To achieve universal education with special emphasis on quality and gender equality, Africa and India will collaborate in the following areas:

- Sharing experiences and building capacity for educational policy planning and administration through the effective utilization of financial and statistical information on education;
- Increasing the scholarships available for Africa from the Indian Technical and Economic Cooperation (ITEC) programmes with focus on science, technology and information technology-related courses;
- Sharing of experiences and best practices in "Mid-day Meal Programme";
- Collaboration in the development and production of teaching and learning materials, including equipment for teaching science and technology and textbooks, especially for universities;

- Collaboration in designing and implementation of Open and Distance Education/Learning Programmes with attendant capacity building for personnel required, such as teachers and ICT technicians;
- Establishing programmes for exchange of students and staff through twinning leading African and Indian Universities;
- Cooperation in equipping scientific laboratories and training workshops for Technical and Vocational Education; and
- Cooperation in establishing programmes in capacity building and entrepreneurship for youth through ICT.

Health

Africa and India acknowledge that upgrading and streamlining healthcare systems and increasing access to healthcare for the people of Africa and India is a critical issue and agree to increase cooperation in the field of health promotion and healthcare systems through the following areas of cooperation:

- Sharing experiences, information and expertise on traditional systems of medicine within recognized intellectual property regime;
- Training and capacity building for health professionals and physicians;
- Sharing experience and information on healthcare systems development and community health programmes;
- Linking the centers of excellence in the health sector, such as research and training institutes, etc.;
- Focus on cooperation in devising and implementing programmes for enhancing universal access to adequate medical services, including developing the telemedicine infrastructure and technology to enable patients to receive quality health services, such as medical diagnostic and other services to which they would not ordinarily have access due to distance and/or limitation in the availability of specialists;

- Strengthen the indigenous manufacturing capacities and to make available affordable and quality pharmaceutical products, especially essential medicines. This may also include exchange of technical experts and collaborative efforts;
- Enhance cooperation in controlling HIV/AIDS, TB, Malaria and other communicable diseases;
- Cooperation in combating the proliferation and dumping of counterfeit medicines;
- Local production of oral rehydration therapy.

Water and Sanitation

In both Africa and India, many communities lack access to adequate and safe drinking water, as well as basic sanitation resulting in prevalence of diseases related to poor hygiene and environmental sanitation. In order to achieve the MDGs and the Johannesburg Declaration on Sustainable Development and Plan of Action, efforts have to be doubled particularly during 2008, the International Year of Sanitation. In this connection, cooperation could focus on sharing experiences and promoting programmes in the following areas:

- Development of sanitation infrastructure, particularly in urban and sub-urban settings;
- Urban development, in particular, combating the mushrooming of slums and shanty towns;
- Waste management; and
- Putting in place appropriate framework for water quality control and water treatment.

Culture and Sports

Recognizing the need to enhance mutual understanding and friendship between different nations and ethnic groups and achieving common prosperity and progress of mankind, as well as underlining the importance of cultural exchanges and cooperation, Africa and India resolve to enhance cultural relations between the two sides. To this end, focus will be given to the following areas:

- Encourage people-to-people contacts and exchanges to deepen the traditional friendship between the two sides;
- Strengthen contacts among young people through encouraging and supporting exchange of students among schools and universities;
- Encourage the visit of Professors under the bilateral cultural exchange programmes at prestigious universities in Africa and India and encourage creating/maintaining chair of African/Indian studies; -
- Encourage bilateral cultural exchange programmes of performing art troupes and art exhibitions;
- Foster closer linkages in the film industry sector and encourage holding of film festivals, as well as increase interaction and cooperation for the film industry of Africa and India; and
- Cooperation in the area of sports.

Poverty Eradication

A significant percentage of the population in Africa and India live below the poverty line and many of the working poor lack social protection.

Unemployment and underemployment, particularly for the youth, resulting in internal and external migration are contributing to unplanned rapid urbanization. These are serious issues for both Africa and India and both can cooperate to resolve these problems in the following areas:

- Strengthening cooperation in the framework of the implementation of the Millennium Development Goals (MDGs);
- Cooperation in the implementation of poverty alleviation strategies;
- Sharing experiences in employment creation and business management;
- Development of social security systems; and
- Sharing of best practices in development of credit unions, especially in rural settings.

TOURISM

As a significant industry that provides economic benefits and promotes friendship and socio-cultural understanding among nations, Africa and India hereby resolve to continue to promote the growth of tourism, as well as expand people-to-people exchanges in their two regions to further promote understanding, trust and cooperation between their peoples. To this end, focus will be given to the following areas:

- Promotion of close interaction between relevant authorities in Africa and India to facilitate coherence of policies and initiatives related to tourism development;
- Adoption of appropriate measures to prevent all threats to tourism, which may have direct impact on tourism;
- Strengthening of partnership with the private sector especially travel agencies, hotels, airlines and other tourism related establishments, as well as the media, with a view to advancing tourism development between the two regions; and
- Promotion of general tourism and offering joint tourism packages, including eco-tourism, to utilize the geographical diversity of the two sides.

INFRASTRUCTURES, ENERGY AND ENVIRONMENT

Recognizing that energy and infrastructure is fundamental to the economic growth of developing countries and acknowledging that infrastructural development and environmental sustainability are some of the priority areas of NEPAD, Africa and India agree to place energy, infrastructure and environmental sustainability as one of the key areas of cooperation and commit ourselves to the following areas:

- Development of public-private partnerships in infrastructure development;
- Cooperation in the development of transport and telecommunications networks;
- Cooperation in the field of exploration and exploitation of natural resources, as well as value addition;

- Creation of enabling environment for investment and development of renewable and non-renewable energy sources;
- Cooperation and capacity-building in best practices and adaptation on the impact of climate change and desertification;
- Exchange of experiences on recent advances on alternative energy sources and sustainable land management;
- Development of cooperation in fibre optic cables construction around and within Africa for broadband access network specifically for landlocked countries; and
- Technical cooperation for Clean Development Mechanism (CDM).

AFRICA-INDIA FRAMEWORK FOR ENHANCED COOPERATION

The draft Africa-India Framework for Enhanced Cooperation, the final version of which will be released at the close of the Second Africa-India Forum Summit in Addis Ababa on 25 May, builds upon the Africa-India Framework for Cooperation, signed in Delhi in 2008.

Broadly speaking, there are seven areas of cooperation – now to be enhanced cooperation – between Africa and India. These are: economic cooperation; political cooperation; cooperation in science, technology, research and development; cooperation in social development and capacity building; cooperation in health, culture and sports; cooperation in tourism; cooperation in infrastructure, energy and environment; and cooperation in the area of media and communications.

The draft 2011 framework does slightly flesh out several of the broad strokes painted in the 2008 framework, by laying out concrete goals, and mentioning tangible examples of what has been achieved so far. For example, in terms of agriculture, specific commitments have been made to "cooperate for increasing agricultural output and achieving the Millenium Development Goal of halving the proportion of people who suffer from hunger and malnutrition by 2015". In terms of social development and capacity-building, mention is made of the Pan-Africa E-Network Project, which uses tele-education and tele-medicine to improve capacity across Africa.

Indian investment and involvement in Africa has previously largely been conducted at the private corporate level, rather than been led by the government. But since the 2008 India-Africa summit, there has clearly been political will to take this engagement to a higher level. The framework statements are thus important, to set down what India, and all the countries in Africa, intend to achieve through mutual engagement.

But of course, these statements provide nothing more than a framework: more critical to developing relations between the two countries are the Joint Plans of Action, which set out how to implement some of the general commitments laid out in the frameworks. The first of these was formulated in Delhi in 2010 – two years after the agreed deadline. In the draft 2011 framework, the India-Africa representatives undertake to produce the new plan of action more speedily. "Without prejudice to India's ongoing and future programmes at the bilateral, REC and other levels, it is agreed to jointly revise, within a period of six months, the Joint Plan of Action to fully reflect the Africa-India Framework for Enhanced Cooperation. This Joint Plan of Action will also incorporate a follow-up mechanism which will ensure the effective implementation of programmes and activities agreed in the Plan."

While there has been much goodwill, and many promises of continued friendship, evident in the lead-up to the 2011 India-Africa Forum Summit, the true test of what is achieved will only be visible in the implementation down the line.

PLAN OF ACTION OF THE FRAMEWORK FOR COOPERATION ON THE INDIA-AFRICA FORUM SUMMIT

In order to deepen the India-Africa strategic partnership to promote sustainable development, and to implement the outcomes of the First India-Africa Forum Summit, the two sides have jointly developed this Plan of Action, with a view to implementing the thematic areas that are contained in the Framework for Cooperation.

The Plan of Action is established for a period of 4 years and will be subjected to review, adaptation and enhancement during and after that period.

ECONOMIC COOPERATION

Agriculture

To enhance agricultural education, science and research, India will provide 25 PhD and 50 Masters' scholarships per annum for four years to African students in agriculture in Indian Universities/ Institutions. The scholarships will cover different disciplines in agriculture. In order to ensure equitable distribution, the AU Commission will coordinate the process of selecting the prospective candidates in conjunction with the Government of India and its embassies in Africa.

India will also provide:

- Customized short-term trainings related to transferable skills focusing on training of trainers who will transfer expertise to stakeholders at national level
- Targeted visits of Indian professionals for field demonstrations based on mutually agreed objectives and mission with beneficiary stakeholders
- On-the-spot consultations and in-country trainings
- • Provision of essential hardware and software in field demonstrations
- Exchange of literature, seed, and planting materials, as well as sharing of best practices in agriculture
- The areas to be covered under this programme will endeavour to include management of livestock and fisheries; management of commodity boards; irrigation and water conservation; and capacity building in the area of agro-processing.

Trade, Industry and Investment

The two sides recognize the need to expand two-way trade, greater market access and investment facilitation and agree to the following:

India will establish an India-Africa Institute of Foreign Trade based on the model of the Indian Institute of Foreign Trade. The institute will provide professional education in the field of International trade and management including studies pertaining to the public and private sectors in Africa. In addition, the Indian Institute of Foreign Trade (IIFT) will provide customized capacity building programmes on international trade and business over a four-year period through the existing bilateral arrangements. This will provide capacity building as the process for the establishment of an India-Africa Institute of Foreign Trade is pursued.

India will also establish an India-Africa Diamond Institute on the model of the Indian Diamond Institute in an African country. The Institute will help to develop African capacities and skills in processing, polishing, and grading raw diamonds.

India's Duty-Free and Tariff Preference (DFTP) Scheme for Least Developed Countries (LDCs) in Africa, which has been widely welcomed and which allows access for African goods and services to the growing Indian market, will be continued. Information sharing on the DFTP scheme has been carried out through various fora and will be enhanced under this Plan of Action.

To enhance private sector interaction and building of entrepreneurship and business-to-business linkages, the following initiatives will be undertaken:

Preparation of an India-Africa Business Guide to highlight opportunities on both sides for trade and investment, through the Chambers of Commerce of the two sides

Organization of Business Councils or meetings at the Regional level between Indian and African economic operators, in order to examine business opportunities offered by both economies

Upgrading industrial supply-side capacities and enhancing competitiveness; and exchange of best practices between African and Indian Investment Promotion Agencies

Small and Medium- Scale Enterprises (SMEs)

Small and Medium-Scale Enterprises are at the core of economic development through the private sectors of Africa and India. They contribute to exports, transfer of technology, employment generation, development of regional trade and entrepreneurship. In this respect and to promote the development of capacities and support transfer of technology, the following actions will be undertaken:

India will establish ten (10) vocational training centres in Africa through the National Small Industries Corporation. Thereafter, it will support existing vocational training institutions in Africa.

India will offer generous Lines of Credit on concessional terms to a large number of African countries; undertake programmes for development of capacity building in Africa and support the Chambers of Commerce in India to hold India-Africa Annual Conclave and other similar initiatives.

Programmes to provide enabling infrastructure and conducive operating environment for SMEs and Small and Medium-Scale Industries (SMIs) in Africa will be created as well as joint ventures between African and Indian SMEs including the development of business guides for the establishment of SMEs in Africa and India as a means of youth employment.

Finance

Recognizing that finance is critical to the implementation of the Plan of Action, India announced at IAFS 2008 that it will provide about 5.4 billion United States Dollars in Lines of Credit to African countries and institutions over the 5-year period. A separate provision of 500 million USD to develop capacities in Africa, of which nearly half is committed to this continental level Joint Plan of Action is envisaged.

These financial provisions will support the integration of Africa through:

- Provision of regional infrastructure among other programmes
- Provision of support for capacity building and development of a Pan-African Stock Exchanges
- Consultations between African Ministers of Finance and Economic Development and their Indian counterparts to share experiences

- Sharing of experiences on the mobilization of domestic savings and the strengthening of Micro-Finance institutions in Africa

Regional Integration

Regional integration is an important objective for Africa and various efforts to harmonize the Regional Economic Communities (RECs) through the promotion of integrated projects are ongoing. India has subsisting engagements with many of the RECs and has developed an implementation process for this purpose. Consequently, India agrees to consider financial support to mutually agreed integration programmes carried out by the African Union and the RECs, especially those of inter-regional and continental importance. India will provide a line of credit of USD 300 million to support regional integration infrastructure projects through the AU.

Political Cooperation

Bearing in mind that peace, security and development are inter-linked, the two sides agree to:

Peace and Security

Enhance the capacity of African Governments, institutions and various stakeholders in the implementation of UN Resolution 1325 on women's role in the peace process

Cooperate in efforts to combat illicit drug trafficking and abuse, as well as small arms and light weapons

Cooperate in developing and implementing training of trainers towards enhancing the civilian component of peacekeeping operations.

Civil Society and Good Governance

Strengthen the African Court on Human and People's Rights through sharing best practices, capacity building of the court and provision of equipment and the mobilization of resources for the activities of the court

Promote the interaction of legal experts/lawyers through the Bar Associations, and cooperation in legal research methodology and on emerging international legal issues and regulatory framework that support outsourcing

Exchange experiences on best practices, research and human resources within the framework of decentralization and local governance alongside the conference of Ministers of Public Services and Administration and ECOSSOC.

Science, Technology, Research And Development

Science and Technology

Conscious of the fact that science, technology, research and development are fundamentals and major catalysts for socio-economic activities, the two sides agree to the following:

- Proposals for enhancement of research, development and scientific exchanges involving programmes and events to discuss issues of policy transfer of technology mechanisms through the institutional strengthening of three institutions and capacity building will be undertaken
- India-Africa Science and Technology Conference will be organized to plan an agenda
- India will support institutional strengthening in areas of mutual interest
- India will provide training in areas like HIV, TB and Malaria.

India will support Africa for its research and development efforts through specific fellowships named after CV Raman which will be implemented bilaterally. These will cover medium term and long term support for researchers and post-doctoral fellows

Consideration will be given to the proposal for the training of journalists in scientific journalism.

Information and Communication Technology (ICT)

Recognizing the contribution made by Information Technology to the economic development of Africa and India:

Both sides welcome the establishment of the Pan-African e-network project which supports the developmental goals of African countries in the education, health and communication sectors.

Both sides agree to the early completion and implementation of this important project.

India will establish an India-Africa Institute of Information Technology which would bridge the gap between academia and industry, and serve as a think-tank for the professional development of IT and provide capacity building and education for the growth of IT in Africa.

India will support the African Union's initiative in this sector and support capacity building to this end through the ITEC programme. Africa's desire to have India participate in the implementation of the inter-connection of all African capital cities with broadband network by 2012 and work with Africa to build continental and national e--strategies including the development of all e--applications would be jointly developed by both sides.

COOPERATION IN SOCIAL DEVELOPMENT AND CAPACITY BUILDING

Recognizing the importance of human capacity enhancement in the attainment of socio-development objectives, the two sides agree to the following:

Education

i. India will establish an India-Africa Institute of Education Planning and Administration, which will provide academic and professional guidance to agencies and institutions engaged in educational planning and administration in Africa.

ii. India will consider collaborative development of high quality open source Overseas Development Learning training materials for teachers and various categories of school managers.

iii. India will develop training workshops on local and low cost production of educational materials

iv. India will assist in the development of TVET programmes aligned with labour market demands for both formal and informal economies, and global economic trends.

Health

- India will organize an India-Africa workshop on traditional medicine to highlight the commonalities in approach and sharing of experience.
- Both sides will strengthen public and private sectors collaboration in the areas of pharmaceutical production and procurement in Africa and India in the framework of pharmaceutical manufacturing plan for Africa
- Both sides will support collaboration in research and development in traditional medicine and practices in Africa and India
- Both sides agree to share experiences, specialized expertise and best practices in healthcare systems development and community health programmes
- India will collaborate with Africa in training and continuing education for health professionals; the Pan-African e-network tele-medicine component supports CME and the training of health professionals in various sectors already part of ongoing bilateral and regional programmes.

Water and Sanitation

- India will organize seven training programmes in specialized areas by reputed training/research/academic institutions in India. Up to 50 participants per course will be invited through the African Union.
- India will also support African institutions and initiatives in the field of integrated water management through proposals to be mutually decided.
- India will fully support Africa in attaining the MDGs in the areas of water and sanitation

Culture and Sports

Africa and India will endeavour to jointly:

- Promote film and TV cultural programme exchanges
- Organize joint international training for trainers in the field of cultural goods protection and cultural industries

- Jointly study the establishment of regional laboratories for doping control in Africa and India
- Organize joint international trainings of trainers in the field of sports management and development, including sports medical care
- Organize youth cultural and sports festivals through events like Africa-India Week and by tapping the talent of the large African student presence in India through the Indian Council for Cultural Relations.

Poverty Eradication

- Support for the goal of poverty eradication through the following specific programmes will be undertaken
- Organization of seminars/exhibitions across Africa, including through public/private partnerships
- Construction of prototype low-cost houses in 5 African countries, one per region
- Exchange of cost-sharing experiences in the construction of demonstration houses in 5 African countries, one per region.
- Both sides agree to share best practices in the development of credit unions, especially in rural settings
- Promotion of micro-finance projects in Africa.

TOURISM

Recognizing that tourism provides economic benefits and promotes friendship and socio-economic understanding among nations, the two sides agree as follows:

- India will sponsor a study towards the harmonization of policies and norms in the tourism sector in cooperation with relevant institutions in Africa
- Both sides will strengthen partnership with the private sector especially travel agencies, hotels, airlines and other tourism related establishments, as well as the media, with a view to advancing tourism development between the two regions

- Both sides will promote general tourism and offering joint tourism packages, including eco-tourism, to utilize the geographical diversity of the two sides.

INFRASTRUCTURE, ENERGY AND ENVIRONMENT

Recognizing that infrastructure, energy and environment are fundamental to the economic growth of developing countries, the two sides agree as follows:

i. Training programmes for up to 50 African participants (annually) at the National Institute for Training of Highway Engineers (NITHE) will be provided by India.
ii. Energy: Note that India has actively engaged with Africa through the India Africa Hydrocarbon Conferences and welcomes India's commitment to work with Africa to process its resources including by establishing refineries in some countries.
iii. Define together with the RECs, the regional power pools and national governments concrete projects in the field of hydropower, wind and bio-energy in African countries, which have high potential
iv. Cooperation to explore renewable sources of energy in Africa.

Transport

Maritime Transport

- Develop and promote mutual assistance and cooperation in the area of maritime safety and security, prevention and protection of the main environment and port users
- Work for the creation of regional coast guard networks (North, West, Central, East and South) and surveillance facilities
- Develop Africa's training in the area of maritime and harbour administration
- Collaborate and exchange information in the area of maritime transport, harbour management, safety, security and preventing, controlling and combating pollution,

particularly through training, exchange of skills and knowledge programmes

- In all these areas more specific proposals will be developed by experts from the two sides.

Air Transport

- Coordination of the respective external air transport policies
- Identification and· development of hubs for air bridge to support airlines operations between the two regions and beyond.
- The African side will provide a concept note on these in order to create a dialogue between African and Indian authorities.

Land Transport

- Status Quo Assessment of the Trans African Highway (TAH) Network
- Development of a road safety strategy for the African continent.
- The African side will develop and provide India with concept notes on both projects.

Environment

i. Elaboration of specific programs to combat desertification and climate change which constitute major challenges for the international community

ii. Sharing of experiences on projects for carbon development mechanisms

iii. TERI's MOU with ECA and support to the Africa Climate Policy Centre is also recognised. The Indian initiative to have an African section at the Delhi Sustainable Development Summit annually organized by TERI in February in New Delhi initiated since 2009 will be utilized to foster closer engagement among the environmental policy makers in India and Africa.

MEDIA AND COMMUNICATION

Bearing in mind that closer linkage in the field of media and communication will generate greater synergy in their relationship, the two sides agree to:

i. Cooperate in human resource training in the area of modern corporate communications using modern technology (ICT) and the development of language skills

ii. Provide assistance in the production of documentary videos, which are effective in disseminating information on specific missions or interventions.

iii. Other programmes in this area could be undertaken through existing ITEC programmes and through the Public Diplomacy Division in India. These would be discussed between the African Union Commission and the Permanent Mission of India to the AU.

iv. Similarly, an exchange of media delegations, editors' conferences and training of media persons will form part of the initiatives that India is taking in Africa. These will be undertaken regionally and bilaterally.

With respect to the institutions to be established in Africa, namely, India-Africa Institute of Foreign Trade; India-Africa Diamond Institute; India-Africa Institute of Information Technology; India-Africa Institute of Education Planning and Administration; Pan-African Stock exchange and India-Africa Vocational Training Centres, the host countries undertake to facilitate their establishment and sustenance including:

i. Land for the Institutions

ii. Building infrastructure

iii. Budgetary provision for recurring costs

iv. Governance structures for administration and running of the Institutions

v. Business plan for future development and sustainability.

vi. On its part India will establish and equip the institutions and maintain them for a period of three years.

8

India: It's Time for 'Act Africa'

"When the five-day India-Africa Forum Summit takes place in India from October 26 (2015), the two sides along with the industry honchos are expected to deliberate on the need for greater cooperation in agriculture and agro-processing, which would have a positive impact on the food security situation in Africa and India. Analysts feel that, to boost Africa's agricultural production, the Indian industry can help in training and transfer of technology as it imports pulses from the African continent, as recommended by diplomats from both sides."

These developments shed light on a few questions pertaining to India-Africa relations, especially vis-à-vis China:

How have India-Africa-China relations evolved over time? What are India's economic interests in Africa in comparison to China's linkages? What measures can Delhi take to bridge the trade gap between India and Africa?

Distance no barrier: Thriving historical linkages

India-Africa ties took shape across the vast Indian Ocean since the 4th century. But Africans in India really flourished as traders, artists, rulers, architects and reformers between the 14th Century and 17th Century. One outstanding personality was Ethiopian born Malik Ambar, who came as a slave but rose to be a Regent of one of the South Indian Sultanates. He proved to be an unbeatable nemesis for the mighty Mughals and finally laid the foundation of Maratha power which would rise to its zenith with Chatrapathi Shivaji. Ambar is believed to be the father of guerrilla warfare in India since he used his Maratha cavalry to harass the Mughals with great effect. Africa supplied not only great leaders but vital resources. East African iron was exported to India for the manufacture of famous swords. Centuries later, Mahatma Gandhi inspired African countries, who were resisting the shackles of colonialism and apartheid, with peaceful dialogue and non-violence.

Chinese linkages were no less prominent. In the early years of the Ming Dynasty, between 1405 and 1433, China launched one of history's most remarkable and mysterious naval enterprises: Admiral Zheng set out in fleets of technologically unparalleled "treasure ships" to destinations as far as the Horn of Africa. However these missions were not aimed at territorial conquest or resource trade. They merely reflected the Chinese desire to exchange high-level visits and gifts or "tributes". The nature of ties changed in the 1950s-1970s when China was keenly interested in propagating Communism throughout the African Continent, and even supplied military hardware for this purpose. It gradually obtained a key objective: the recognition of the 'One China' policy. Communist propaganda has since then waned, but military and trade ties remain strong, and are far ahead of India's tryst with Africa.

The Indian Elephant races with the Dragon

India-Africa trade is set to touch USD 100 billion this year, up from around USD 70 billion in 2013 and a major leap from barely USD 5 billion about a decade ago. While Indian exports to Africa include petroleum products, automobiles, pharmaceuticals and telecom equipment, imports are crude oil, gold, raw cotton, precious stones and textile yarn. Besides, India's diamond-cutting industry – the world's largest – depends on rough diamonds from Africa, while uranium in Niger, Uganda and Tanzania is vital for India's nuclear power industry. Despite the depth of cooperation, India-Africa trade is dwarfed by China's presence in Africa.

China has moved far beyond India, by becoming Africa's largest trade partner in 2009. Beijing needs economic relations with Africa chiefly for importing crude oil, making the resource rich continent China's second largest energy supplier. Africa also exports other resources to China, namely iron ore, metals, other commodities, as well as a small amount of food and agricultural products. At the same time, China exports a range of machinery and transportation equipment, communications equipment, and electronics to African countries.

However some barriers in Africa- China do remain. Africa has been affected by the unpredictable Chinese financial scenario: Currencies in African countries with strong exports to China, like South Africa (gold and wine), Angola (oil), and the Zambia (copper) have already fallen following Beijing's move to devalue the yuan. On the other hand, Africa can rely on India with its resilient economy.

Despite the detriments observed, China-Africa trade has received a significant boost since the Forum on China-Africa Cooperation (FOCAC) was established in 2000. Since this multilateral cooperation institution was setup, trade has jumped from USD 50 billion in 2000 to over USD 200 billion in 2012. However, the African side has its own fears and reservations regarding the influx of Chinese goods and labour and export of African resources: At the fifth FOCAC Ministerial Meeting in Beijing, South African President Jacob Zuma remarked that "Africa's commitment to China's development has been demonstrated by the supply of raw materials, other products and technology transfer. This trade pattern is unsustainable in the long term. Africa's past economic experience with Europe dictates a need to be cautious when entering into partnerships with other economies." The evidence is clear as seen in the nascent and vulnerable African industries being hit by China's aggressive exporting of machinery and manufactured goods. Textile, shoe and ferrochrome steel makers are especially harmed. Besides, the corporate social responsibility programs operated by Chinese companies are "passive" rather than "active." In this light, the 6th FOCAC meeting in 2015 will possibly witness an elevated devotion on Beijing's part towards (African priorities), including agricultural development, industrialization, training, job creation and technology transfer through investment in manufacturing industries.

On the other hand the very first India-Africa Forum Summit at Delhi in 2008 focused on agriculture and human resources, besides technology and energy. IAFS-II resulted in the Addis Ababa Declaration of 2011. It highlighted a range of issues beyond bilateral trade: U.N. reforms, Africa's place in world affairs, climate change, countering terrorism, the Doha Round and South-South cooperation. The announcement of India's new funding for additional commitments — USD 5 billion for lines of credit, USD 700 million for new institutions and training programmes, and USD 300 million for the Ethiopia-Djibouti railway line — was an apt response to African expectations. The IAFS-III to be held in Delhi this year will have a unique line of action: inviting all 54 members of Africa, unlike earlier summits. This will help to enhance India's image in Africa considerably.

However India has always remained ahead of China in the sphere of positive public perception. One factor behind this is that India markets to Africa according to the domestic needs: Although Africa has a large population of 1.1 billion, there is less viability as a strong market due to prevalence of low income. In this light India is going to export to the predominant agricultural sector, for instance supplying tractors for small farms. On the other hand, Chinese trade with Africa remains Sino-centric. For instance, the goods exported to Africa are priced so low that it affects the local manufacturers. This in turn causes job displacement. There are also concerns about the Chinese presence, in terms of unfair labour practices and environmental concerns. On the other hand, Indian presence in welcomed in Africa, as it generates a significant number of local employment opportunities. According to a Financial Times report, companies such as Mahindra say they hire about 90 per cent of their employees locally, with the aim to upping that to 95 per cent and more. The report adds that instead of only selling finished goods, Indian conglomerates are already producing certain products in Africa. This implies the opening of more avenues for employment in Africa's manufacturing sector. Employment is not limited to the African side alone. Andhra Pradesh signed an agreement with East African nations to send 500 farmers to work as entrepreneurs and landowners. This will help to offset the difficulty faced back home due to droughts and lack of fertile land. Thus India and Africa share a symbiotic relationship in the crucial human resources sector.

Government consulting is another area where India can exercise its expertise. This is necessary, as many of the states in Africa need direction while consolidating their unstable economies. Communication will not be a barrier to such ventures. The colonial legacy of both parties leaves little cultural or language barriers. But China cannot boast of the same people to people affinity. There are reports of the Chinese people's racial prejudice towards Africans and ignorance about their imperialist dominated past.

India's specialization in ICT also gives it an edge over Chinese presence in Africa, via the Pan Africa e-network which was kicked off in 2006. The USD 1 billion project, in tandem with the 54 members of the African Union, aims to connect the African states to a satellite and fibre optic network. This network has been a boon for telemedicine programmes and online education. The brainchild of former Indian President A.P.J. Abdul Kalam, the pan African e-network enables doctors in India to offer consultation as well as training to their counterparts in Africa. The advantages garnered in e-education are numerous. The ease of access for African students to classroom sessions in India enables a sound teacher-student ratio when compared to the often crammed African university classrooms. The superior quality of the online internationally recognized courses have no room for cheating. Besides, they expose Africans to Indian culture and learning attitudes.

India also bypasses China in the realm of peacekeeping operations. Since India needs crucial oil and gas supplies from Sudan, South Sudan, Libya and Nigeria, apart from energy interests in Angola and the Ivory Coast, it has led to led to India contributing significant peacekeeping troops to the continent. India has deployed 2200 peacekeeping troops to the United Nations Mission in South Sudan (UNMISS) alone, while China deploys approximately the same number all across the continent. Significantly, Indian companies have a 25 per cent stake in two South Sudan oil companies, and an oil pipeline. Other Indian peacekeeping operations include past and ongoing deployments in Namibia, Liberia, Angola, Congo, Ethiopia- Eritrea, Mozambique, Somalia, Rwanda and Sierra- Leone. The approach of peacekeeping is also different. For instance, China's contributions to UN peacekeeping missions have generally been non-combat peacekeepers in medical and engineering roles. This may be to protect and sustain China's investment projects. On the other hand India, while also protecting its economic interests, believes in goodwill as well as presenting itself as a strong contender for a permanent seat in the UN Security Council.

While peacekeeping remains India's stronghold, China has surged far ahead in terms of aid. Some experts refer to China's financing strategy as the "Angola model," by which Beijing provides low-interest loans to countries with low credit ratings, and in turn receives favorable rights to develop oil and mining projects. While exact figures are hard to pinpoint, it is estimated that China engages in 1,673 projects in 51 African countries and has committed USD 75 billion in official finance. However African leaders are almost three times more likely to spend Chinese development aid in areas where they have ethnic ties, casting doubt on the humanitarian effectiveness of Beijing's strict "hands-off" policy in the continent. According to AidData, most of that aid went to areas where national leaders were born, indicating a strong political bias. Interestingly, China handles foreign aid via its Ministry of Commerce, unlike India, where aid is a function of the Development Partnership Administration arm of the Ministry of External Affairs. This shows the difference in implied intentions while contributing aid. Chinese overseas firms are known to survey the ground reality in their areas of operation, and report back to the home country. Beijing shapes its aid strategy accordingly. India follows a more humanitarian approach while granting aid. In fact, Africa is the largest recipient of Indian aid. In 2011 India committed USD 5 billion in aid to Africa. It is estimated that Indian aid to African countries in 2014-2015 is Rs. 350 crores. An assessment of the nature of aid given demonstrates that India is keen to help Africa build its vocational skills, educational and hospital infrastructure, IT, agriculture, river basin management, green energy and even surveillance and radar equipment.

The humanitarian nature of India's aid is not sufficient to tide over the reality of China's clout in Africa, especially in infrastructure. From the days of when the Tazara Railway was built to the present day high speed rail networks, China has chugged a long way in building Africa's infrastructure. In 2014, China announced that it expects to raise its direct investment in the continent to USD 100 billion by 2020, mainly in infrastructure development which will be channeled through various Chinese lending agencies, including the newly established BRICS Bank. The AIIB will also lend to African states. However Chinese backed infrastructure projects are criticized for their inferior standards and disregard for ecological damage. Political turmoil in the recipient state is also ignored. On a different note, India is serving as a role model for democracy in Africa, where for instance many states are keen to emulate Electronic Voting Machines (EVMs) system in order to avoid electoral malpractices and coups. India must take advantage of these small yet significant milestones to widen its influence in Africa.

Staying ahead in the African Safari

India can capitalize on the positive public perception it enjoys in the continent. It is observed that Kenya has a higher positive perception of China, while South Africa ranks lower. This appears ironical at first, given that South Africa is China's largest African trade partner, with trade valued at more than USD 20 billion. Perhaps the high level of trade has led to competition with local producers and sellers, thus denting China's image. India must not ignore Africa's interest in Prime Minister Modi's 'Make in India' campaign. As proposed, they must be encouraged to export to India, make in India and sell in Africa. This will ensure positive relations on a government-government, business- business and people-people level.

In addition, active Corporate Social Responsibility can be teamed with peacekeeping efforts to achieve humanitarian ends. India, in its own small way can include the democracy quotient while building relations from a bottom-up approach. It can help to offset opposition from authoritarian regimes. It will be a difficult path, but India cannot afford to be a silent spectator as it rises to be an economic powerhouse in a few decades. True, diplomatic foreign policy dictates that India should not interfere, but perhaps the key lies in mediation and building political awareness. It will be feasible to put India's diplomacy with Africa, which has stronger roots than China's, to good use and create a favourable political atmosphere for future business opportunities. Indian entrepreneurs can team with African traders in less trodden yet promising paths such as rural industries, indigenous products and fashion designing. Incentives can be offered to Indians engaging with Africa. Indian diamond traders can be encouraged to lead the way for the rest of the world to buy only 'conflict-free' diamonds, thus forcing African states in turmoil to seek conflict resolution.

India may not have the economic resources that China does to engage with Africa, but it does have the treasures of democracy, sectors such as IT, and entrepreneurial spirit. These may serve to give Delhi a lion's share of Africa's goodwill. The IAFS's continued emphasis on agriculture demonstrates that India acknowledges that the primary economy of both sides needs due diligence, unlike the Chinese focus on resources and manufacturing, which is presenting its own set of problems. India has, in the past and the present, been a vital part of Africa's peace movement and security. This aspect can translate into rich dividends as India moves forward with its large Western cousin. In time, India can be one of the lamps that helps to illuminate the continent emerging from the shadow of under development and make Africa a true Indian ally, in every sense of the word.

BOOSTING TRADE, SECURITY TIES ON AGENDA OF INDIA-AFRICA SUMMIT

Tapping unbounded opportunities and expanding two-way engagement in varied sectors with African continent, where China has been ramping up its influence, will be the major focus of upcoming India-Africa Forum Summit that will see participation by 54 nations.

Heads of State of a significant number of countries are likely to participate in the four-day congregation beginning October 26, the biggest diplomatic event to be hosted by India in the last three decades, seen as its effort to consolidate the historical ties with the continent, endowed with large reservoirs of minerals and hydrocarbons. On October 26, India will host top officials of the African nations while on October 27, External Affairs Minister Sushma Swaraj will host her African counterparts. The summit meeting will be held on October 29 in which heads of state and government will participate.

On October 30, bilateral meetings have been scheduled. A total of around 1,000 delegates including Heads of Government, ministers, officials and business leaders are expected to descend on Delhi for the event. The influential African Union will also participate in the event. Boosting trade, enhancing security cooperation to combat threat of terrorism and exploring ways to deal with scourge of poverty, disease, illiteracy and hunger will be areas of discussions.

To expand trade, the summit is likely to delve on India's association with various African blocs including the Economic Community of West African States (ECOWAS), Southern African Customs Union (SACU) and the Common Market for Eastern and Southern Africa (COMESA) as these forums play a crucial role in trade and investments. The leaders are also likely to deliberate on mitigating challenges of climate change and collectively promote the socio-economic advancement of the citizens of both sides.

India has been having a cordial relationship with African nations with most of them supporting New Delhi's endeavour to become a permanent member in an expanded UN Security Council.

The government believes a vibrant India and a resurgent Africa have a vision of a close partnership and that the summit will provide a platform to develop a new paradigm of cooperation.

India-Africa summit will see biggest gathering of African nations, says Narendra Modi

The upcoming Third India-Africa Forum Summit is "going to be one of the biggest gatherings of African countries outside Africa" and is a reflection of the desire on both sides to engage more intensively, Prime Minister Narendra Modi said.

In a series of tweets and later a statement, Modi said "as minds meet and hands work together, the IAFS-III could be a landmark event in our journey towards further cementing strong ties between India and Africa".

"India is proud to host the 3rd India Africa Forum Summit from 26-29 October 2015 in New Delhi. This time the level of engagement has been scaled up significantly and we have invited leaders from all 54 African countries and the African Union.

"The Summit is going to be one of the biggest gatherings of African countries outside Africa, which is a reflection of the desire on part of both Africa and India to engage more intensively in our quest for a better future.

"India and Africa have a historic relationship based on mutual respect, trust and solidarity. In recent times, our relationship has witnessed progress and has grown into a mutually beneficial partnership."

Modi said Indian investments in Africa, which stand at $30 billion, have contributed immensely to job creation here.

He said that in the run up to the summit, many side events are being organised. Trade ministers of India and African countries, accompanied by business delegations, will meet on October 23.

A business exhibition will be organised at the Summit venue on October 27 and 29 by leading Indian chambers of commerce and industry. More than 16,000 schools are participating in various competitions organised by the Central Board of Secondary Education on themes related to India-Africa cooperation, the statement said. Modi said in tweets that Mahatma Gandhi (Bapu) and Africa shared a close bond.

"Exhibition 'Memories of Mahatma' talks about Bapu and his connection with Africa," he tweeted.

Agriculture, blue economy and security are key aspects of India's ties with African countries.

India's trade with Africa now stands at $70 billion. India has provided lines of credit of $7.4 billion so far, which is being utilised in 137 projects across 41 countries.

Airtel deal to sell over 3,500 towers in Africa collapses

Bharti Airtel said the deal to sell over 3,500 telecom towers in Africa to Eaton Towers has lapsed and stands terminated.

"The agreements for sale of tower assets in Africa between Bharti Airtel Malawi Holdings B.V. & ors. and Eaton Towers (Lilongwe) Ltd & ors. has lapsed and therefore stands terminated," Bharti Airtel said in a regulatory filing.

Last year in September, Airtel announced that it has sold over 3,500 telecom towers in Africa to Eaton Towers.

As part of the deal, Airtel was to sell and lease back over 3,500 towers to Eaton in 6 countries across its African operations under a 10-year contract. The company had said the agreement would allow Airtel to focus on its core business and customers, enable it to deleverage through debt reduction, and would significantly reduce its on-going capital expenditure on passive infrastructure.

Airtel in June said its agreement with Helios Towers Africa for sale of its tower assets in Tanzania and Tchad stands terminated. The company in July last year signed a deal with Helios Towers Africa (HTA) for sale of 3,100 towers in four countries across its African operations, which span across 17 nations.

The company had not mentioned names of the countries but sources had said the deal was signed for Tanzania, Tchad, Congo and Democratic Republic of the Congo. Now the deal with Tanzania and Tchad stands terminated, the agreement with HTA for Congo and Democratic Republic of the Congo is still intact, sources said.

While poverty in Africa has declined, number of poor has iIncreased

Poverty across the continent may be lower than what current estimates suggest, though the number of people living in extreme poverty has grown substantially since 1990, according to the latest World Bank Africa poverty report.

Poverty in a Rising Africa, the first of two upcoming reports on poverty in Africa, documents the data challenges facing the region and reviews the status of Africa's poverty and inequality, both monetary and nonmonetary, taking these data challenges into account.

"The main messages which emerge from this effort to assess poverty in Africa are both encouraging and sobering," said Kathleen Beegle, World Bank program leader and co-author of the report. "Although the data show that the share of the African population in extreme poverty did decline, major poverty challenges still remain, especially in light of the region's rapid population growth."

According to latest World Bank estimates, the share of Africans who are poor fell from 56% in 1990 to 43% in 2012. The report argues that the poverty rate may have declined even more if the quality and comparability of the underlying data are taken into consideration. However, because of population growth many more people are poor, the report says. The most optimistic scenario shows about 330 million poor in 2012, up from about 280 million in 1990. Poverty reduction has been slowest in fragile countries, the report notes, and rural areas remain much poorer, although the urban-rural gap has narrowed.

Other key findings of the report are:

Nonmonetary dimensions of poverty have been improving, but the challenges remain enormous. Compared with 1995, adult literacy rates are up by four percentage points and the gender gap is shrinking. Newborns can expect to live six years longer and the prevalence of chronic malnutrition among under five-year-olds is down six percentage points to 39%. At the same time, despite substantial improvement in school enrolment, the quality of schooling is often low and more than two in five adults are still illiterate.

Reinvigorating Africa's primary educational achievements is urgent. Paradoxically, citizens in resource-rich countries have worse outcomes in human welfare indicators, conditional on income. This finding underscores that while economic growth is critical for poverty reduction, it is not sufficient.

The picture on African inequality is complex. Seven of the 10 most unequal countries in the world are in Africa, most of them in southern Africa. Excluding these countries and controlling for GDP levels, inequality is not higher in Africa than elsewhere in the world. The household survey data do not reveal a systematic increase in inequality across countries in Africa. But the number of extremely wealthy Africans is increasing. Differences between urban and rural areas and across regions are large. Intergenerational mobility in education and occupation has improved, but remains low.

The report concludes with a plea to strengthen Africa's poverty data. While the availability, comparability and quality of data to track non-monetary poverty has improved, in 2012, 25 of Sub-Saharan Africa's 48 countries had conducted at least two household surveys over the past decade to track monetary poverty, and many of these surveys are not comparable over time. On October 15, the World Bank and its partners announced stronger support to complete household-level surveys every three years in the world's poorest countries, including several in Africa, to address huge data gaps that have previously stunted poverty-fighting efforts.

"Better data will make for better decisions and better lives," said Luc Christiaensen, World Bank lead economist and co-author of the report. "It is not just about quantity, the quality of the data also matters. The report offers examples of missed opportunities when surveys are not conducted with quality standards. Maintaining and accelerating the momentum of progress of the past two decades requires collective efforts."

CENTRAL AFRICA

UN agency delivers food aid to thousands displaced by recent violence in CAR

The World Food Programme (WFP) announced today that aid workers have reached more than 30,000 newly displaced people in desperate need of food in the Central African Republic's capital, Bangui, where the situation remains "tense and volatile" after a new surge in violence. "It is critical that WFP has the necessary resources to come to the aid of people who are most vulnerable and have been repeatedly affected by a crisis that erupted two years ago," said Bienvenu Djossa, WFP Country Director in the Central African Republic (CAR).

According to WFP, nearly 900,000 people are still displaced or have taken refuge in neighbouring countries since the start of the conflict in 2013 and the agency and its partners aim to assist 1.2 million people in areas worst-affected by conflict and hunger.

The agency urgently requires $21 million to continue providing vital assistance to families in need through to the end of the year.

"More than 40,000 people have been forced to flee their homes in a matter of days," according to Mr. Djossa.

"The situation remains tense and volatile, but WFP has been able to reach over the past week those most in need, people who have been cut off from any assistance for days, and living in difficult circumstances in over 20 displacement sites," Mr. Djossa said.

He went on to say that even before this latest escalation in violence, "about one in four people were in need of urgent food assistance, and were struggling to recover from the widespread disruption the conflict caused to their lives."

France says it's discussing new Central African UN sanctions list

France said it was working with partners at the United Nations Security Council to impose new sanctions on individuals threatening peace and blocking political transition in the Central African Republic (CAR).

CAR has been in turmoil since Seleka Muslim fighters briefly seized power in the majority Christian country in 2013. They later handed power to an interim government but still control swathes of the north.

Elections are scheduled for October 18 but are expected to be postponed for technical and security reasons.

Armed groups and politicians on Wednesday boycotted the start of a political forum in the former French colony. There has been a surge in violence in the capital, Bangui, since late September, sparked by the murder of a Muslim man, which has seen 77 people killed and 400 injured.

"We are favourable to the adoption of new UN Security Council sanctions on those who threaten peace and stability and prevent the political transition process," Foreign Ministry spokesperson Romain Nadal told reporters in a daily briefing.

"We are working in this direction with our partners on the Security Council."

Nadal declined to give further details.

A French diplomatic source refused to give any prospective names, but said the sanctions would cover travel bans and the freezing of assets.

So far, five individuals have been placed under the UN sanctions, including former president Francois Bozize and Seleka leader Noureddine Adam in 2014. The Belgian branch of the CAR's diamond trading company, Kardiam, and three other people linked to the three-year-old conflict were added in August.

A 10 500-strong UN mission in the CAR, known as Minusca, was deployed to shore up the precarious stability established under a transitional government after France intervened in December 2013.

Paris still has 900 troops on the ground used as a rapid reaction force in support of Minusca.

Three killed in violence in Central African Republic

Inter-communal fighting has killed at least three people in the capital of Central African Republic, residents and the United Nations said.

Several others were wounded and houses burned during last week's night's violence in Bangui's PK5 neighbourhood, the U.N. Mission in Central African Republic said. Mission spokesman Hamadoun Toure said peacekeepers arrived and the fighting stopped.

Resident Sam Gounoumoundjou said the fighting between Muslim ex-Seleka rebels and the Christian militia group known as anti-Balaka began after an attack on Muslim boys playing soccer.

"The clash began with a simple act of provocation, an attack with Kalashnikovs on a group of young Muslim boys playing soccer on a field not far from Yakite, a non-Muslim stronghold," he said. The ex-Seleka rebels and anti-Balaka, however, denied responsibility for fighting.

Sectarian clashes between rival Christian and Muslim militias have flared recently. Similar fighting in the capital in late September broke out after a young Muslim's dead body was found near a mosque. The fighting then killed at least 71 people and injured 400, according to a new count from the Ministry of Public Health.

Central African Republic erupted into widespread sectarian violence after the Muslim Seleka rebels overthrew the president in 2013 and the Christian anti-Balaka militiamen formed to combat them.

Doctors without Borders said that its compound in Bangassou in the Mbomou province was attacked; seriously injuring a staff member whose condition is stable after emergency surgery.

Four staff members were kidnapped and released after 30 minutes, the group said.

"I strongly condemn this attack and call on all armed groups to respect the life and freedom of movement of humanitarian workers who are providing assistance to people affected by the crisis," said Humanitarian Coordinator Aurelien A. Agbenonci.

The U.N. also condemned the attack.

New religious violence in Central Africa leaves one dead, 10 injured

At least one person was killed and 10 injured in fresh sectarian clashes in a flashpoint neighbourhood of the Central African Republic's capital of Bangui, military and hospital sources said.

The violence in the largely Muslim district of PK-5, accompanied by gunfire, forced thousands of residents to flee to other parts of the city.

Many returned to their homes on Friday morning as calm was restored, an AFP correspondent said.

"These new clashes broke out following the death of a young Muslim who was killed by suspected anti-balaka members," said a military source, referring to the largely Christian militia. The anti-balaka "then launched attacks on PK-5 that were repulsed by armed Muslims."

The clashes left one person dead and 10 injured, a hospital source said. Some residents however put the death toll at three.

The return of violence to the district follows clashes in late September that left 61 dead and more than 300 wounded before

French troops and UN peacekeepers intervened to restore calm. Both outbreaks of violence were sparked by the killing of a Muslim in PK-5.

A former French colony which gained independence in 1960, the Central African Republic was shaken by months-long violence between Christians and Muslims in 2013, triggered by the ousting of then president Francois Bozize, a Christian, by mainly Muslim Seleka rebels.

The country was due to stage presidential and legislative elections on October 18, but the polls have been postponed because of delays in registering voters.

One in 10 Central Africans — 460,000 people — have sought refuge outside the country, mainly in Cameroon, Chad, DR Congo and Congo, since 2013.

NORTH AFRICA

Global LNG prices steady on North Africa and Middle East demand

Asian liquefied natural gas (LNG) prices for December delivery were steady this week as large tender awards by Egypt and Jordan offered support in the midterm, with Egypt's first cargoes from the tender due before the end of the year.

The price of Asian spot cargoes for December delivery was unchanged from the previous week at $6.80 per million British thermal units (mmBtu).

"Egypt's deals will start by the end of the year, Jordan in January. We're not that far from January so if those who won did not have cargoes to fill the amount being tendered then they will be coming out in the market to look for it," said a trader.

Egypt is to import 55 cargoes of LNG, equal to about a tenth of its annual gas demand, via a tender awarded to seven companies including Trafigura, Vitol, Noble Group , EDF Trading, Gas Natural, PetroChina and Shell.

Traders said that Jordan has awarded half of its four-year, up to 78-cargo LNG buy tender to Shell, covering deliveries in 2016 and 2017.

Elsewhere in the Middle East, the Dubai Supply Authority (DUSUP) is holding a private tender to buy between 4-6 liquefied natural gas (LNG) cargoes each in 2016 and 2017, and is nearing the final stages of the process with an award expected soon, trade sources said.

In the more mature import markets, including Japan and Korea, traders said there were pockets of demand, but that there was no major buying interest.

Earlier this week, data showed state-run Korea Gas Corp (KOGAS) September domestic gas sales fell 7.4 percent year on year, while Japanese power companies used 3.92 million tonnes of LNG in September, down 12.8 percent from a year earlier.

On the supply side Trinidad is set to close a tender next week for the sale of one liquefied natural gas (LNG) cargo loading on Dec. 19, trade sources said.

A narrow price gap between the European benchmark NBP gas price and the Asia LNG price made re-loads a possibility for those looking to optimise cargoes.

"Storage is quite OK in Europe so re-loading is a possibility," said a trader. (Reporting by Sarah McFarlane; editing by Adrian Croft)

Mauritania to send ground boots to Yemen, military source

Some 500 Mauritanian military forces are gearing up to join Saudi Arabia-led military coalition in Yemen to combat Houthi rebels, military sources said.

"Soldiers of the armed forces who are ready to be sent to Saudi Arabia, completed over the past weeks their military training at Atar military school located in the centre of the country," the sources said.

The information emerged as Saudi Deputy Defence Minister Muhammad Ben Abdallah Al-Ayesh visited the Mauritanian capital this week. He was received on Tuesday by the Mauritania President Mohamed Ould Abdel Aziz.

The Saudi official also met the Mauritanian Minister of Defence and the Chief of the army Mohamed Ould Cheikh Mohamed

Ahmed to discuss modalities related to the operation. Saudi Arabia is leading an international campaign against Yemen Houthi rebels. The international military coalition shelled the rebels' positions for several weeks and recorded significant gains on the ground.

The rebels were pushed out of major parts of the territory but fights still rage on.

Egypt-UNSC: Cairo vows to endeavour to bring stability in conflict zones

Egyptian Foreign Minister, Sameh Shoukry, said his country's actions within the Security Council will be orientated towards bringing stability in conflict zones including Libya, Syria, Iraq, Yemen and mostly the Palestinian-Israeli conflict.

The Egyptian Foreign Minister made the statement Thursday after his country was elected to sit as a non-permanent member of the United Nations Security Council for two years as of January 2016. Present at the vote in New York, Shoukry said Egypt, as a non-permanent member of the Security Council will also seek to bring support for Africa and to affirm African sovereignty and regional integrity.

The Egyptian official conferred with his Senegalese counterpart, Mankeur Ndiaye, also present in New York, on the situation in the continent. Both men stressed the need for the 15-member Security Council to address the health challenges facing Africa. Egypt, the only North African candidate, won the seat with 179 votes out of 193 vote participants. This will be the fifth time since the creation of the UN that Cairo will be sitting at the UN Security Council.

Egypt was elected alongside with Senegal, Ukraine, Japan and Uruguay. The five incoming members will replace outgoing Chad, Nigeria, Jordan, Lithuania, and Chile.

India-Africa summit: Morocco provides an alternative African voice for India

With preparations in full swing for the upcoming India-Africa Forum Summit, it's time for New Delhi to renew ties with old African friends and establish synergy with new African partners.

With the likes of South African President Jacob Zuma, Egyptian President Abdel Fattah el-Sisi, Zimbabwe President Robert Mugabe and Nigerian President Muhammadu Buhari attending, the summit is being touted as the largest-ever gathering of African leaders in India. A total of 52 African countries have confirmed participation, making the event between October 26 and 29 an ideal platform for New Delhi's new Africa push.

India-Africa ties are steeped in historical linkages and shared cultural bonds. That a sizeable Indian-origin population resides in several African nations bears testimony to generations of people-to-people contacts. However, at the level of the government this resource has never been exploited to its full potential. As a result, the goodwill that India enjoys in Africa has rarely been converted into hard strategic gains.

Contrast this with China's robust presence in Africa today. Beijing has made significant inroads into the continent on the back of massive infrastructure development projects. China's overall trade with Africa stands at $200 billion compared to India's $70 billion (2013 figures). However, African nations, although grateful for the Chinese projects, have started becoming wary of their overdependence on Chinese investments, which in many cases compel them to barter away their natural resources.

This puts India in a sweet spot in terms of its relations with Africa. This is precisely why New Delhi must use the India-Africa Forum Summit as a springboard to elevate its ties with the continent. One of the things it must do is to scout for new African partners. And one such crucial ally can be Morocco. This North African constitutional monarchy's sovereign, King Mohammed VI, will be in attendance at the summit - a rare diplomatic privilege and opportunity for New Delhi to boost ties with Rabat.

It's pertinent to note that Morocco has been named as the most competitive economy in North Africa by the latest World Economic Forum report. Given Morocco's strategic location on the western edge of North Africa with a substantial Atlantic costline just a stone's throw away from Europe, Morocco could be India's economic entry point into both Francophone Africa and European economies. Morocco, much like India, is blessed with a substantial young labour force. But what really gives Morocco the edge in comparison to other North African nations is its leadership.

Morocco was one of the few nations in North Africa to use the pro-democracy Arab Spring wave to its advantage. Under the guidance of King Mohammed VI, Morocco adopted a new Constitution that strengthened constitutional rights, enshrined gender equality and equal representation for women and committed to an ambitious regionalisation plan that will see greater autonomy to local bodies. In fact, King Mohammed VI himself devolved much of his powers to the elected Moroccan parliament.

In addition to such democratic reforms, Morocco today is at the forefront of combating Islamic terrorism through a sound multi-dimensional approach. Not only is Morocco a key contributor to UN sponsored forums on fighting the scourge of transnational terrorism, including on the important question of dealing with foreign fighters — as necessitated by the rise of the Islamic State terror group — but Rabat is also pioneering an innovative counter-radicalisation programme based on promoting moderate Islam. As part of the latter, Morocco has been training foreign imams in the values of moderate Islam to counter the jihadi virus that has infected several constituencies in the Middle East and North Africa region. In fact, only recently several Salafists in Morocco who were arrested in connection with terrorism have applied for pardon and reconciliation after going through a de-radicalisation process.

Taken together, both in terms of economic cooperation and security collaboration, Morocco can be an important lead for India in Africa. This will certainly broaden India's engagement in Africa, especially in Francophone Africa. Plus, King Mohammed VI's vision and Morocco's position outside the Africa Union provide New Delhi an alternative and fresh African voice that will surely enrich India's strategic depth in Africa.

SOUTHERN AFRICA

Mozambique: Refugees shun Europe for South Africa

As the sun dips behind the giant brown hills that separate South Africa and Mozambique, a slim young man is busy doing final mechanical checks on a Toyota Land Cruiser at a house that clings to the side of the mountain.

Wearing a white polo shirt, track suit and dark sunglasses, Eduardo is a well-known human trafficker in the town of Ressano Garcia, a sleepy border crossing 97km away from the capital, Maputo.

A newly married father of one, Eduardo said he joined this illicit trade not to make money, but to answer God's call. He sees himself as doing a job that heads of states and the international community should be doing - moving people in danger to safer, more prosperous surroundings.

"I feel not good when I hear what happened to them in their countries," Eduardo told, requesting his full identity not to be disclosed for fear of arrest. "I help them because I know they are suffering in their countries. They then move to other countries because here in Mozambique, even we don't have jobs."

In a town where most young men his age are unemployed, Eduardo sees his business not just as rescuing refugees, but also providing job opportunities to many people who otherwise might have turned to violent crime to make a living.

Deeply religious, Eduardo said he has been people-smuggling for the last three years and the job itself satisfies him immensely.

"I have got a better life because of this job. I feel good because I'm doing something good," he said.

Mozambique, a former Portuguese colony of some 25 million people, has one of the fastest growing economies in the world but almost all the refugees and migrants are headed to South Africa, the second-biggest economy in the continent.

With large numbers from Sub-Saharan Africa finding the Mediterranean route too expensive and dangerous, South Africa has become an attractive and easier option. Hundreds seeking a better life across the border pass through this town every month.

During the day, refugees stay out of sight fearing police arrests. But as the sun sets and vehicle traffic on the town's only tarmac road dwindles, they venture out of safe houses - under the watchful eye of their smugglers - to try their luck at the wire fence that separates the two southern African countries.

In one of the many refugee hideouts in this part of Mozambique are three men who have travelled by road and boat for more than two months, managing to cross three international borders. They paid $250 each to Eduardo to take them across the border into South Africa.

Penniless and visibly exhausted as they waited to complete the last leg of a journey that started in the south-central Somali town of Beletweyne, the men didn't have many nice things to say about the people who got them here. Security forces are a major threat to their passage.

"We caught 280 illegal migrants since the start of this month," Inacio Dina, spokesman for Mozambique's interior ministry, told. "We repatriated them to the countries of their origin. We will continue catching and deporting them until there are no more illegal people in our country."

Dina added the authorities are also hunting for the human traffickers. "In relation to traffickers and those involved in that illegal trade, our police force are working hard to detect them and they will be brought before the law."

As the world's attention focuses on the Mediterranean Sea and the refugee crisis in Europe, both traffickers and refugees in Mozambique agreed more needs to be done to help their situation.

"People with power, presidents and leaders, need to help them. Their problems are bigger than we can fix. We can only do a small thing for them," Eduardo said.

Namibia has no system for rewarding national sports heroes

The Namibian Government especially the Ministry of Sport, Youth and National Service does not have a system in place to reward athletes who represent the nation at international sporting events.

There has been a barrage of criticism directed at government after it emerged that the majority of Namibian para-athletes are wallowing in poverty despite excelling at major events such as International Paralympic Committee (IPC) Athletics World Championships and All Africa Games.

A classic example is that of Ruben Gowaseb who won gold for Namibia at the 14th Special Olympics World Summer Games in Los Angeles, USA held from July 25 to August 2, 2015. A public debate erupted about the treatment of the country's disabled athletes after it emerged that Gowaseb was deprived the customary hero's welcome usually accorded to athletes who have done the country proud upon arrival at Hosea Kutako International Airport.

Instead the marathon runner was transported by bus from the airport and had to literary walk home after he and fellow athletes were dropped off at the Special Olympics Centre at the Katutura Youth Complex.

Many people took to social media to vent their anger towards sport administrators, citing how disability sport was playing second fiddle to able bodied sports citing the handsome rewarding of the national soccer team, the Brave Warriors, when they won the COSAFA Cup earlier this year in South Africa.

After winning the 2015 Council of Southern Africa Football Association (COSAFA) in May, President Hage Geingob announced a cash reward of N$1.2 million for the 24 national football team players for doing the nation proud.

However, there is an isolated case of para-athlete and Olympic gold medallist Johanna Benson who was showered with numerous rewards including a house, a street named after her and a diplomatic passport for her exploits at 2012 Paralympics Games.

The Director of Sport in the Ministry of Sport, Youth and National Service, Shivute Katamba has confessed to The Southern Times that there is no system in place, on how to remunerate Namibian athletes, while dismissing assertions that disability sport is lowly rated.

"We rate our athletes with dis-abilities very high. They give our country an identity. And currently we submitted a proposal to the deputy minister, and the permanent secretary, and we are also reviewing our act and policies, because currently there is no system as to how to reward them, according to their achievements, be it gold, silver or group achievements," Katamba said.

"These are our brothers and sisters and should be treated as equals," said the government official.

"These are our own people. If people don't know people like Ananias (Shikongo) can operate a switchboard and can use a computer, in fact we have had a switchboard operator here, who was blind, and he worked here for more than 20 years".

He conceded that poverty amongst athletes was a national concern, and should not just be upon the ministry to remedy.

"We as a nation should hold hands from the corporate sector and government and come to their aid," he said.

In 2013, Shikongo won a silver medal at the World Championships in Lyon, France in the T11 100m category.

He is among a group of para-athletes who are preparing to represent Namibia at the 2015 IPC Athletics World Championships in Doha, Qatar from October 21-31.

"We are world champions but we live in poverty," were the words gold medallist Ananias Shikongo about the predicament faced by the local para-athletes, adding that they are depended on monthly State grants.

"All they tell us is that, we are happy, you have done us proud. We even take taxis, and even pay taxi for our fellow friends. The government doesn't even avail transport for us. When we arrive at the airport we didn't even receive any welcome, and we have to hustle for transport. We are world-champions, but we live in poverty," he said.

Police Commissioner launches community awareness campaign in Malawi

Deputy Commissioner of Police Southern Region and Officer-In-Charge for Thyolo District, Teleza Nankhuni has launched a massive community sensitisation campaign aimed at strengthening relationships between the Police and community in combating crime.

The campaign comes in the light of a recent surge in criminal activities being committed in the district.

Speaking at the opening ceremony in Ndalama Village, one of the infamous hot beds for criminals, Nankhuni explained to the people the importance of security to the development of the district and the entire country.

She mentioned that thieves recently stole batteries at communications provider Airtel tower leading to disturbances in network, subsequently bringing down people's business. In addition, the OC cited breaking into of Chipiku stores leading to the fore close of the chain of shops in the district as typical examples of how security and development go hand-in-hand.

She then disclosed that Police and estate controllers have partnered to man a 24 hour road block, a move the people welcomed saying most illegal things move at night. Initially the roadblock was only mounted during daylight.

Further she told the community a police unit will be established in the area soon.

"We have partnered with Estate Controllers to man a road block 24 hours in order to stop seepage of illegal things into or out of our district. The relationship between us (Police and Community) is important because these unscrupulous people live among us, hide them and next they will rob or worse still kill you," she said.

She pleaded to the community to enhance their patrols so that murders should not even take place. Referring to the recent mutilation of a 35 year old man, Nankhuni warned that this should be the last time this happens in her jurisdiction and will adopt aggressive measures to see to it that people are safe in their areas.

Among other issues discussed were increase of the unlawful wounding, suicide, gender based violence and juvenile offenders.

In the past two weeks, Thyolo Police has brought in 11 children, ages ranging from 10 years to 16, arrested for theft, burglary and robbery, a situation she said was worrisome to the department.

Zimbabwe: Councils demand 5 Percent of national revenue

Government is working on a framework to guide the disbursement of money allocated to departments that fall under the Ministry of Local Government, Public Works and National Housing in line with provisions of the new Constitution.

Section 301 of the new Constitution provides for the allocation of at least 5 percent of national revenue to the local government, to help establish provincial and metropolitan councils among other functions.

Addressing the 11th Treasurers and Internal Auditors Conference in Kariba recently, principal director (rural local authorities) Mr Christopher Shumba welcomed the constitutionally guaranteed five percent allocations.

"The constitutionalisation of the local government sector and the allocation of at least 5 percent to the sector from the national fiscus, is indeed a welcome development," said Mr Shumba.

The Ministry of Local Government, Public Works and National Housing is working with Treasury and other stakeholders towards the finalisation of the framework that shall guide the disbursement of the funds in question.

Government used to give grants to local authorities for capital projects and to meet service delivery. However, it was replaced by the Public Sector Investment Programme to fund capital development projects when revenue began to decline following the imposition of sanctions by the West.

Chief financial advisor in the ministry Mr Alpha Nhamo said consultations on the framework were in progress with stakeholders such as UN agencies joining hands with local partners.

He said the framework would look at modalities to disburse funds using an agreed formula that ensured all local authorities benefited.

"The formula looks at population density, the extent of need in the various councils and also infrastructure," he said.

The formula would be anchored on statistics from ZimStats for accuracy.

EAST AFRICA

Djibouti's new deal with East African nation will expand its port's capacity

Ethiopia and Djibouti have signed a deal worth $1.55 billion for the construction of a 550km refined petroleum products pipeline linking the two countries. The 20-inch pipeline which will transport diesel, petrol and jet fuel from Damerjog port in Djibouti to Awash terminal in central Ethiopia has been contracted to Black Rhino Group and Mining Oil & Gas Services (MOGS). Construction work is scheduled for completion in 2018.

The pipeline project includes an import facility with a storage capacity of 950,000 barrels in Damerjog, linked by a 20-inch diameter pipe to a depot in Awash. Oil products are currently transported over 800 kilometres by road from Djibouti port to Addis Ababa. This new pipe is capable of transporting 240,000 barrels of fuel a day.

Djibouti's port is situated at the realm of one of the world's busiest shipping lanes. Therefore this project will bolster its position as a shipping hub by expanding the capacity of its port. The project is also set to increase the scale of oil products import and the overall productivity of Ethiopia's supply chain by reducing the cost of transportation.

"The pipeline will increase energy security, aid economic development and reduce harmful emissions," said Brian Herlihy, Chief Executive Officer of Black Rhino, which is owned by funds managed by Blackstone Group LP. He also added that partners, who are set to work under a 30-year concession, will do so in agreement with the governments of Ethiopia and Djibouti.

MOGS Chief Executive Officer, Errol Gregor explained that the Horn of Africa project will sustain the momentum of economic growth and growing fuel demand in both Djibouti and Ethiopia. However this can only be achieved by both enabling high quality energy and ensuring that there is a steady energy supply at good cost points.

In order to meet the demand for oil products, the Ethiopian Petroleum Supply Enterprise (EPSE) will import three million tonnes in fiscal year 2015/16. EPSE's chief executive officer Tadesse Hailemariam said the importation of three million tonnes of refined oil products represents an increase of 7.14 per cent from the 2.8 million tonnes recorded in the 2014/15 fiscal year.

He also added that EPSE plans to build about 160 retail outlets in the country, with a storage capacity of 250,000 litres of petroleum products. There are currently about 660 petrol stations in the country.

Kenyatta roots for free movement within East Africa

President Uhuru Kenyatta has asked the East African Legislative Assembly (EALA) to hasten legislation of the Common Market Protocol.

He said the legislation will accelerate regional integration and anchor the free movement of people, goods, capital and services within the region.

"We must allow our people to take their skills wherever they will be best rewarded. Why confine the energy and innovation of our young people to the countries of their parents?" President Kenyatta posed.

Mr Kenyatta emphasized that the ultimate goal of political union will not be achieved if people are not allowed to move freely across the region.

He commended EALA members for the work that has already gone into making the Common Market Protocol a reality but expressed the need for the process to be concluded during the current term of EALA.

The assembly runs on five-year terms. The current term - which started in 2013 - will end in 2017.

He said leaders must create laws, institutions and frameworks that will help region face the future together, adding that Kenya will play its part in that great task.

To entrench the region's integration, President Kenyatta expressed the need to communicate the benefits of the union to the people.

"Too often, the integration of East Africa is taken to be merely a political matter - a job for politicians, not ordinary people," President Kenyatta noted.

He added: "Some might say that this is not really a problem, for integration will be quicker if we leave it to the authorities. But they are wrong. We can avoid division by giving East African citizens a more direct say in the task of integration."

Rapid progress

The President expressed satisfaction that there was rapid progress in the region's joint infrastructure projects.

He cited the signing of agreements for the Standard Gauge Railway, witnessed by regional leaders, and the commissioning of the Taveta-Arusha road as examples of the joint projects.

"These projects are representative of the hard work that has gone into knitting the nations of the community together by road, rail and air. The rewards are already apparent: we see shorter travel times, and more investment in the region," he said.

Balala urges East Africa unity on mining laws

Mining Cabinet secretary Najib Balala has urged African states to work together to guarantee stability of investments in the region.

Speaking during the opening of the Eastern Africa Mining and Energy Conference in Nairobi, Balala also said it will now take 91 days for those applying for licences to know the fate of the application.

He said there is no need for states to compete against one another, adding that those with mining resources should have uniform legal regimes.

"These regimes are fundamental in enhancing transparency, thus avoiding corruption and opaqueness in the mining sectors," said the CS.

He said resources need to transform people's lives by transferring benefits accruing from them to the citizens, calling on the region to work with the licensed international and local companies to ensure there is dialogue in resolving issues.

Uganda's State minister for Mineral Development Peter Lokeris said the region needs to exploit and explore abandoned resources. He said states must ensure indigenous people benefit directly from mining, warning that focusing on companies and not the indigenous people will be counterproductive.

"We are ready to export pipeline in Eastern Africa and we encourage African nations to consult each other before passing mining laws," he said.

Tanzania elections: Lessons for East Africa

Seeking to reassure Kenya's Jubilee administration, Kikwete said that CCM candidate Dr John Pombe Magufuli will co-operate with the country's leadership led by President Uhuru Kenyatta if he wins that country's presidential contest.

The concerns by Kenya's leadership arise from the close friendship between the Tanzania ruling party candidate and Kenyan opposition leader Raila Odinga, a relationship said to have started when both of them were roads ministers for their respective countries. Pointing to his own friendship with another opposition leader and former Kenyan vice president Kalonzo Musyoka, Kikwete said this had not affected his relationship with the Kenyan leadership. Hopefully, Kikwete' reassurances calmed the nerves of Kenyan leaders.

And it is not just Kenya that's uneasy. Tanzania is East Africa's largest country by land size as well as population. It has for many years provided sanctuary to thousands of people fleeing war, famine and political oppression in neighbouring countries.

It played a critical role in getting rid of Ugandan dictator Idi Amin Dada way back in the 1970s. Above all, Tanzania is extremely important to the region's economy. It is Kenya's largest trading partner, having overtaken Uganda.

The country's northern town of Arusha is important internationally, providing the seat for such organs as the East African Community and the African Court on Human and Peoples' Rights.

When Kenya - against all expectations going by its previous largely peaceful record - went up in flames following the disputed presidential election of December 2007, the whole region was horrified.

Tanzania, too, has enjoyed relatively peaceful elections, save for occasional tensions in the autonomous islands of Zanzibar and Pemba. An implosion in Tanzania is a highly unlikely possibility.

The country has shown great maturity, with none of the inclinations to change the constitution and cling to power that are becoming increasingly prevalent among African leaders. Still, it remains to be seen whether the ruling party CCM would willingly hand over power and support the country's new leadership if it were to lose elections. The opposition stands its best chances ever under former Prime Minister Edward Lowassa.

That would be another score for the country, replicating the victory by Kenya's National Rainbow Coalition (NARC) that propelled former president Mwai Kibaki to power in 2002. So far, there is no reason to doubt that CCM will rise to the occasion and do the honourable thing if the result will not favour the party.

The Tanzanian polls are particularly important given recent events in the region that have put democracy to the test. Burundi is the worst culprit, with President Pierre Nkurunziza plunging his country into crisis by insisting on an unconstitutional term in office. Uganda is already witnessing rising political thuggery and intolerance, which climaxed with the indignity shown toward women politicians recently, with police shamelessly stripping them in public.

With the intimidation having started so early, it is anybody's guess that it will hardly be possible to describe next year's elections there as free and fair by any stretch of the imagination. Rwanda has already moved to extend President Paul Kagame's tenure.

While it is not in doubt that the country has made enormous progress under Kagame's stewardship, true leadership is meant to result in the strengthening of institutions that can outlive a leader. When we instead seek to extend a specific leader's tenure, it is an admission that the country is still walking a tightrope.

Kenya, too, isn't faring well. There have been clear efforts by the Jubilee administration to water down the 2010 constitution and to concentrate power in the presidency - the very cancer that necessitated the crafting of a new constitutional order.

Moreover, the dangerous talk about who "fixed" Deputy President William Ruto at the International Criminal Court, where the case against him has taken a turn for the worse with the admission by judges of testimony that had been recanted by witnesses, puts the country's political stability in a very precarious position. Should Ruto lose the case at The Hague, what will his supporter's make of it, and what will be the consequences for Kenya's as well as the region's stability?

The scenario could be scaring, to say the least. The political leadership of the region, in the foreseeable future, will therefore be upon Tanzania. And that's why the region must watch the country's politics and coming general election closely - both for leadership and inspiration.

WEST AFRICA

US turn to West African oil as shale output slows

US oil refineries are turning back to old suppliers in West Africa as the growth in shale production slows, reigniting a transatlantic trade in crude cargoes that had withered during the tight oil boom.

The number of barrels of West African crude shipped to the US is at its highest level in almost two years, as strong refining margins and attractive prices have seen US plants snap up cargoes. The move comes as traders and investors are watching for signs the US shale oil boom has peaked, after growth of more than 1m barrels a day each year between 2011 and 2014 helped create a global oil glut.

It may also throw a lifeline to producers of light, sweet crude in West Africa, who had largely lost access to North American buyers since the surge in output of similar quality oil from shale fields such as North Dakota's Bakken and the Eagle Ford in Texas.

"Demand for light, sweet crude [in the US] is outstripping supply," said Amrita Sen, head of oil research at Energy Aspects in London. "It's likely these imports will continue at least for the next six months."

While the volumes are not expected to recover to the levels seen before 2010, when Nigeria and Angola at times sent almost half of their oil exports to the US, it may contribute to tightening supplies in other regions.

West African producers have often been forced to discount their high quality oil to win new customers in Asia and Europe over the past five years.

Data from energy intelligence group Genscape shows in addition to US crude oil imports from Nigeria and Angola — the two largest African producers — US plants in the second half of this year have taken more cargoes from smaller producers such as Cameroon and Gabon.

Among the importers since July is refiner Phillips 66, which has purchased crude from Gabon and Angola for its New Jersey refinery. Philadelphia Energy Solutions has also taken Nigerian crude for its plant on the US east coast, according to the US Energy Information Administration. Some barrels are also going to the US Gulf Coast.

Genscape said for the first six months of the year a maximum monthly total of between 3m barrels and 6.6m barrels arrived from countries on Africa's west coast.

In July and August this increased to 8m barrels and 9.6m barrels respectively. While September imports dipped to 6m barrels, October numbers already show a jump to 10m barrels — the highest since November 2013.

West Africa Medic Summit begins in Lagos

Stakeholders in the region's healthcare industry have converged in Nigeria's most populous city, Lagos for the Medic West Africa Exhibition and Congress (MWA).

The summit comes at a time experts believe that patients, in partnership with their health care provider, should have a say in the way their care is administered and managed.

Organisers said this partnership would improve health outcomes and facilitate the treatment process in West Africa. Paelon Memorial Clinic (PMC) is organising the event at the Eko International Convention and Exhibition Centre.

"In PMC, we take the time to listen, educate and inform our patients about every step of their treatment process," said PMC Dr Sylva Cole, Partner and Anaesthetist.

"We honour our patient's wishes and we even encourage them to request for a second opinion if they need the reassurance. In patient care, we put protocols in place for patients to carefully select their practitioner, and discuss and make suggestions regarding their treatment process and terms of care,"

More than 350 of the industry's leading local and international manufacturers and distributors will showcase the latest innovative healthcare products and services to more than 4,000 attendees during the three-day exhibition. Medic West Africa also comprises of the largest IVD & medical laboratory event in West Africa, MEDLAB. Both Medic West Africa and MEDLAB West Africa are free-to-attend.

This year's Medic West Africa event will feature free-to-attend industry master classes conducted by the industry's leading company's healthcare trade professionals.

Ghana to become biggest gas investment hub in West Africa

Ghana is to become the biggest gas investment hub in West Africa following the conclusion of negotiations to start the $7bn OCTP Sankofa Gas Project in the country.

The project which has been endorsed by the World Bank and the International Finance Corporation, IFC, will strategically position Ghana as a force to reckon with in the oil and gas industry.

The investment in the Sankofa project is coming on board after the inauguration of the $1bn Ghana Gas project to supply about half of the country's daily LPG requirements.

Speaking at the Meet the Press series in Accra, the Minister of Petroleum, Emmanuel Armah Kofi Buah said Cabinet has given approval for the inter-connection of the Ghana Gas Pipeline to the West Africa Pipeline to ensure that Gas is made available without hitches.

INDIA-AFRICA TRADE: CONTINUOUS SUNSHINE

The dynamic relationship between India and Africa is built on a shared future, common natural resources, similar demographics and large domestic markets. As both regions aim to increase bilateral trade five-fold to USD 500 billion by 2020, it will be critical for Governments, Industry and other key stakeholders to focus on greater market access, availability of trade finance and simplification of bilateral business processes and tax regime.

The Third Africa-India Forum Summit is now scheduled to be held in New Delhi on October 26-30, 2015 and the Indian Government wishes to make the summit a wider ranging participatory and result-oriented one. Instead of simply enhancing goodwill measures, the third summit is to focus on utilising trade and investment opportunities to propel economic growth in these two regions, and expectations are high this time.

African continent presents an opportunity to invest, trade and build economic partnerships. There are definitive advantages to be derived from robust, low cost and enduring solutions for investment, infrastructure, social, education, health etc. that India has developed that may be effective under similar socioeconomic conditions in Africa. India too stands to gain immensely from all these aspects. Besides gains from trade, India can derive benefits mainly by creating partnerships in the areas of food security, energy security and non-fuel mineral resources.

At the moment African business community has no significant presence in India, except for a few in banking business like FirstRand Bank (FRB) and State Bank of Mauritius (SBM). However, interests are expressed by the African business community to invest in India, particularly in sectors like food and hospitality. To facilitate such possible business partnerships and ventures there is a need for assistance and active intermediation from the Indian government.

Key Future Potential Growth Sectors in Africa

The biggest opportunity of future growth is probably in the consumer-facing sectors like consumer goods, telecom and banking apart from others. By the end of 2008, these sectors started growing two to three times faster than those in OECD countries.

India has a golden opportunity to initiate partnerships with African nations in agriculture where it can benefit from the increased African output while contributing positively to Africa in terms of technical assistance, skill building, and research and development in agriculture.5 Africa will benefit in terms of increased output by using idle capacity, mainly unused arable land.

Food and beverage spending is projected to expand the most in absolute terms, compared to any other consumer good category. However, with continuous development usually the spending pattern shifts towards higher quality goods. If consumption actually rises along with an increase in household income at the current rate then rapid increases are expected in retail banking, telecom and housing.

African Development Bank estimates that if Sub-Saharan Africa (SSA) could achieve infrastructure development similar to that of Mauritius, then annual GDP growth in entire region may rise by 2.3 per cent. Africa needs $93 billion every year to create infrastructure for supporting growth and meeting development goals – two third for new investments and the rest for maintenance. African governments spend an average of $45 billion per annum on infrastructure, two third of which is domestically mobilised from taxes and user charges. Most of the new capital investment comes from external sources. For the specialised private or public sector infra and construction companies in India there are huge opportunities in infrastructure and constructions projects in different parts of Africa.

Productions of different industries in different countries have substantially slowed down due to the overall slowdown in world economy, but still extractive industries will continue to support growth in 2015 and 2016 in most of the African resource-rich countries. According to estimates, the volume growth rate of the continent's oil, gas, and most minerals can be between 2 and 4 per cent per annum in future. Even at current prices, the value of resource production has the potential to touch $540 billion in 2020, rising from an approximate $430 billion currently.

Africa and India: A New Frontier for Mutual Prosperity

India and Africa share many things in common, including heritage, culture and ancient trade. Broad cornerstones of future partnerships will be:

Partnership in agriculture: While India can help Africa in agricultural capacity building, Africa can help India in ensuring future food security.

Resource based partnership: India would do well to explore sustainable ways to contribute to the African growth story while benefitting in terms of its own energy security.

Non-resource based partnership: While some African countries may need financing, others may be looking for partnerships in skill and capacity building. Depending on the difference in economic structures, India can build partnerships with both categories. Social sector cooperation and investment: Education, healthcare and housing sectors present a huge opportunity for cooperation and investment.

EXPLORING INVESTMENT OPPORTUNITIES: MUTUAL BENEFITS

Indian Investment in Africa

Indian government-backed initiative to engage with Africa should provide ample opportunities for Indian outward FDI as well, and no Indian engagement with Africa will be complete without mutual exchange of direct investment. The first ever outward Indian FDI went to Africa – a textile mill established by the Birla Group in Ethiopia in 1959. Indian multinationals have ventured into both green-field and existing investments – in telecom, energy, computer services, power and automobile sectors, among others.

Major Reasons Behind Rising Trend of Indian Investment in Africa

Government policies, coupled with moderate but consistent economic growth, have given confidence to Indian companies to invest abroad through FDI route. Bilateral investment treaties (BIT) and double taxation treaties (DTT) also encourage better flow of FDI in host countries. Host country policies, like changes in corporate tax rates, other fiscal incentives and other privatisation policies, also influence OFDI. Along with political and cultural factors, other factors influencing outward FDI include comfort in English language and geographical location.

Composition of Indian FDI in Africa

Indian investment in Africa has been in primary commodities such as oil, gas and mining. In manufacturing sectors, automobile and pharmaceutical firms historically invested in different African countries. Pan-African investments are also made by prominent Indian telecom, chemical, metal and fertiliser companies.

Africa: New Destination for Investment and Capital Flow

According to Financial Times, Africa is the fastest growing destination for FDI. In 2014, the capital investment coming into the region grew by 65 per cent to an estimated US$ 87 billion, while the global green-field FDI market expanded by only 1 per cent. The number of projects in Africa increased by 6 per cent. Apart from investments in resources, there have been strong FDI inflows into real estate, hospitality and construction in 2014 along with consumer facing sectors like technology, media and telecom, financial services, consumer products and retail. There has also been visible enthusiasm about agricultural sector based investment activities in 2014.

Africa's Outward FDI: Possibilities and Realities

In today's financially integrated world, capital, even from an early stage economy, creates aspirations for itself. It is important to note that African outward FDIs include intra-continent investment of African capital which is the second largest source of FDI in Africa. Employing a part of country's financial resources outside remains essentially a policy decision, and an issue of political economy in any particular country. However, there are African countries in advanced stages of development such as South Africa, where companies are quite keen on investing not only inside but also outside the continent.

Outward Investing African Countries and India as the Potential Destination

In a financially integrated world, foreign investment is increasingly transforming itself into a two-way affair because of global aspirations of transnational capitals. High-profile countries like Mauritius show steady outflow of FDI ; Democratic Republic of the Congo has shown quite a big jump in FDI outflows in the last three years; Tunisia, Burkina Faso, Guinea, Senegal, Togo, Cameroon, Gabon, Zambia and Zimbabwe show sporadic outflows. Algeria, Egypt, Libya, Morocco, Liberia, Nigeria, Angola, and South Africa have shown steady and quite high outflows of FDI in recent times. Some of these FDIs from Africa have the potential to come to India.

Towards a New Era of Investment between Africa and India

Given the enduring relationship with Africa, India is in a perfect position to initiate a mutual organic growth partnership. The relationship has to be built not only on economic fundamentals, but also on mutual trust. With India's clear intention to contribute to the capacity and skill building in Africa, the cornerstone of the relationship must be trade and investment. With relatively free flowing capital and enhanced facilitation on both sides, India and Africa can contribute to each other's growth story. It will feed positively into economic multiplier mechanism and boost economic development in both regions.

Bibliography

Austen, Ralph: *African Economic History: Internal Development and External Dependency*. Portsmouth, NH: Heinemann, 1987.

Diawara, Manthia: *In Search of Africa and India Relations.* Cambridge, Mass.: Harvard University Press, 1998.

El-Khawas, Mohamed A., and Barry Cohen: *The Kissinger Study of Southern Africa.* Westport, Conn.: L. Hill, 1976.

Getz, Trevor R.: *Cosmopolitan Africa, c. 1700–1875.* African World Histories. Oxford: Oxford University Press, 2013.

Goodwin, Stefan: *Africa in India: Antiquity into the Age of Global Exploration.* Lanham, MD: Lexington, 2009.

Lemarchand, René: *Indian Policy in Southern Africa: The Stakes and the Stance.* Washington, D.C.: University Press of America, 1981.

Meriwether, James Hunter: *Proudly We Can Be Africans: Black Americans and Africa, 1935–1961.* Chapel Hill: University of North Carolina Press, 2002.

Minter, William: *King Solomon's Mines Revisited: Western Interests and the Burdened History of Southern Africa.* New York: Basic Books, 1986.

Morgan, Kenneth: *Slavery and the British Empire: From Africa to America.* Oxford: Oxford University Press, 2008.

Northrup, David: *Africa's Discovery of India, 1450–1850.* New York: Oxford University Press, 2014.

Nwaubani, Ebere: *The United States and Decolonization in West Africa, 1950–1960.*Rochester, N.Y.: University of Rochester Press, 2001.

Parker, John, and Richard Rathbone: *African History: A Very Short Introduction.* Oxford: Oxford University Press, 2007.

Philips, John Edward: *Writing African History.* Rochester, NY: University of Rochester Press, 2005.

Postma, Johannes: *The Atlantic Slave Trade.* Westport, CT: Greenwood, 2003.

Wright, John: *The Trans-Saharan Slave Trade.* London: Routledge, 2007.

Index

❑❑❑